The Political Economy of Prosperity

Why do some nations and cities attain high levels of economic and social prosperity? What makes them so successful? The kinds of factors habitually cited in answer to these questions explain why nations improve their economic and social performance but not why a small group of nations (or cities) perform much better than the rest. Economists stress efficient markets, effective industries and functional factors like transport, health, education, and infrastructure. Political scientists emphasize honest and democratic government. This book argues that three further factors are key: paradoxes, patterns, and portals.

To an unusual degree, the world's most prosperous economies and societies think and act paradoxically. At their core are enigmatic, puzzle-like belief systems that elicit cooperation via abstract patterns rather than personal connections. They are often accompanied by high levels of autodidactic, self-directed learning and intense creation in the arts and sciences. These factors, when combined, facilitate large-scale interactions between strangers and, in so doing, they energize markets, industries, cities, and publics. Pattern-based political economies are especially prominent in the portal cities, regions, and nations that are concentrated along the world's maritime circumference in North America, East Asia, North-Western Europe, and Australasia. It is only by integrating additional cognitive, cultural, creative, and geographic elements that we can truly understand the successes of prosperous economies.

This book represents a significant contribution to the literature on political economy, economic growth, and prosperity.

Peter Murphy is Adjunct Professor in the School of Humanities and Social Sciences at La Trobe University, Australia, and Adjunct Professor at the Cairns Institute at James Cook University.

Routledge Frontiers of Political Economy

For more information about this series, please visit: www.routledge.com/books/series/SE0345

The Political Economy of Prosperity

Successful Societies and Productive Cultures

Peter Murphy

Routledge
Taylor & Francis Group

LONDON AND NEW YORK

First published 2020
by Routledge
2 Park Square, Milton Park, Abingdon, Oxon OX14 4RN

and by Routledge
52 Vanderbilt Avenue, New York, NY 10017

Routledge is an imprint of the Taylor & Francis Group, an informa business

First issued in paperback 2021

British Library Cataloguing-in-Publication Data
A catalogue record for this book is available from the British Library

Library of Congress Cataloging-in-Publication Data
A catalog record for this book has been requested

ISBN: 978-1-138-58125-8 (hbk)
ISBN: 978-1-03-208697-2 (pbk)
ISBN: 978-0-429-50680-2 (ebk)

Typeset in Bembo
by Apex CoVantage, LLC

Sometime in the late 1990s, I was a visiting academic at the University of Michigan at Ann Arbor. After a nice stay at the university, I had to fly out from the airport some distance away. So I booked a limousine service, and a very capable driver turned up on time. It was a long trip and so we chatted. It turned out he was a young Pakistani who had got lucky and received one of the 50,000 green cards the United States gives out every year in a lottery. He was supporting himself by driving while doing a business course at a community college. He struck me as very energetic and engaged. Eventually, I asked him what he thought of the United States. He replied that he liked America a lot. 'You see sir,' he said, 'everything works. Everything works.' That in one sentence sums up successful modernity. You find it in places where 'everything works'. I often think about the conversation with that gentleman. This book is dedicated to him.

Contents

Tables

Acknowledgments

My thanks to John Rundell for a number of thought-provoking discussions about Ireland, Trevor Hogan for a long conversation about the river systems of China and related matters, and David Roberts for his observations about Australian cities. I also want to thank an anonymous reviewer of the proposal for this book who made an astute suggestion about the organization of chapters. The advice was good and I followed it.

I am appreciative of the editors of Australia's *Quadrant* magazine. They encouraged me to experiment in print with some of the ideas that appear in this book. *Prosperity* includes material from 'The Anglosphere's Quiet Revolution', *Quadrant*, January-February 2017, and 'The Rage Against Modernity's Miracles', *Quadrant*, October 2018.

My greatest debt of gratitude is to Christine Mintrom, for a shared life filled with wry wonder and repartee – an economy of laughter in miniature.

1 Prosperity

Growth

Prosperity is a recent historical phenomenon. In 1800, the 17 countries for which we have reasonable estimates had an average GDP per capita of US$1,656 (in constant 2011 dollars) – US$4.50 a day.[1] In 1850, across 35 countries, the average was US$2,034. In 1900, it was US$3,538 covering 44 countries. In 1950, it was US$3,769 including 140 countries. In 2016, a recorded 169 countries had an average GDP per capita of US$18,631 – US$51 a day. The productive capacity of the world in two centuries had multiplied by a factor of least ten. Considering how few countries in 1800 we have reliable figures for, it is almost certain that the world's overall productive capacity grew considerably more than tenfold in two centuries.

This remarkable achievement compares with the record of virtually no growth in the centuries between the time of the Roman Empire and 1500.[2] In year 1 CE, 13 component parts of the Roman Empire had an average GDP per capita of US$1,175 – US$3.20 a day. In 1500, nine countries for which estimates exist had an average GDP per capita of US$1,778 – virtually unchanged in 15 centuries.[3] In a handful of countries after 1500, there is the first inkling of accelerating growth. The United Kingdom and the Netherlands each enter the nineteenth century with a level of economic prosperity two-and-a-half times the recorded average.[4] By 1851, Switzerland's annual product per head is US$5,349, twice the recorded average. By 1860, Australia had reached twice the world average, the United States the same by 1920 (Tables 1.1 and 1.2).

These are modernity's exception societies. They pioneered a template for economic and social prosperity. Crucial to that template are growth-generating, self-organizing systems. This growth model 'takes off' in the settler societies in the nineteenth century; in Sweden in the late nineteenth century; in Japan, Germany, Norway, Denmark, and Finland in the early twentieth century; and in Ireland, Iceland, Singapore, Hong Kong, Taiwan, and Israel in the second half of the twentieth century (Tables 1.1 and 1.2).

There are a number of wealthy societies – though, strictly speaking, not prosperous societies – that are wealthy because they are resource-dependent states (Table 1.3). The current study brackets those states, principally because most

Table 1.1 Economic growth, 1820–2016: high-performing nations/territories

Year	Australia		Austria		Belgium		Canada	
	Real GDP per capita, 2011 US$	Rate of growth prior decade	Real GDP per capita, 2011 US$	Rate of growth prior decade	Real GDP per capita, 2011 US$	Rate of growth prior decade	Real GDP per capita, 2011 US$	Rate of growth prior decade
1820	941		2,112				1,530	
1830	1,542	**164%**	2,425	115%			1,691	111%
1840	2,496	**162%**	2,626	108%			1,965	116%
1850	3,589	**144%**	2,861	109%	3,029		2,249	114%
1860	5,259	**147%**	3,082	108%	3,761	**124%**	2,453	109%
1870	5,947	113%	3,229	105%	4,415	117%	2,866	117%
1880	7,786	**131%**	3,604	112%	5,028	114%	3,071	107%
1890	8,099	104%	4,236	118%	5,623	112%	4,023	**131%**
1900	7,292	90%	4,997	118%	6,121	109%	4,924	122%
1910	9,465	**130%**	5,705	114%	6,666	109%	6,877	**140%**
1920	8,658	91%	4,183	73%	6,499	97%	6,531	95%
1930	8,554	99%	6,217	**149%**	8,167	**126%**	8,137	**125%**
1940	11,203	**131%**	6,865	110%	7,483	92%	9,080	112%
1950	13,466	120%	6,426	94%	8,960	120%	12,333	**136%**
1960	15,972	119%	11,302	**176%**	11,404	**127%**	14,804	120%
1970	21,845	**137%**	16,900	**150%**	17,406	**153%**	20,382	**138%**
1980	26,184	120%	23,856	**141%**	23,733	**136%**	27,359	**134%**
1990	31,200	119%	29,292	123%	28,210	119%	31,921	117%
2000	39,200	**126%**	36,363	**124%**	34,231	121%	38,108	119%
2010	45,684	117%	40,450	111%	37,791	110%	41,326	108%
2016	48,845	107%	41,445	102%	38,766	103%	43,745	106%

Year	CH/Switzerland		Denmark		Germany		Finland	
	Real GDP per capita, 2011 US$	Rate of growth prior decade	Real GDP per capita, 2011 US$	Rate of growth prior decade	Real GDP per capita, 2011 US$	Rate of growth prior decade	Real GDP per capita, 2011 US$	Rate of growth prior decade
1820			2,288					
1830			2,390	104%				
1840			2,566	107%				
1850			3,175	**124%**	2,884		1,543	
1860	5,456		3,129	99%	3,312	115%	1,546	100%
1870	6,709	123%	3,599	115%	3,715	112%	1,845	119%
1880	7,996	119%	3,920	109%	4,023	108%	1,870	101%
1890	11,269	**141%**	4,534	116%	4,904	122%	2,236	120%
1900	13,763	122%	5,420	120%	6,029	123%	2,701	121%
1910	16,063	117%	6,657	123%	6,763	112%	3,086	114%

Year	CH/Switzerland		Denmark		Germany		Finland	
	Real GDP per capita, 2011 US$	Rate of growth prior decade	Real GDP per capita, 2011 US$	Rate of growth prior decade	Real GDP per capita, 2011 US$	Rate of growth prior decade	Real GDP per capita, 2011 US$	Rate of growth prior decade
1920	15,324	95%	7,173	108%	5,647	83%	2,988	97%
1930	19,812	**129%**	9,596	**134%**	8,027	**142%**	4,316	**144%**
1940	18,989	96%	9,193	96%	10,914	**136%**	5,214	121%
1950	21,147	111%	12,475	**136%**	7,840	72%	6,886	**132%**
1960	29,063	**137%**	15,833	**127%**	15,565	**199%**	10,087	**146%**
1970	39,438	**136%**	22,793	**144%**	21,896	**141%**	15,505	**154%**
1980	43,814	111%	27,361	120%	28,512	**130%**	20,964	**135%**
1990	50,132	114%	33,155	121%	32,178	113%	27,306	**130%**
2000	52,804	105%	41,548	**125%**	37,776	117%	32,957	121%
2010	58,267	110%	43,178	104%	41,576	110%	37,643	114%
2016	59,662	102%	44,836	104%	44,689	107%	37,239	99%

Year	France		Hong Kong		Ireland		Iceland	
	Real GDP per capita, 2011 US$	Rate of growth prior decade	Real GDP per capita, 2011 US$	Rate of growth prior decade	Real GDP per capita, 2011 US$	Rate of growth prior decade	Real GDP per capita, 2011 US$	Rate of growth prior decade
1820	1,867							
1830	1,959	105%						
1840	2,349	120%						
1850	2,627	112%						
1860	3,113	119%						
1870	3,086	99%						
1880	3,488	113%						
1890	3,909	112%						
1900	4,731	121%						
1910	4,878	103%						
1920	5,309	109%						
1930	7,455	**140%**			5,859			
1940	6,650	89%			6,172	105%		
1950	8,531	**128%**	3,466		6,983	113%	7,841	
1960	12,170	**143%**	4,321	**125%**	8,660	**124%**	10,111	**129%**
1970	18,771	**154%**	7,855	**182%**	12,537	**145%**	13,684	**135%**
1980	24,292	**129%**	14,510	**185%**	17,272	**138%**	22,632	**165%**
1990	29,031	120%	23,745	**164%**	23,899	**138%**	26,538	117%
2000	33,967	117%	30,196	**127%**	43,959	**184%**	31,742	120%
2010	36,141	106%	42,836	**142%**	49,178	112%	36,134	114%
2016	37,124	103%	48,330	113%	56,597	115%	42,085	116%

(Continued)

Table 1.1 (Continued)

Year	Israel		Japan		Korea (South)		Luxembourg	
	Real GDP per capita, 2011 US$	Rate of growth prior decade	Real GDP per capita, 2011 US$	Rate of growth prior decade	Real GDP per capita, 2011 US$	Rate of growth prior decade	Real GDP per capita, 2011 US$	Rate of growth prior decade
1820								
1830								
1840								
1850								
1860								
1870			1,160					
1880			1,359	117%				
1890			1,592	117%				
1900			1,856	117%				
1910			2,052	111%				
1920			2,668	**130%**	841			
1930			2,912	109%	808	96%		
1940			4,523	**155%**	1,232	**152%**		
1950	4,192		3,023	67%	1,178	96%	12,333	
1960	6,938	**166%**	6,273	**208%**	1,691	**144%**	14,629	119%
1970	12,053	**174%**	15,286	**244%**	2,989	**177%**	19,139	**131%**
1980	16,344	**136%**	21,130	**138%**	5,674	**190%**	22,999	120%
1990	19,442	119%	29,567	**140%**	12,004	212%	33,835	**147%**
2000	25,136	**129%**	32,988	112%	21,420	**178%**	47,973	**142%**
2010	28,482	113%	34,990	106%	31,321	**146%**	53,877	112%
2016	31,701	111%	37,465	107%	36,103	115%	57,006	106%

Year	Netherlands		Norway		New Zealand		Singapore	
	Real GDP per capita, 2011 US$	Rate of growth prior decade	Real GDP per capita, 2011 US$	Rate of growth prior decade	Real GDP per capita, 2011 US$	Rate of growth prior decade	Real GDP per capita, 2011 US$	Rate of growth prior decade
1820	3,395		2,614					
1830	3,429	101%	2,724	104%				
1840	4,090	119%	3,038	112%				
1850	4,266	104%	3,068	101%	1,885			
1860	4,334	102%	3,569	116%	3,643	**193%**		
1870	4,992	115%	4,117	115%	5,104	**140%**		
1880	5,268	106%	4,729	115%	6,169	121%		
1890	5,733	109%	5,233	111%	6,184	100%		
1900	5,990	104%	6,141	117%	7,078	114%	2,780	
1910	6,807	114%	7,231	118%	8,754	**124%**	3,445	124%
1920	7,593	112%	8,958	**124%**	9,289	106%	2,437	71%
1930	10,081	**133%**	10,929	122%	8,168	88%	3,845	**158%**
1940	8,694	86%	12,167	111%	10,375	**127%**		
1950	10,790	**124%**	16,360	**134%**	13,924	**134%**	4,504	

Year	Netherlands		Norway		New Zealand		Singapore	
	Real GDP per capita, 2011 US$	Rate of growth prior decade	Real GDP per capita, 2011 US$	Rate of growth prior decade	Real GDP per capita, 2011 US$	Rate of growth prior decade	Real GDP per capita, 2011 US$	Rate of growth prior decade
1960	14,911	**138%**	21,705	**133%**	15,586	112%	4,367	97%
1970	21,534	**144%**	30,213	**139%**	18,425	118%	8,384	**192%**
1980	26,460	123%	45,426	**150%**	20,331	110%	17,148	**205%**
1990	31,062	117%	55,640	122%	22,539	111%	28,576	**167%**
2000	40,385	**130%**	75,434	**136%**	27,284	121%	42,646	**149%**
2010	44,066	109%	80,892	107%	31,635	116%	59,263	**139%**
2016	45,600	103%	82,814	102%	34,295	108%	6,5729	111%

Year	Sweden		Taiwan		United Kingdom		United States	
	Real GDP per capita, 2011 US$	Rate of growth prior decade	Real GDP per capita, 2011 US$	Rate of growth prior decade	Real GDP per capita, 2011 US$	Rate of growth prior decade	Real GDP per capita, 2011 US$	Rate of growth prior decade
1820	1,500							
1830	1,557				3,481	107%	2,364	114%
1840	1,662	107%			3,940	113%	2,583	109%
1850	1,818	109%			4,248	108%	2,825	109%
1860	2,058	113%			4,988	117%	3,425	121%
1870	2,272	110%			5,716	115%	3,736	109%
1880	2,501	110%			5,879	103%	4,866	**130%**
1890	2,763	110%			6,711	114%	5,184	107%
1900	3,519	**127%**			7,446	111%	6,252	121%
1910	4,296	122%	1,249		7,567	102%	7,586	121%
1920	5,075	118%	1,404	112%	6,881	91%	8,485	112%
1930	7,159	**141%**	1,876	**134%**	8,504	**124%**	9,490	112%
1940	8,202	115%	1,849	99%	10,716	**126%**	11,307	119%
1950	11,385	**139%**	1,355	73%	10,846	101%	15,241	**135%**
1960	14,677	**129%**	2,002	**148%**	13,512	**125%**	18,058	118%
1970	21,483	**146%**	3,753	**187%**	16,829	**125%**	23,958	**133%**
1980	25,234	117%	7,782	**207%**	20,211	120%	29,613	**124%**
1990	29,749	118%	14,703	**189%**	25,679	**127%**	36,982	**125%**
2000	35,261	119%	25,761	**175%**	31,619	123%	45,887	**124%**
2010	42,753	121%	37,253	**145%**	34,722	110%	49,267	107%
2016	44,659	104%	42,165	113%	37,334	108%	53,015	108%

Source: Maddison Historical Statistics, Groningen Growth and Development Centre, University of Groningen, 2018, real GDP per capita in 2011 US$. www.rug.nl/ggdc/historicaldevelopment/maddison/.

Percentages in bold and grey highlights: nations and territories with above average (greater than 123%) growth per decade.

Note: Switzerland pre-1900 data from Maddison, The World Economy: A Millennial Perspective, Table B–21. World GDP per capita, 20 Countries and Regional Averages, AD 0–1998. CH/Switzerland stands for Confoederatio Helvetica/Switzerland.

Table 1.2 Rate of economic growth, global, 1820–2016

National GDP per capita calculated as a percentage of the average GDP per capita of all nations with a recorded or estimated GDP per capita, 2011 US constant dollars

Year	Average real GDP per capita 2011US$	Rate of growth prior decade	High-growth (HG) decades	No. of nations with estimated or recorded GDP per capita	Australia	Austria	Belgium	Canada	Switzerland	Denmark	Germany	Finland
1820	1,453	N/A		49	65%	145%		105%		157%		
1830	**1,995**	**137.2%**	**HG 1820s**	17	77%	122%		85%		120%		
1840	2,174	109.0%		19	115%	121%		90%		118%		
1850	2,030	93.4%		35	177%	141%	149%	111%		156%	142%	76%
1860	**2,644**	**130.3%**	**HG 1850s**	30	**199%**	117%	142%	93%	**206%**	118%	125%	58%
1870	2,101	79.5%		66	283%	154%	210%	136%	319%	171%	177%	88%
1880	**3,114**	**148.2%**	**HG 1870s**	34	250%	116%	161%	99%	257%	126%	129%	60%
1890	3,111	99.9%		44	260%	136%	181%	129%	362%	146%	158%	72%
1900	3,502	112.5%		44	208%	143%	175%	141%	393%	155%	172%	77%
1910	4,070	116.2%		46	233%	140%	164%	169%	395%	164%	166%	76%
1920	3,860	94.8%		50	224%	108%	168%	169%	397%	186%	146%	77%
1930	**4,633**	**120.0%**	**HG 1920s**	56	185%	134%	176%	176%	428%	**207%**	173%	93%
1940	5,176	111.7%		52	216%	133%	145%	175%	367%	178%	**211%**	101%
1950	3,767	72.8%	1930s level	139	358%	171%	**238%**	**327%**	561%	331%	208%	183%
1960	5,078	134.8%		148	315%	**223%**	225%	292%	572%	312%	307%	**199%**
1970	**7,716**	**151.9%**	**HG 1960s**	150	283%	219%	226%	264%	511%	295%	284%	201%
1980	**12,468**	**161.6%**	**HG 1970s**	167	210%	191%	190%	219%	351%	219%	229%	168%
1990	11,515	92.4%		167	271%	254%	245%	277%	435%	288%	279%	237%
2000	**14,248**	**123.7%**	**HG 1990s**	168	275%	255%	240%	267%	371%	292%	265%	231%
2010	**17,150**	**120.4%**	**HG 2000s**	168	266%	236%	220%	241%	340%	252%	242%	219%
2016	18,598	108.4%		168	263%	223%	208%	235%	321%	241%	240%	200%

Year	Average real GDP per capita 2011US$	Rate of growth prior decade	High-growth (HG) decades	No. of nations with estimated or recorded GDP per capita	France	Hong Kong	Ireland	Iceland	Israel	Japan	Korea	Luxembourg
	Global	*Global*	*Global*	*Global*	_National GDP per capita calculated as a percentage of the average GDP per capita of all nations with a recorded or estimated GDP per capita, 2011 US constant dollars_							
1820	1,453	N/A		49	128%							
1830	**1,995**	**137.2%**	**HG 1820s**	17	98%							
1840	2,174	109.0%		19	108%							
1850	2,030	93.4%		35	129%							
1860	**2,644**	**130.3%**	**HG 1850s**	30	118%							
1870	2,101	79.5%		66	147%					55%		
1880	**3,114**	**148.2%**	**HG 1870s**	34	112%					44%		
1890	3,111	99.9%		44	126%					51%		
1900	3,502	112.5%		44	135%					53%		
1910	4,070	116.2%		46	120%					50%		
1920	3,860	94.8%		50	138%					69%	22%	
1930	**4,633**	**120.0%**	**HG 1920s**	56	161%		126%			63%	17%	
1940	5,176	111.7%		52	128%		119%			87%	24%	
1950	3,767	72.8%	*1930s level*	139	**226%**	92%	185%	**208%**	111%	80%	31%	**327%**
1960	5,078	134.8%		148	240%	85%	171%	199%	137%	124%	33%	288%
1970	**7,716**	**151.9%**	**HG 1960s**	150	243%	102%	162%	177%	156%	**198%**	39%	248%
1980	**12,468**	**161.6%**	**HG 1970s**	167	195%	116%	139%	182%	131%	169%	46%	184%
1990	11,515	92.4%		167	252%	**206%**	**208%**	230%	169%	257%	104%	294%
2000	**14,248**	**123.7%**	**HG 1990s**	168	238%	212%	309%	223%	176%	232%	150%	337%
2010	**17,150**	**120.4%**	**HG 2000s**	168	211%	250%	287%	211%	166%	204%	183%	314%
2016	*18,598*	*108.4%*		*168*	*200%*	*260%*	*304%*	*226%*	*170%*	*201%*	*194%*	*307%*

(Continued)

Table 1.2 (Continued)

Year	Global Average real GDP per capita 2011US$	Global Rate of growth prior decade	Global High-growth (HG) decades	Global No. of nations with estimated or recorded GDP per capita	Netherlands	Norway	New Zealand	Singapore	Sweden	Taiwan	UK	USA
					National GDP per capita calculated as a percentage of the average GDP per capita of all nations with a recorded or estimated GDP per capita, 2011 US constant dollars							
1820	1,453	N/A		49	234%	180%			103%		223%	143%
1830	**1,995**	**137.2%**	**HG 1820s**	17	172%	137%			78%		175%	119%
1840	2,174	109.0%		19	188%	140%			76%		181%	119%
1850	2,030	93.4%		35	210%	151%			90%		209%	139%
1860	**2,644**	**130.3%**	**HG 1850s**	30	164%	135%	93%		78%		189%	130%
1870	2,101	79.5%		66	238%	196%	138%		108%		272%	178%
1880	**3,114**	**148.2%**	**HG 1870s**	34	169%	152%	**243%**		80%		189%	156%
1890	3,111	99.9%		44	184%	168%	198%		89%		216%	167%
1900	3,502	112.5%		44	171%	175%	199%	79%	100%		213%	179%
1910	4,070	116.2%		46	167%	178%	202%	85%	106%	31%	186%	186%
1920	3,860	94.8%		50	197%	**232%**	215%	63%	131%	36%	178%	**220%**
1930	**4,633**	**120.0%**	**HG 1920s**	56	218%	236%	241%	83%	155%	40%	184%	205%
1940	5,176	111.7%		52	168%	235%	176%		158%	36%	**207%**	218%
1950	3,767	72.8%		139	**286%**	434%	200%	120%	**302%**	36%	288%	405%
1960	5,078	134.8%	1930s level	148	294%	427%	370%	86%	289%	39%	266%	356%
1970	**7,716**	**151.9%**	**HG 1960s**	150	279%	392%	307%	109%	278%	49%	218%	310%
1980	**12,468**	**161.6%**	**HG 1970s**	167	212%	364%	239%	138%	202%	62%	162%	238%
1990	11,515	92.4%		167	270%	483%	163%	**248%**	258%	128%	223%	321%
2000	**14,248**	**123.7%**	**HG 1990s**	168	283%	529%	196%	299%	247%	181%	222%	322%
2010	**17,150**	**120.4%**	**HG 2000s**	168	257%	472%	191%	346%	249%	**217%**	202%	287%
2016	*18,598*	*108.4%*		*168*	*245%*	*445%*	*184%*	*353%*	*240%*	*227%*	*201%*	*285%*

Source: Maddison Historical Statistics, Groningen Growth and Development Centre, University of Groningen, 2018, real GDP per capita in 2011 US$. www.rug.nl/ggdc/historicaldevelopment/maddison/.

Note: Switzerland pre-1900 data from Maddison, *The World Economy: A Millennial Perspective*, Table B–21. World GDP per capita, 20 Countries and Regional Averages, AD 0–1998. "National GDP per capita calculated as a percentage of the average GDP per capita of all nations": percentages in **bold** indicate the beginning of multiple decades of high-level performance by a nation.

Table 1.3 Resource-dependent states, 2016

Rank	Nation/territory	Natural resources rents, as a percentage of GDP	Rank	Nation/territory	Natural resources rents, as a percentage of GDP	Rank	Nation/territory	Natural resources rents, as a percentage of GDP
1	Liberia	49.9	26	*Middle East & North Africa*	16.8	51	*Heavily indebted poor countries (HIPC)*	*11.2*
2	Kuwait	44.7	27	Turkmenistan	16.7	52	Malawi	11.1
3	Iraq	42.4	28	Equatorial Guinea	16.5	53	*Small states*	10.5
4	Congo, Democratic Republic	32.7	29	Ghana	16.4	54	Chile	10.5
5	Suriname	29.0	30	Papua New Guinea	16.3	55	Lao PDR	9.5
6	Saudi Arabia	27.2	31	Iran, Islamic Republic	16.0	56	Brunei Darussalam	9.2
7	Oman	26.8	32	Chad	15.7	57	Gambia, The	9.1
8	Mauritania	26.2	33	Uganda	15.3	58	Zimbabwe	8.8
9	Congo, Republic	24.9	34	United Arab Emirates	15.3	59	Kyrgyz Republic	8.4
10	Mongolia	23.2	35	Zambia	15.1	60	*Sub-Saharan Africa (excluding high income)*	*8.3*
11	Guinea	21.8	36	Kazakhstan	15.0	61	*Least-developed countries: UN classification*	*8.3*
12	Sierra Leone	21.8	37	Niger	14.1	62	*Sub-Saharan Africa (IDA & IBRD countries)*	*8.3*

(Continued)

Table 1.3 (Continued)

Rank	Nation/territory	Natural resources rents, as a percentage of GDP	Rank	Nation/territory	Natural resources rents, as a percentage of GDP	Rank	Nation/territory	Natural resources rents, as a percentage of GDP
13	Qatar	21.1	38	Algeria	13.7	63	*Sub-Saharan Africa*	*8.3*
14	Azerbaijan	20.5	39	Gabon	13.5			
15	Burkina Faso	20.4	40	Central African Republic	13.5			
16	Timor–Leste	20.2	41	*Middle East & North Africa (IDA & IBRD countries)*	*13.4*			
17	Solomon Islands	20.2	42	*Middle East & North Africa (excluding high income)*	*13.3*			
18	Togo	19.8	43	Angola	13.2			
19	Guinea–Bissau	19.3	44	Mali	12.6			
20	Guyana	19.3	45	*Low-income countries*	*12.1*			
21	Arab World	18.8	46	Ethiopia	12.0			
22	*Fragile & conflict-affected situations*	*18.0*	47	Madagascar	11.8			
23	Somalia	17.7	48	Other small states	11.5			
24	Burundi	17.5	49	Russian Federation	11.5			
25	Mozambique	17.2	50	Uzbekistan	11.4			

Source: World Bank, World Development Indicators, 2016.

The natural resources rent is the total revenue generated from the extraction of natural resources less the cost of extracting those resources. The resources states are defined here as states whose natural resources rent is 8 percent or greater of GDP. Why the 8 percent threshold? Because above that point are clustered least-developed countries, heavily indebted poor countries, low-income countries, and the poorest land mass, sub-Saharan Africa.

resource-dependent states are poor rather than wealthy. States that rely heavily on the sale or export of resources are mostly low-income countries. There are a handful of resource-reliant states that are rich. However, their wealth is more the result of geological accident than the fruit of systemic human activity. It's the latter that is the basis of prosperity.

A handful of modern societies figured a way to harness human activity in a manner that mixed human purpose, order, and freedom in a historically unprecedented manner. This model proved to be exportable to would-be medium-income countries. After 1950, the model to varying degrees spread across the globe. The number of middle-income countries increased accordingly.[5] In 1950, the median GDP per capita for all countries was US$2,570; in 2016, it was US$12,464 (in constant 2011 dollars). Accompanying the growth of the middle-income countries, with levels of prosperity fivefold what they were 70 years before, was a mild increase in the difference between the median level of national prosperity and the upper level. In 1950, Switzerland had the highest GDP per capita (US$21,147). The median for all other countries was US$2,570, 12 percent of the Swiss figure. In 2016, Norway was the highest, with US$82,814 per capita.[6] The global median was 15 percent of Norway's level, and the global average was 22 percent of Norway's GDP per capita.

GDP per capita is a standard measure of prosperity. It is a useful shorthand for prosperity. But how useful? To what extent does GDP per capita capture not only the economic prosperity of a nation but also its social prosperity? What use is the wealth of a nation if that wealth is not also reflected in the longevity and literacy of the population and the moderate distribution of income across the nation? Consequently, the present study draws on social components of prosperity as well as economic ones. Yet, for all that, the difference between countries ranked by GDP per capita and countries ranked by multiple social and economic factors is not huge. Without the growth of real GDP per capita, the considerable blessings of modern life are simply not possible.

Circular causality

Prosperity exists. What explains it? The first thing to be said is that prosperity is not the result of a single factor. We cannot understand it if we try and isolate a sole dominant driver that is the 'cause' of it, any more than we can say that there is an 'independent variable' that strongly 'correlates' with prosperity. Prosperity cannot be reduced to a single cause. Rather, it is multifactorial. Many things co-create it. Social facts are complex. Reducing them to one or two driving forces misconstrues their nature.

As a consequence, among the multiple factors that are significant in shaping prosperity, none of them strictly speaking is the 'cause' of prosperity or

(more cautiously put) an 'independent variable' strongly 'correlated' with prosperity. Social causation does exist. But it does not work in the manner of a
law-like relationship. It is not the case that *if* X exists *then* prosperity follows.
Nor can we simply say that factor X is 'strongly correlated' with prosperity,
because social causation is circular. Social causes have effects. But those effects
are also in turn causes. Markets, for example, stimulate industries, propelling
their rise. But emerging industries also create new markets. A buoyant labor
market increases real wages, making larger houses more affordable. But, conversely, dense expanding cities stimulate productivity increases, allowing the real
wages in labor markets to grow. The cause is the effect; the effect is the cause.
Social causation is circular in nature.

Circular causation can be best understood as a pattern. It is like a color
wheel, a set of contrasting colors that are complementary. Contrasts operate
through oppositions; ratios and proportions organize oppositions into pleasing
complementarities. The pair 'contrast-complement' neatly sums up the kind of
ambidextrous 'contrary-harmonic' factors that animate prosperous economies
and societies.

Prosperity is not reducible to one causal factor or decisive variable. Rather,
it is a product of a number of significant factors. Each factor influences the
other. Every factor is a cause and an effect. All of the significant factors are
organized in a pattern-like manner. They contrast with each other; they complement each other. They are the effect of each other and the cause of each
other. Though it might sound complex, in reality those who participate in
modern social systems grasp this state of affairs fairly easily. This is because
human beings readily think in pattern terms. This is a deeply embedded
human cognitive capacity.

Patterns are formed by contrasts. Patterns organize oppositions into leg-
ible wholes. Black-and-white, void-and-mass, large-and-small, high-and-low,
foreground-and-background are typical kinds of complementary oppositions.
Patterns use devices like proportion, symmetry, rotation, homology, and ratio
to structure these oppositions in ways that are clear and easy to interpret and
understand. Via patterns, complexity is turned into a kind of simplicity. 'Pattern-and-ratio' constitutes one of two principle ways in which persons in successful modern societies orientate themselves. 'Pattern-and-ratio' provides the
basis for ordered liberty – the most satisfying and most productive way of living
in a modern society.

'Pattern-and-ratio' is not the only way that human beings classify things –
including themselves. They do so by rules (procedures, lists, sequences, registers,
and inventories), ranks (high-low, better-lesser, hierarchies, grades, statuses, and
identities), intervals (degrees of difference, more-less, larger-smaller), and ratios
(geometric means, harmonic means) (Table 1.4). 'Rules-and-hierarchies' is the
second principle way that persons in modern societies orientate themselves.
The paradigms of 'pattern-and-ratio' and 'rules-and hierarchies' compete for
the soul of modern societies.

Table 1.4 Social organization of polarities

Scale	Association of polarities a and b	Property	Mathematical operator	Relation	Operation	Statistical measure of central tendency
Nominal	Group name, identity, taxonomy of a and b	Classification, membership	$a =, \neq b$	Equal, not equal	Group	Mode
Ordinal	Rank, grade, hierarchy, status, social ladder-rung of a and b	Comparison, level	$a >, < b$	Higher (greater) than, lower (less) than	Sort	Median
Interval	Degrees of difference in the quantity or volume of a and b	Difference, range, extent, variance	$a +, -b$	Plus, minus	Measure	Mean, deviation
Ratio	Equilibrium, harmonization, counterpoise of a and b	Proportional relation of magnitude, amount	$a\ \phi, \propto, /b$	Golden ratio, proportion, ratio	Balance	Geometric mean, coefficient of variation

Source: Though it departs from it and is repurposed here, the taxonomy in Table 1.4 is indebted to the schema of measurement developed for the sciences by Stevens (1946).

Systems

Successful modernity has a strongly functional character. It generates inter-acting self-organizing systems. These, when combined, generate prosperity. Underlying this is pattern thinking. Pattern thinking combines opposites in pleasing ways. The intellectual version of this is paradox. Patterns are the stuff of everyday systems. Paradox is the stuff of the highest peaks of creation. Both run in parallel. Both are pivotal aspects of successful modernity. Highly proficient modern markets are inconceivable without the expectation of buyers that those who are sellers can provide goods or services that are simultaneously lower in price *and* higher in quality and the corresponding belief on the part of sellers that this is possible. This kind of pattern thinking suffuses successful economies and societies. Just as the price system is crucial to modern economies, so are engineering systems. The maxim of the engineer is to produce more outputs with less inputs. This is the technological criterion of efficiency – just as lower prices for higher quality goods is the market criterion of economy. Both are paradoxes.

Systems dominate modern life. This is in contrast to premodern societies. Systems are self-organizing. They lack central direction.[7] They evolve and adapt spontaneously. Millions even billions of persons participate in them every day. Each person makes decisions individually, none of which by itself determines the shape or direction of the system. But collectively these untold number of decisions coalesce into patterns of action. Individuals in turn respond to these patterns. They adapt their decision making and choices to take account of the prevailing social pattern. These responses, when combined, then reshape the patterns of the system. Mutual adaptation occurs, in this case at both the level of system and the level of individual.

Modern societies are built around five key systems: markets, industries, cit-ies, publics, and households. A sixth, lean government, is not so much a self-organizing system as a necessary complement of the quintet of self-organizing systems. These systems interact. Each is a system in itself and an environment for another system.[8] Each causes effects in the others. Those effects in turn act back upon the initial system. Causes have effects; effects act as causes. The result is upward and downward spirals of action and interaction.

The systems that dominate modern life are functional. The opposing twin of function is hierarchy. This includes both premodern social hierarchies and modern organizational hierarchies. Hierarchies organize societies via statuses. Persons belong to ranks. Ranks are structured like a set of Matryoshka nesting dolls. Hierarchies are stacked inside hierarchies, running from the extended family through the wider society onto the state. Premodern societies are typi-cally composed of a series of nested hierarchies. Each of these hierarchical units has to perform tasks and achieve goals. To that extent, hierarchies are functional. But their function is subordinate to that of status. Every rank, from the modest to the grand, has to obey a higher authority. This is true whether we are talking about a kin, clan, band, tribal, patrimonial, patron–client, or feudal society. Some mobility may occur between smaller and larger hierarchies and between up and down hierarchies. Societies transform from one kind of hierarchical stacking order to another. But the hierarchic principle of up-and-down, ascending-and-descending dominates. This is continued in modern societies where hierarchies are fused with rules and procedures. As the degree of functionality increases, so does the extent of organization-style rules and norms. As legal-rationality expands, so do organizational ranks and status positions that pivot on the production and documentation of rules and procedures, taxonomies, and modern group identities.

The alternative to a hierarchical society is a functional society that is based not on rank but rather on system. This is not a black and white distinction. There are a small number of premodern societies where we see some evidence of function competing with rank. This principally occurs in the case of ancient and medieval cities.[9] A functional society focuses on practical outcomes – that is, on matter-of-fact achievements or successes. Such practical successes do not have to be grand, nor do they have to be ostentatious. If the members of a rank society are concerned with recognition, gradation, and social station, the denizens of a functional society are more content to be anonymous and draw their sense of well-being from the general background atmosphere of economic and social prosperity. Their projection of the good life expresses itself less in affectations of rank and conspicuous displays of status than in the unruffled enjoyment of a generalized prosperity that rapidly translates all scarce objects into common ones. Today, it takes an average of eight years for a food item that appears on an haute-cuisine menu to appear in fast-food restaurants. Functional societies are much less concerned with reputation and good name, that is, with status, than hierarchical societies. Like a figure in a Vermeer painting, persons in a functional society focus on the conscientious performance of tasks. Doing a task well is a source of pleasure and happiness. At the general social level, task-driven behavior yields huge social dividends. It creates prosperity.

Self-organizing social systems are anonymous. They operate autonomously. They can't be planned by a central intelligence. Laws and rules can usefully condition the behavior of systems. Law is important because it can enforce contracts, restrain cartel and monopoly abuses, encourage the easy entry of competitors into markets, secure private property, and ensure the stability of the monetary system.[10] That said, the positive law of the state is only secondary compared to the non-state or natural laws inherent in a competitive market economy.[11] The point of the former is to support the latter. The operating principle of the state is different from that of markets. One of the paradoxes of markets is that (to an extent) they rely on the law of the state. This though is often conflated with attempts to direct the behavior of systems and engineer specific outcomes – planning and dirigisme. These attempts universally end in failure or worse.

In no small part this is because billions of people participate every day in markets and other systems including industries, cities, and publics. The number and nature of these system interactions and transactions is innumerable just as they are unpredictable. But that does not mean they are chaotic. Over time, systems manifest clear patterns: from cycles to equilibria, ratios to proportionality. No single person, group, agency, or institution establishes these. Instead, very large numbers of persons acting anonymously in autonomous social systems set these in motion unwittingly. Today, after two centuries of the wide-ranging development of such systems, they involve the larger part of humanity to one degree or another.

Creation

The complement of autonomous systems is the institution of creation. Creation is small in the way that systems are large. The smallness of the numbers of those who participate in the institution of creation makes it considerably less anonymous. Creation nonetheless works autonomously. Like systems, creation is difficult to direct or organize through 'rules-and-hierarchies'. That has never stopped governments and social groups from trying. Creation is the process of idea generation. It occurs across the arts and sciences but also across religion, free-floating metaphysics, and beyond. Over the long term, its fruits gradually filter into social systems, affecting how they operate and the expectations of their participants. Creation is a form of cognition. It is a way of thinking that entails 'contrast-and-complementarity', the union of opposites that characterizes the fruits of the human imagination. Although it might appear to stand at a distance from these, imagination is the precursor to all kinds of ways of enhancing productivity, efficiency, flow, adeptness, and efficacy essential to modern economies. It is the starting point for conceptualizing machines, methods, industries, products, designs, and myriad other economic phenomena.

There are relatively few persons who actively participate in the act of creation irrespective of the social domain. The act of creation is often confused with the act of transmission. These two are not the same. The transmission or diffusion of ideas is commonplace. The invention of an idea is rare. While few people engage in the act of creation, there are multiple levels of creation. The first level mixes together creation and transmission. For instance, there exist quite large book industries and patent industries, mostly clustered in a handful of countries. Books and patents typically mix the recycling of ideas with the invention of ideas. Mostly, they lean toward transmission rather than creation. We can also isolate the much rarer creative component: so rare in fact that in the past 3,000 years we have had barely more than that number of significant creative figures. Rarer still is the number who have explicitly engaged with the core engine of creation: paradoxy.

Successful societies are anchored in paradoxical worldviews. Historically, these include heterodox religions such as Taoism and Zen Buddhism in East Asia or Calvinism in England, Switzerland, the Netherlands, and the United States. Secular parallax worldviews play a similar role. William Shakespeare and Winston Churchill are good examples of the latter. Religious heterodoxies and public parallaxologies are dotted with rich pithy ambidextrous epigrams and formulations. Axioms such as 'what should be shrunken must first be stretched', 'whatever is desired cannot be had; what is not desired comes of its own', 'Nature's God', 'in order to be sure one must be unsure', 'time is money', 'no gain without pain', 'if men were angels. . .' are ways of thinking about the world that share a common kind of cognition, one that coalesces opposites. The 'opposites-attract' style of thinking encourages creative combination and the generation of patterns. On a social scale, this undergirds innovation, large-scale systems of exchange, and order that does not need rules – crucial traits in modern dynamic economies. It also guards us against the fact that conscious, purposeful, intentional actions (like legislation or strategic planning) often have unintended or unexpected consequences. As the nineteenth-century economist William Jevons famously observed, an increase in a society's energy efficiency can lead to the unexpected opposite: an increase in that society's energy consumption.

'Do more with less' and 'creative destruction' are influential examples of fruitful economic paradoxes. High-performing modern industrial-capitalist societies are typically energized by these kinds of paradoxes. The paradoxes can be comic, tragic, ironic, enigmatic, religious, or secular. Energy, drive, and propulsion arises from objects and events that are simultaneously tense and relaxed, taut and slack. The world's most prosperous economies and societies think and act paradoxically. Buried deep in their core are enigmatic, puzzle-like belief systems. These elicit interaction and cooperation via abstract patterns rather than codified rules or personal connections. Such patterns are more closely related in character to aesthetic forms than regulations or procedures, decrees or instructions. They combine antitheses. Pattern behavior is often accompanied by high levels of autodidactic, self-directed learning. Such factors when combined facilitate large-scale interactions between strangers. In so doing, they energize markets, industries, cities, and publics.

Notes

1 Groningen Growth and Development Centre, Maddison Historical Statistics, 2018, real GDP per capita in 2011 US$. All the GDP per capita figures that follow are in constant 2011 dollars. Gross domestic product (GDP) per annum is a measure of economic activity: the total value of goods produced and services provided in a country in a given year. In contemporary national accounting, this can be calculated for example by adding together the value of personal consumption spending, government consumption spending and gross investment, private gross investment, and net exports (the value of exports less imports). Maddison's calculation of historic GDP is explained in his paper 'Measuring and Interpreting World Economic Performance 1500–2001', https://crawford.anu.edu.au/pdf/edges/Maddison.pdf

2 The Roman data we have encompasses the Roman equivalents of today's Turkey, Tunisia, Portugal, Jordan, Israel, Iraq, Iran, Greece, France, Spain, Egypt, Switzerland, and Belgium. Groningen Growth and Development Centre, Maddison Historical Statistics, 2018, real GDP per capita in 2011 US$.

3 Belgium, Germany, Egypt, Spain, France, Italy, Poland, and Sweden, Turkey. Maddison Historical Statistics, Groningen Growth and Development Centre, University of Groningen, 2018, real GDP per capita in 2011 US$.

4 GDP per capita 2011 dollars: $3,277 UK (1800) and $3,334 Netherlands (1807).
5 Groningen Growth and Development Centre, Maddison Historical Statistics, 2018, real GDP per capita in 2011 US$.
6 That is Norway bar Qatar. Like elsewhere in this study, natural-resources-dependent states, Qatar included, are excluded from the study. Natural-resources-dependent states are defined as states whose total natural resources rent as a percent of GDP is 8 percent or greater. Natural resource dependency creates vast economic and social distortions. Sometimes, the distortions mean unnatural levels of wealth – wealth not commensurate with effort. In the majority of cases, the opposite applies. Located at rates above 8 percent we find the UN-classified least-developed countries in the world and the most heavily indebted poor countries in the world. Qatar in 2016 had a GDP per capita of $156,299. Qatar's total natural resources rent as a percent of GDP was 21.1 percent. Norway's was 5.8 percent. World Bank, World Development Indicators, 2018.
7 The best-understood of the self-organizing systems are markets. For an account of the spontaneous order that markets create, see Röpke, 1971 [1937].
8 Luhmann, 1995 [1984].
9 Murphy, 2001.
10 This was the argument of the twentieth-century German economic school of *ordoliberalism*. See Eucken, 1982 [1952]; Böhm, 1982 [1933].
11 Böhm, 1982 [1933].

Bibliography

Böhm, F. 1982 [1933]. "The Non-State <Natural> Laws Inherent in a Competitive Economy". In *Standard Texts on the Social Market Economy: Two Centuries of Discussion*, 107–114. New York: Fischer.

Eucken, W. 1982 [1952]. "A Policy for Establishing a System of Free Enterprise". In *Standard Texts on the Social Market Economy: Two Centuries of Discussion*, 115–132. New York: Fischer.

Luhmann, N. 1995 [1984]. *Social Systems*. Stanford, CA: Stanford University Press.

Murphy, P. 2001. *Civic Justice: From Ancient Greece to the Modern World*. Amherst, NY: Humanity Books.

Röpke, W. 1971 [1937]. *Economics of the Free Society*. Chicago, IL: Henry Regnery.

Stevens, S.S. 1946. "On the Theory of Scales of Measurement". *Science* 103, no. 2684: 677–680.

2 Space–time

Space

Pattern-based political economies are prominent in the portal cities, regions, and nations that are concentrated along the world's maritime circumference. The English geographer Halford Mackinder divided the world into three zones: the 'pivot' (Russia, Iran, Central Asia), the 'inner crescent' (China, India, and Europe), and the 'outer insular crescent' (UK, Japan, Southern Africa, Australasia, North America).[1] Mackinder's theory was geo-political. However, his categories, suitably adapted, also apply (perhaps even more strongly) to the geography of economics, wealth, and prosperity. Contemporary high-performing societies are overwhelmingly located either on the 'outer crescent' maritime circumference of the Eurasian landmass in North America, East Asia, North-Western Europe, and Australasia or on the portion of the coastal rim of the 'inner crescent' and the major river and lake systems that connect to it.

Geography does not determine prosperity. But that precept applies not only to the specific case of economic geography. While social causes exist, no social cause determines anything in a non-reciprocal way. Social causation is not a one-way street. Every cause is an effect and every effect is a cause. Some cause-effects are more important than others, but each is still circular. So geography is less of a strict determinant of economic and social prosperity and more a condition of its possibility. It is an important one nonetheless.[2] A classic case is Africa – its coasts have few harbors for the kinds of ports that have been the lynchpins of international trade and communications for the past five centuries.[3] The existence of ports, coasts, harbors, and river systems is not 'the cause' or even 'a cause' of prosperity so much as it is an explanation for its absence. Not having these factors in abundance is like missing some essential connective tissue in the world system.

As it was in 1800, 1900, and 2000, most of the world's wealth is concentrated on the world's maritime circumference and the major river basins that link to the world-rim. Today that means the following:

Outer crescent: Britain and the settler societies (the Anglosphere)
Inner crescent: Europe's North-Sea-Rhine-Po 'vital axis' – extending from the Benelux countries through the Rhineland and Switzerland to Northern

Italy with its Vienna (Danube), Paris (Seine), Lyon (Rhone), Munich (Isar-Danube), and Hamburg (Elbe) satellites

Outer crescent: The Nordic countries

Outer crescent: Maritime East Asia's island, archipelago, and city-states – Japan, Taiwan, Hong Kong, and Singapore

Inner crescent: Maritime East Asia's sea-girt 'inner crescent' South Korean peninsula and China's Shanghai, Tianjin, Jiangsu, Zhejiang, Fujian, Guangdong, and Shandon provinces

In the 1500s the Mediterranean Sea was still a major conduit for trade. By the nineteenth century sea trade had been replaced by ocean trade. But while everything changes, nothing changes. Consider the two most upwardly mobile contemporary economies: Israel and Slovenia. One borders the Mediterranean; the other, the Adriatic. Italy may be falling out of the top-25 most prosperous nations but its two near-neighbors show signs of falling upwards into that important tiny upper-bracket of countries. Repetition is common in the story of prosperity. In the second half of the twentieth century, ocean-going transport was replaced by air travel for people (though not for goods). Yet if we look at the pattern of the world's most visited cities, today mostly by air travel, we see that underlying this, little has changed. These cities are clustered on the world maritime rim in a pattern that would be immediately recognizable to a denizen of the nineteenth-century British Empire, the world's great ocean-straddling thalassic empire (Table 2.1).

Table 2.1 Port traffic, international visitors, 2016–2017

	Port	Country	Region	Location	TEUs 2017 *	Nation/ territory, city	Overseas visitors, millions 2016
1	Shanghai	China	East Asia	Yangtze Delta	40,233	Thailand, Bangkok	21.47
2	Singapore	Singapore	Southeast Asia	Malacca Strait	33,666	United Kingdom, London	19.88
3	Shenzhen	China	East Asia	Pearl River Delta	25,208	France, Paris	18.03
4	Ningbo-Zhoushan	China	East Asia	Yangtze Delta	24,607	United States, New York	12.75
5	Hong Kong	China	East Asia	Pearl River Delta	20,770	UAE, Dubai	15.27
6	Busan	South Korea	East Asia	Korean Strait	20,493	Singapore, Singapore	12.11
7	Guangzhou	China	East Asia	Pearl River Delta	20,370	Malaysia, Kuala Lumpur	12.02
8	Qingdao	China	East Asia	Yellow Sea	18,262	Turkey, Istanbul	11.95

Port	Country	Region	Location	TEUs 2017 *	Nation/ territory, city	Overseas visitors, millions 2016
9 Dubai	United Arab Emirates	Western Asia	Arab Peninsula	15,368	Japan, Tokyo	11.7
10 Tianjin	China	East Asia	Yellow Sea	15,040	South Korea, Seoul	10.2
11 Rotterdam	Netherlands	Northern Europe	North Sea	13,734	Hong Kong, Hong Kong	8.37
12 Port Klang	Malaysia	Southeast Asia	Malacca Strait	11,978	Spain, Barcelona	8.2
13 Antwerp	Belgium	Northern Europe	North Sea	10,451	Netherlands, Amsterdam	8
14 Xiamen	China	East Asia	Taiwan Strait	10,380	Italy, Milan	7.65
15 Kaohsiung	Taiwan	East Asia	Taiwan	10,271	Taiwan, Taipei	7.35
16 Dalian	China	East Asia	Yellow Sea	9,707	Italy, Rome	7.12
17 Los Angeles	United States	North America	West Coast	9,343	Japan, Osaka	7.02
18 Hamburg	Germany	Northern Europe	Elbe River	8,860	Austria, Vienna	6.69
19 Tanjung Pelepas	Malaysia	Southeast Asia	Malacca Strait	8,261	China, Shanghai	6.12
20 Laem Chabang	Thailand	Southeast Asia	Gulf of Thailand	7,670	Czech Republic, Prague	5.81

Source: Lloyd's List Top 100 Ports 2018, Maritime Intelligence https://lloydslist.maritimeintelligence. informa.com/one-hundred-container-ports-2018; Mastercard Global Destination Cities Index 2016 https://newsroom.mastercard.com/wp-content/uploads/2016/09/FINAL-Global-Destination-Cities-Index-Report.pdf *Container Traffic, in thousand twenty-foot equivalent units (TEUs).

In short, the world's wealth and prosperity clusters. These clusters considered as an entire set are neither Western nor Eastern, neither European nor Asian. They don't constitute a common language group. Nor are they composed of a common colonizing or previously colonized group of countries. Rather, it is the category-bending maritime rims and littoral-fluvial arteries of East Asia, North-Western Europe, and the settler societies of Australasia and North America that dominate the world's prosperity (Table 2.2). What distinguishes the settler societies is that they were seeded foremost as colonies of economic and social settlers rather than as part of empires of political control. When the latter motives clashed with those of the former, the latter lost out.

The littoral-rim group includes the island states of Britain, Ireland, New Zealand, Japan, Taiwan and Singapore, Baltic-framed Scandinavia, the South Korean peninsula, and the island continent of Australia with its economy concentrated principally on its coastal rim. The second – littoral-fluvial – cluster is composed of economically powerful coastal peripheries that are echoed, like a geometric fractal, by interior riparian portals dotted along connecting river and lake systems. The latter grouping is found in North America, Europe, and China.

Table 2.2 High GDP per capita metropolises 2014, 2 million or above population, 2010 PPP US$

City	Population size, millions	Nation	GDP per capita, US$ 2010	Zone
London	11.7	United Kingdom	58,243	Outer crescent circumferential and fluvial (Oceanic, North Sea, Thames River)
Greater Sydney	4.8	Australia	43,214	Outer crescent
Greater Melbourne	4.5	Australia	40,335	circumferential
Greater Brisbane	2.3	Australia	39,851	
Toronto	6.7	Canada	41,800	Outer crescent fluvial (Great Lakes)
Vancouver	2.4	Canada	40,824	Outer crescent circumferential (Pacific West Coast)
New York (Greater)	20.1	United States	71,862	Outer crescent circumferential (East Coast)
Los Angeles (Greater)	17.6	United States	54,632	Outer crescent circumferential (West Coast)
Chicago	9.6	United States	59,224	Outer crescent fluvial (Great Lakes)
Washington (Greater)	8.9	United States	68,146	Political capital; outer crescent circumferential
Dallas	7.1	United States	62,215	Outer crescent fluvial (Trinity River)
Houston	6.6	United States	71,576	Outer crescent circumferential (Gulf of Mexico)
San Francisco (Greater)	6.6	United States	88,562	Outer crescent circumferential (West Coast)
Philadelphia (Greater)	6.4	United States	62,180	Outer crescent circumferential, fluvial (East Coast, Delaware River)
Miami (Greater)	6.1	United States	45,179	Outer crescent circumferential (East Coast, Gulf of Mexico)
Atlanta	5.3	United States	54,079	Outer crescent circumferential (dry port + wet port, Port of Savannah)
Phoenix	4.5	United States	43,603	Outer crescent fluvial (Colorado River Basin)
Detroit (Greater)	4.4	United States	49,846	Outer crescent fluvial (Great Lakes)

City	Population size, millions	Nation	GDP per capita, US$ 2010	Zone
Boston	4.3	United States	74,376	Outer crescent circumferential (East Coast)
Seattle	3.7	United States	75,078	Outer crescent circumferential (West Coast)
Minneapolis	3.4	United States	62,821	Outer crescent fluvial (Mississippi River)
San Diego	3.3	United States	58,518	Outer crescent circumferential (West Coast)
Denver	2.7	United States	63,027	Outer crescent fluvial (South Platte River, Missouri River Basin)
St. Louis	2.6	United States	49,931	Outer crescent fluvial (Missouri River Basin)
San Antonio	2.3	United States	43,708	Outer crescent fluvial (Missouri and Mississippi River confluence)
Orange	2.3	United States	46,069	Outer crescent circumferential (West Coast)
Portland	2.2	United States	61,416	Outer crescent circumferential (West Coast)
Sacramento	2.2	United States	45,361	Political capital
Las Vegas	2.1	United States	41,260	Outer crescent fluvial (Colorado River Basin)
Cincinnati	2.1	United States	54,754	Outer crescent fluvial (Mississippi River Basin, Ohio River)
Cuyahoga (Greater Cleveland)	2.1	United States	55,751	Outer crescent fluvial (Great Lakes)
Vienna	2.8	Austria	46,779	Inner crescent fluvial (Danube River Basin, terminates in the Black Sea)
Brussels	2.6	Belgium	54,186	Political capital
Prague	2.1	Czech Republic	44,881	Inner crescent fluvial (Vltava River, southern part of the Elbe River Basin, terminates in the North Sea north of Hamburg)

(*Continued*)

Table 2.2 (Continued)

City	Population size, millions	Nation	GDP per capita, US$ 2010	Zone
Paris	11.9	France	61,469	Inner crescent fluvial (Seine River, terminates in the English Channel at Le Havre)
Milan	5.1	Italy	51,217	Inner crescent fluvial (Po River Basin, terminates in the Adriatic Sea)
Rome	4.4	Italy	41,849	Political capital
Hamburg	3.2	Germany	52,494	Inner crescent circumferential (Elbe River-North Sea-Baltic Sea Canal)
Munich	2.8	Germany	68,938	Inner crescent fluvial (Danube River Basin, terminates in the Black Sea)
Stuttgart	2.7	Germany	57,288	Inner crescent fluvial (Neckar River, part of the Rhine River Basin, terminates in the North Sea)
Frankfurt am Main	2.6	Germany	61,403	Inner crescent fluvial (Rhine River Basin, terminates in the North Sea)
Amsterdam	2.7	Netherlands	58,850	Inner crescent circumferential (North Sea)
Warsaw	3.1	Poland	48,592	Political capital
Madrid	6.5	Spain	42,102	Political capital
Barcelona	4.0	Spain	43,858	Balearic and Mediterranean Seas
Bern	*0.4*	*Switzerland*	*51,815*	Inner crescent fluvial (Switzerland intermodal between Rhine, Rhone, Po, and Danube River Basins; lake-dominated topography)
Basel	*0.5*	*Switzerland*	*70,399*	
Geneva	*0.6*	*Switzerland*	*63,515*	
Zurich	*1.3*	*Switzerland*	*64,140*	
Stockholm	2.2	Sweden	59,470	Outer crescent circumferential (Baltic Sea, egress to Atlantic Ocean)
Copenhagen	2.0	Denmark	52,672	
Oslo	*1.3*	*Norway*	*61,473*	
Helsinki	*1.4*	*Finland*	*49,252*	
Tokyo	35.3	Japan	42,551	Outer crescent circumferential (Pacific Ocean, Sea of Japan, East China Sea)
Higashiosaka	16.9	Japan	35,820	
Toyota	8.5	Japan	41,837	
Fukuoka	2.7	Japan	31,761	
Sapporo	2.2	Japan	30,964	

City	Population size, millions	Nation	GDP per capita, US$ 2010	Zone
Seoul	23.9	South Korea	33,254	Inner crescent
Gimhae	4.6	South Korea	28,549	circumferential (Japan
Dalseong	2.5	South Korea	21,327	Sea, Yellow Sea, egress to Pacific Ocean)
			2013 GDP per capita (2010 PPP US$)	
Shenzhen	3.1	China	121,304	Pearl River Delta, coastal, egress to the South China Sea and Pacific Ocean
Guangzhou	8.3	China	48,120	Pearl River city, egress to Pearl River Delta, South China Sea and Pacific Ocean
Xiamen	2.0	China	39,837	Coastal city, egress to Taiwan Strait, East China Sea, South China Sea, Pacific Ocean
Shanghai	14.3	China	39,172	Yangtze River Delta zone, coastal city, egress to the East China Sea
Beijing	13.2	China	38,477	Political capital, proximity to the Yellow River Basin, Bohai Sea and Yellow Sea
Tianjin	10.0	China	37,176	Coastal city, egress to Bohai Sea, Yellow Sea and Pacific Ocean
Dalian	5.9	China	33,598	Coastal city, egress to the Bohai Strait, Yellow Sea and Pacific Ocean
Nanjing	6.4	China	32,358	Yangtze River Delta zone
Mainland China	1357.0	China	12,367	

Source: Metropolitan areas dataset, OECD.Stat; National Bureau of Statistics China, China Statistical Yearbook 2014, 25–2 Main Economic Indicators of Provincial Capitals and Cities Specially Designated in the State Plan (2013); OECD National Accounts Statistics: PPPs and exchange rates.

Time

Space and place, geography and city, play significant tacit background roles in the creation of prosperity – both its possibility and its reality. However, prosperity does not express itself only in space. Time also is important. For prosperity has a history. And like the geography of prosperity, its history is not universal. High levels of prosperity develop during distinct time periods. 'High levels' in this instance means typically two to three times (occasionally more) the international average GDP per capita (Table 1.1). A small number of countries and clusters of countries have achieved this. To arrive at this rarified point, such countries typically move along two pathways. The first pathway is that of the hare. The second pathway is that of the tortoise. A third pathway – a boomerang pathway – is also worth noting, for what it reveals about the other two.

Hares

The hare route to prosperity entails dramatic consistent high growth over four successive decades or more (Table 1.1). High growth is defined here as 124 percent or higher growth in GDP per capita per decade. The first country to achieve this was Australia between 1820 and 1860. Finland did it between 1940 and 1990, France 1940 and 1980, Hong Kong 1950 and 2010, Ireland 1950 and 2000, Japan 1950 and 1990, South Korea 1950 and 2010, Norway 1940 and 1980, Singapore 1960 and 2010, Taiwan 1950 and 2010, and the United States 1960 and 2000. Germany's great growth period occurred from 1920 to 1980, interrupted by the catastrophe of World War II, from which it quickly recovered, courtesy of the American Marshall Plan.

High growth has gradually become a form of political legitimation, perhaps today the most powerful single form of political legitimacy. It is noticeable that when the party is over – when successive decades of high growth stop – political headaches begin. France is a good example. Nearly four decades on from its uber-growth phase, France today is sharply divided politically between its rural and rural-industrial areas in decline and its urban areas, considerably more prosperous but without the kind of growth rates to absorb the long-term rural and regional decline.

The United States for most of its history was a tortoise rather than a hare economy. That changed in 1960. After high growth stopped in 2000, a version of the rural-urban, poorer-prosperous divide opened up. In the 2010s, these divides acquired a populist-anti-populist political coloring. But this was a symptom of a deeper phenomenon, the uneven nature of the development and economic growth of the large metropolis compared with markedly less dense and less economically intense rural and rural-industrial areas (Table 2.3).

Table 2.3 Gap between national and major city GDP, 2012 GDP per capita (US$ 2010)

Rank	Nation/Territory, City	Plus or (minus), largest city GDP per capita compared to national-territory GDP per capita (US$)	Rank	Nation/Territory, City	Plus or (minus), largest city GDP per capita compared to national-territory GDP per capita (US$)
1	Germany, Berlin	(3,393)	16	Slovenia, Ljubljana	10,510
2	Australia, Sydney	(1,011)	17	Greece, Athens	10,762
3	Korea, Seoul	(919)	18	Switzerland, Zurich	10,833

Rank	Nation/Territory, City	Plus or (minus), largest city GDP per capita compared to national-territory GDP per capita (US$)	Rank	Nation/Territory, City	Plus or (minus), largest city GDP per capita compared to national-territory GDP per capita (US$)
4	Canada, Toronto	(441)	19	Ireland, Dublin	11,533
5	Hong Kong, Hong Kong	0	20	Italy, Rome	12,695
6	Singapore, Singapore	0	21	Estonia, Tallinn	12,773
7	Norway, Oslo	113	22	Finland, Helsinki	13,005
8	Austria, Vienna	4,069	23	Hungary, Budapest	14,274
9	Chile, Santiago	5,268	24	United Kingdom, London	17,646
10	Japan, Tokyo	5,502	25	Czech Republic	18,947
11	Mexico City, Mexico	5,513	26	Sweden, Stockholm	20,219
12	Netherlands, Amsterdam	5,952	27	France, Paris	23,325
13	Belgium, Antwerp	6,712	28	Poland, Warsaw	24,169
14	Denmark, Copenhagen	7,271	29	United States, New York	23,878
15	Portugal, Lisbon	9,958	30	Slovak Republic, Bratislava	30,192

Source: OECD Stats, Metropolitan areas: GDP from cities, 2018.

Table 2.4 Cities and productivity, United States, 2010

Average productivity per worker

United States US$113,000	**Large Metro Areas** US$119,000	Small Metro Areas US$99,000	Non-Metro Areas US$101,000

Source: Brookings Metropolitan Project, 2015, Figure 2.4. Larger metropolitan areas are more productive, 2010.

The population density and interactive intensity of the former, the big cities, substantially outstrips the latter.[4] This is measurable in the relative productivity growth of both over time (Table 2.4). Productivity is the single most important factor in generating economic growth. Periods of national uber growth paper over the phenomenon of uneven development and the gap between big cities and more sparsely populated rural and regional areas.

Tortoises

Not all high-achieving countries grow in a hare-like style. Many behave more like tortoises. They expand in a steady fashion. These countries rely on persistence rather than explosive dashes to achieve high levels of prosperity. The tortoises include Austria, Denmark, the Netherlands, New Zealand, the United Kingdom, the United States (until more recently), and Switzerland.

Switzerland is a 'perhaps tortoise' because we don't have good statistics on the country before 1860. For one of the world's great economies, Switzerland has been remarkably shy in tracking itself statistically. In any event, since 1860 it has been a very high-performing tortoise. As for the other tortoises, they exhibit a characteristic tortoise-economy mix of stronger and milder decades of per capita GDP growth without an uber phase of multiple sequential decades of propulsive high growth. One of the shared characteristics of this group is that they start the nineteenth century (or in New Zealand's case, the 1840s) with high levels of prosperity for the times. A subgroup of tortoises – Belgium, Denmark, Canada, New Zealand, and Switzerland – benefited from exiting World War II with their economies relatively intact compared with many others. New Zealand notably held on to that advantage till 1970 and then relinquished it.

The tortoise path means that a handful of nations at the beginning of the nineteenth century or by the mid-nineteenth century were already relatively wealthy. Their subsequent achievement was to maintain a steady pattern of middling growth decade after decade over the long term. This is important for two reasons. First, it indicates the power of patient dedication to a task over very long periods of time. Second, it indicates that prosperity in a number of cases has deep historical roots. Some of these roots extend back to the late Renaissance era.

All economies – hare and tortoise – undulate. Rates of growth and relative prosperity move up and down over time. This pattern though compares favorably with another more hair-raising kind of long-term undulation. South Africa and Argentina are cases in point. These countries have a pattern of high growth in one decade that they are unable to sustain for multiple decades. And rather than fall into a pattern of persistent growth over time, they follow a high-growth decade with low-growth or negative-growth decades. This start-stop pattern is distinctive. It generates promise followed by disappointment.

Notes

1 Mackinder, 1996 [1904].
2 Landes, 1999 [1998]; Sowell, 2015.
3 Duignan and Gann, 1975, 296.
4 Bouchet, Liu and Parilla, 2018.

Bibliography

Bouchet, M., S. Liu and J. Parilla. 2018. *Global Metro Monitor 2018*. Washington, DC: Metro Policy Program, Brookings Institution.

Duignan, P. and L.H. Gann. 1975. *Colonialism in Africa 1870–1960*, Volume 4. Cambridge: Cambridge University Press.

Landes, D. 1999 [1998]. *The Wealth and Poverty of Nations*. London: Abacus.

Mackinder, H. 1996 [1904]. "The Geographical Pivot of History". In *Democratic Ideals and Reality*, 175–194. Washington, DC: National Defense University Press.

Sowell, T. 2015. *Wealth, Poverty and Politics: An International Perspective*. New York: Basic Books.

3 Axiomodernity

Exceptional modernity

Prosperity is a modern phenomenon. Nothing prior in human history compares with it. For millennia, most human beings lived on the equivalent (in contemporary dollars) of three dollars a day or less. In year 1 of the Common Era, we have plausible estimates of GDP per capita for 14 countries – a large number of them provinces of the Roman Empire. The average GDP per capita of those country proxies was US$1,175 per annum in 2011 dollars, the equivalent of US$3.20 a day. The wealthiest country proxies were 130 percent of the Roman average. Those are estimates from parts of the (then) most advanced economy in the world. Fast forward a millennia or more. Across the entire 1300s, for Egypt, Italy, France, and Sweden, average per annum GDP per capita was US$1,620 or US$4.40 a day – only a slight uptick in 13 centuries. That remained as a general rule true until 1700 (Table 3.1). It then took until the second half of the nineteenth century for the average of all recorded countries to reach US$2,761 per annum and another century and a half to reach US$18,000 – or US$50 a day in constant dollar terms.

As there are rules in life, so there are exceptions. Thus it was that, after 1300, at first one then two and subsequently a handful of countries or regions began to depart from the towering historic human norm of near-universal poverty. At first the exceptions only proved the 3-dollar-a-day rule. Then after 1800 the exceptions rather than confirming that rule modelled a transformation of the rule to the point today that it is now a 50-dollar-a-day rule rather a 3-dollar-a-day rule, a staggering achievement across billions of people.

That said, throughout this momentous shift, the exceptions did not stop being exceptions. However, their number over time increased and they furnished systemic templates – that is, models to copy – that redefined the international economic median from the low-income one that had lasted millennia to a middle-income one. This was a remarkable, indeed epochal, transformation.

One in ten countries in the world today are exceptions. These are markedly prosperous societies whose GDP per capita is twice the global average or more (Table 1.1). The exceptions are all effective at embedding functional systems in their societies. They have to be. The core of modern prosperity is a series of

Table 3.1 GDP per capita, 1–1799, US\$ 2011. GDP per capita twice the average of all recorded countries

Year	Number of recorded countries	Average of all recorded countries (US\$)	Holland (part country) (US\$)	Italy (US\$)	England (part country) (US\$)	Belgium
1 CE*	14	1,175				
1300–1399	6	1,620		3,196		
1500–1599	12	1,507	3,415	3,050		
1600–1699	16	1,460	4,102	2,814		[2,489]‡
1700–1799	19	1,912	4,491	[3,067]‡‡	[2,819]#	

Source: Maddison Historical Statistics, Groningen Growth and Development Centre, University of Groningen, 2018.

GDP per capita twice the average of all recorded countries.

*Estimates for the ancient equivalents of Italy, Greece, Egypt, Iran, Iraq, Israel, Jordan, Tunisia, Belgium, Switzerland, France, Portugal, Turkey, and Spain.
‡‡169 percent of recorded global average.
‡171 percent of recorded global average.
GDP per capita in England in the eighteenth century was just shy of 150 percent of the recorded global average. The United Kingdom over 1700–1799 had an average per capita GDP of US\$2,679, 140 percent of the recorded global average.

The average dollar value to a recipient of a US welfare benefits package in 2013 ranged from US\$16,984 to US\$43,099 p.a. depending on US state. Source: Tanner and Hughes, The Work versus Welfare Trade off: An Analysis of the Total Level of Welfare Benefits by State, Cato Institute, Washington DC, 2013, Table 5, Welfare Benefits Packages as Percentage of Federal Poverty Level (FPL), 12–13.

systems that to a significant degree are self-organizing. These have developed markedly across the last two centuries: specifically large-scale long-distance markets, high-technology industries, big cities, nuclear households, and intensive reading publics. The art of lean government complements these. That said, functionality – powerful as it is – does not explain exceptionality. What does?

The pathways to exceptional modernity are variable. Some began as far back as the 1500s, others as recently as the last half century. Some nations have bolted to the top; others have sauntered there. From the viewpoint of time, there are multiple pathways to prosperity. From the standpoint of space, there is less variability. Modernity's exceptions share a common geography. They are spatially alike in inverse proportion to the degree that they are temporally divergent. They are all located on the maritime periphery of the Eurasian world-island. That is to say, countries that enjoy exceptional levels of prosperity are concentrated on the maritime rims of Australasia, East Asia, North-Western Europe, and North America and along major river and lake systems that connect to the last three of these rim zones.

On first observation, that common geography might appear to be a peculiar thing. But, as it turns out, to date it has proved to be an almost iron law of exceptional prosperity. Since 1500, the most prosperous societies have been located in four maritime-and-fluvial zones.

What is interesting in addition is that this is not without precedent. Before the modern era, arguably the peak of human civilization was the Axial Age, the period between the eighth century BCE and the third century of the Common Era.[1] This is a period in which money economies and long-distance trade develop along with big cities and the humanities. Three societies stand out: the Mediterranean sea–based states (thalassocracies) of ancient Greece and (originally) ancient Rome; Han China centered on the Yellow River; and the powerful Indo-Gangetic Plain state, the Indian Maurya Empire (and the subsequent the Shunga and Kushan empires). The three imperial states – Indian, Roman, and Chinese – traded with each other.

Trade is one thing. Prosperity, though, is another thing altogether. It is only after 1800, as societies begin to lift themselves above the GDP per capita norm of 3 dollars a day or less, did prosperity on a society-wide scale and eventually on a worldwide scale begin to develop. Nonetheless, the parallel between the Axial Age and the world's most successful modern economies is telling. Partly, the parallel between the two is spatial. It is also material. They are the most materially advanced societies of their time. But as well as spatial and material factors, crucially, the parallel between the two is also metaphysical. Standing behind their materialism, and in decisive ways making it possible, is a kind of metaphysics. Let's call this a metaphysics of creation.

In that spirit, I am going to use the term 'axiomodernity'. I am going to apply it to a series of societies. These societies don't just belong to the modern age or modernity. After all, there exists 'multiple modernities' – some of these are despotic, others are quite broken down. Rather, I am talking here about one specific type of modernity – one particular spatial and temporal slice of it. This slice, axiomodernity, has evolved gradually and on occasions traumatically in four distinct geographical zones: the maritime rims, major fluvial nodes and arteries, and primary river basins of East Asia, North-Western Europe, North America, and Australasia.

The reach of axiomodernity is not synonymous with 'Europe' any more than it is synonymous with 'the West' or with 'Asia' or the entirety of 'the globe'. It is not an artefact of the 'East', of the 'West', or of the 'world system'. Rather, it is a spatiotemporal sliver of the world – though its capacity to produce prosperity has global implications. It generates templates that spread around the world. Notably in the past half-century most of the world that was in a state of absolute poverty has been lifted out of it. Wealth and income in middle-income countries has grown substantially. Yet reaching high-income levels is very difficult. Expectations after the fall of the Soviet Union that some East European countries might rise to the top proved unrealistic. Having been released from the grip of the Soviet Empire they have remained stubbornly outside the most successful cohort.

Why is that? Simply put, material economies underperform if they are unable to routinely, that is to say tacitly, tap into a certain background metaphysics. If geography is a condition of what's possible and what's not, and history is its gradual, checkered unfolding, the question remains: the unfolding of what?

Location on the world's maritime circumference encourages actions at a distance, such as world trade or the republic of science. Those actions in turn encourage economic behavior that is based less on personal relationships or impersonal procedures – on hierarchies and rules – and more on pattern-based interactions. The key thing about patterns is that they integrate opposites. Take as one example the case of markets. Typically, when prices for a good rise, the quantity demanded falls. But if it's a Veblen good – a status good – should prices fall, then demand decreases. In the case of a normal good, if the income of consumers goes up, demand goes up. But for an inferior good, demand will fall. Conversely, if the price of a good goes up, the quantity supplied goes up. But as the price of inputs increases, the quantity of a good supplied decreases. Or as the effectiveness of technology increases, the price of inputs falls with the effect that the quantity of a good supplied at a given price will increase.

These are all subtle kinds of pattern-based interaction. They mesh antitheses together: rises and falls, status and function, income and expenditure, demand and supply, less labor and more output, and so on. That's the economic or social side of things. But pattern is also an aesthetic phenomenon. If we want to explain Japan's modern economic power, rather than begin with markets we can begin with Japan's distinctive Zen-flavored Higashiyama culture that originated in the 1400s. In any event, starting from either or both directions, we eventually get to the same point, namely, that powerful economies interpolate a high degree of 'contrast and complementarity' combined with an innate ability to strike an equilibrium between the two – a union of opposites – as between for example 'supply and demand'.

Using an older conceptual language, we can describe this contrarian-complementarian kind of political economy as an economy of grace. 'Supply and demand' is one of the building blocks of successful modernity along with the union of 'intimacy and distance' in personal behavior, 'foundation and innovation', 'creation and diffusion', 'creation and destruction' in technological industries, 'public and private' in cities, 'reflection and communication' in reading publics, 'exit and loyalty' in relation to organizations, and 'exit and voice' in matters related to government.

Janusian cognition

Fluvial-based societies and key maritime portals located on the world's littoral crescents tend to share a distinctive ethos. The German political theorist Carl Schmitt observed this in his study *Land and Sea*.[2] He advocated for landed states. He particularly had in mind modern Germany, the outcome of the nineteenth-century German Empire, not the old Germany of the Hanseatic cities with their *Fischmenschen*, or sea people.[3] Modern Germany, he argued, was a country whose ethos was earth bound and territorial, not sea going or oceanic. Its orientation was continental not global.

Schmitt observed that mercantile sea powers like England and America developed an elective affinity with Calvinism. This did not mean that they were Calvinist societies. Calvinism never had a large number of followers. Its long-run diffuse cultural impact, however, far exceeded its literal membership. Calvinism was one amongst many heterodox strands of thought in the modern age that produced outlooks conducive to high-growth economies. The particular case of Calvinism illustrates a more general point about how these interesting heterodoxies work and the kind of metaphysics conducive – even if more often than not paradoxically conducive – to materially high-achieving modern societies.

Calvinism's style – including its style of doing business – was distinctive. It encouraged a read-it-for-yourself type of thinking. The Calvinist injunction to 'read the Bible for yourself' echoes through key modern cultures of individual initiative, garage-style technological innovation, and autodidacticism. Calvinism stressed nuclear relationships rather than extended-family-kin connections or political patrimonialism.[4] It was comfortable with strangers.[5] This was the outlook of an economy and society that was mobile not static and sea borne not rooted to the earth. The Calvinist ethic emphasized hard work rather than good works. It valued production as much as consumption; saving as much as spending; labor and industry as much as rest and retirement. It encouraged trust in distant abstractions (prototypically God) instead of reliance on close-to-hand communities, personal connections, and social hierarchies. It preferred the operation of grace to the functioning of law.

All of this pointed, however distantly and in an unintended way, to a modern economy. Without these factors a high-growth economy is not possible. But Calvinism was also an off-spring of its era, the late Renaissance, a period of intense experiment, secular and religious, the age of *paradoxia epidemica*. In no small measure, the enduring legacy of Calvinism's heterodoxy was due to its paradoxy, in particular the way that its worldview blended necessity and volition, predestination and will, grace and law. Calvinists who believed that salvation had been foreordained by God at the time of creation would work tirelessly to signal to others that they were among the few who had been elected by God to be saved. This was deeply paradoxical, and as such it generated incredible energies. It combined intense purposeful this-worldly individual behavior with a view that the larger forces in life have a destiny of their own. It condensed both freedom and necessity, activism and fatalism into a remarkable mobilizing union of opposites.

This is not only energizing or mobilizing but also creative. For the ability to coalesce opposites, compound them, make a union of them, synthesize them, equilibrate, balance, fuse, merge, blend, and bond them lies at the heart of the act of creation. These are the means and media of the imagination. This is true whether we are talking about the little things of everyday problem solving and adeptness through the mid-range of large-scale technology innovation and market proficiency to the most abstract domains of the arts and sciences.

What is implied by what has come before is that modern prosperous societies have a tacit metaphysical framework. That framework can be expressed in secular and/or religious terms, but it is not identical with either. What is important is a metaphysical frame of mind that is woven into the deep background of daily social and economic behavior. Its structure accrues geological-like layers over long periods of time. Among the most important aspects of this frame of mind are ones that are Janusian in nature. These structure thought and behavior in an oscillating swing-shift fashion.

The word 'Janusian' derives from the word for the Roman god Janus. Janus was the god of the doorway, gate or passage between two contrary entities: inside and outside, beginning and end, war and peace. The Romans thought of January as akin to their two-faced god. The month of January looked back to the previous year while simultaneously looking forward to the promise of a new year. Janus was similar in character to Portunus, the Roman god of harbors. Both were associated with shipping, trade, and travel. Both rehearsed in mytho-logical terms a kind of axial 'marine reason'.[6]

Janusian thinking befits a society that began as a Mediterranean thalassocracy and whose trade eventually extended from Londinium to Trapezus, Carthago to Alexandria and Byzantium, and from Myos Hormos (Quseir al-Qadim) to Eudaemon (Aden) to Barigaza (Indian Gujarat), Muziris (Southern India), and the Mouths of Ganges River – across the Mediterranean, North Sea, Pontus (Black Sea), Red Sea, Erythraean Sea (Arabian Sea), and the Bay of Bengal. Indo-Roman trade intersected at various points with the Shanghai and Beijing to Tyre (Lebanon) and Bay of Bengal trade along the Silk Road routes. Rome was not a modern industrial-capitalist society. It did not possess an intensive growth economy. It did not enjoy generalized prosperity – nor did the larger world around it. But the Axial Age achievements of the Roman Empire and its mirror opposite the Han Empire and the Indo-Gangetic empires in between them were substantial. Their achievements – including detribalizing their pol-itics, monetizing their economies, and extending trade across the length of Eurasia – were remarkable and enduring.

Janusian cognition contributes a tacit framework for the oscillating pattern of expansive economies of all kinds. Such cognition does not move *from* a premise *to* a conclusion, as in the case of rationalism. Rather, Janusian cognition enacts a mental passage backwards-and-forwards between opposites. Janus represents a third-party passage between in and out. It is the mythical face on opposite sides of a coin. Janusian cognition is the uncanny resolution of the relation between start and finish, conception and delivery. It fuses movement that has an end with unending motion and the limits of ordinary time with eternity or immortality. It is the intellectual cognate of the Roman god Quirinus who is the armed protector of peace, that is, the peaceful Mars.

Janusian thinking represents the kind of rapid volte face (the act of turn-ing round in order to face in the opposite direction) implicit in the early-nineteenth-century French economist Jean-Baptiste Say's view that supply is not a function of demand but rather demand is a function of supply. This was not intended by Say to explain the supply of goods and services in an every-day sense but rather those rarer moments, crucial for high levels of prosper-ity, when an entrepreneur devises some product, puts it into the marketplace, and generates a massive demand for something for which no demand existed before the supply of the product. That kind of paradox drives modern dynamic economies.

Axiomodernity

If modern high-functioning societies are anchored in paradox, this anchoring has a history. It begins in a particular era. It waxes and wanes and wanes and waxes, in time. Similarly, it has a spatial dimension. That spatial dimension also is not universal. Rather, it 'takes place' principally, and certainly most deeply, on the maritime world rim and along the fluvial arteries that connect to that rim – in North America, East Asia, Australasia, and North-Western Europe. This history and geography is not fixed in stone. Yet it is slow changing. Today low-income nations can lift themselves up into the middle-income bracket. This requires effort but there is also a clear route to it. Adoption of functional systems of markets, industries, cities, and publics is a distinct pathway through modernity. This is not without its vexing issues or manifest resistance. A lot of people don't like functionality. Nonetheless, it is a reasonably straightforward pathway. Mainland China in its entirety, or Indonesia and Malaysia, are good examples of states moving along this course.

On the other hand, entering the high-income cohort of coastal China or Switzerland, Singapore or Australia is much more difficult. In no small measure is this because functionality alone – without a conducive background metaphysics – is not enough. Rather a distinct frame of mind is also necessary (Table 3.2). This frame of mind can be described in various ways: skeptical, wry, ironic, bisociative, non-dualistic, paradoxical – in short ambidextrous.

The ambidextrous frame of mind is not universal. It clusters in specific places. Nor does it come about easily. Sometimes, it is even a response to self-lacerating tragedy. A significant number of high-prosperity societies at some point in their history have experienced severe geo-political divisions and partitions. This does not apply to all of them. Some, like Australia and New Zealand, have a political history that is relatively placid. Others, like Sweden and Denmark, expanded and shrank but for all that they were not partitioned or torn in deep-going ways. Yet a majority of the most prosperous societies at some point in their history have been partitioned societies, whether it is Britain divided between the Anglo-Saxons and Danelaw territory; Germany between East and West Germany; Ireland between British Northern Ireland and the Republic of Ireland; British North America split between Canada and the United States; Singapore exiting its troubled union with Malaya; America severed in civil war; Hong Kong separated from the rest of China in the 'two systems, one country' arrangement; or Taiwan separated from China without formal independence. Aggravated geo-political dualism seems under certain conditions to be a seedbed for forms of economic non-dualism of a particularly energetic and productive kind. Successful societies transcend the suffering of a divided and lacerated condition with a combinative wit.

Table 3.2 Ambidexterity and prosperity

	Australia	New Zealand	Canada	UK	USA
Cluster	*Anglosphere; insular/peninsula state*	*Anglosphere; insular/peninsula state*	*Anglosphere; torn state*	*Anglosphere; torn state; insular peninsula state*	*Anglosphere; torn state*
Greater than twice the world's GDP per capita, decades	1860s-2000s (excluding the 1920s)	1860s-1910s, 1930s-1960s	1950-2016	1810s, 1840s, 1860s, 1880s-1890s, 1930s-1960s, 1980s-2000s	1910s-2000s
High-growth decades	1820s-1850s, 1870s, 1900s, 1930s, 1960s, 1990s	1850s-1860s, 1900s, 1930s-1940s	1880s, 1900s, 1920s, 1940s, 1960s, 1970s	1920s-1930s, 1950s-1960s, 1980s	1870s, 1940s, 1960s-1990s
Paradox social-historical context: partition-union, dualism-combination	Heavy transportation, migration from London and the South-East of England, 1778-1890; the uncanny nature (unfree-free) of the foundation-era emancipist class; lengthy pacific ambidextrous union-separation from the UK, 1823-1931	Lengthy, peaceful union-separation with the UK, from self-governing colony (1841) to sovereign independence (1931)	Union-division of Americans and Canadians; French and English Canadians; Britain and Canada (1763-1931), French-English divide, aka 'the two solitudes' (Hugh McLennan, 1945).*	Union-division of Anglo-Saxons and Normans; English and Celts; Crown and Parliament; Britain and colonies; the island nation and Continental Europe; city-country; London-regions, North-South	War and revolution cut ties to the UK, 1765-1783; UK transmitted four founding migrant cultures to the American colonies: Calvinist, Quaker, Cavalier and Scots-Irish reproduced in America as individualist, industrial, slave and military cultures
Paradox culture component	Urban-centered, mild Anglican Calvinism, neo-classical, ironic, comic, skeptical; the paradox of being an 'island-continent'	Sardonicism, self-deprecating laconicism, use of litotes, 'friendly but reserved', 'yeah nah' non-duality, black comedy	Ironic, satiric, parodic, self-deprecating culture; cultivates doubleness	Wit, irony, sarcasm, humor, satire, understatement, teasing; grace, dexterity and speed of switching between opposites	Not an ironic nation. A neoclassical political balance provides an institutionalized rather than verbal skepticism. Socially, tense amalgams of recurring polarities bound together by

a fierce sense of compensation and retribution

Paradoxy seed-bed	United Kingdom, 1600–1930	United Kingdom, 1600–1930	United Kingdom, 1600–1930	Anglo-Saxon, Renaissance, Neo-Classical, English-Romantic, Edwardian, Calvinist and Pietistic Methodist paradoxia	Classical antiquity; Renaissance paradoxia epidemica; United Kingdom, 1600–1750 translated into institutional balance terms
Characteristic of outlook	'Life is full of alternatives but no choice.' Patrick White, *The Aunt's Story*, 1948; the enigmatic 'walls-ceilings, beach shells-concrete roofs' of Jorn Utzon's The Sydney Opera House, 1973	'It is not easy to look tragic at eighteen.' Katherine Mansfield, *The Doves' Nest and Other Stories*, 1923	'Wealth is not without its advantages, and the case to the contrary, although it has often been made, has never proved widely persuasive.' J.K. Galbraith, 1958	'The whole object of travel is not to set foot on foreign land; it is at last to set foot on one's own country as a foreign land.', G.K. Chesterton, 1909.	'Dissatisfaction with the institutional structure… (is) widespread, but there is no effective means through which this shared attitude can be translated into positive results. Reactions against the excesses of bureaucracy provide the source for bureaucratic expansion.' James M Buchanan, 1975

(*Continued*)

Table 3.2 (Continued)

Cluster	Belgium	Hong Kong	Ireland	Israel	Korea (South)
	Cantonal/ partitioned/ torn state	Cantonal/ partitioned/ torn state; insular/ peninsula state	Cantonal/ partitioned/ torn state; insular/ peninsula state	Cantonal/ partitioned/ torn state	Cantonal/ partitioned/ torn state; insular/peninsula state
Greater than twice the world's GDP per capita, decades	1940s–2000s	1980s–2000s	1980s–2000s	—	—
High-growth decades	1850s, 1920s, 1950s–1970s	1950s–2000s	1950s, 60s, 70s, 80s, 90s	1950s, 60s, 70s, 90s	1950s,1970s–2000s
Paradox social-historical context: partition-union, dualism-combination	Till 1830 ruled by France, Holy Roman Empire, Austria, Spain, the Netherlands; once 'the battlefield of Europe'; a union of division between Dutch-speaking Flemish and the French-speaking Walloons—and the residents of Brussels	Ceded by China to the UK in 1842; from whence it became an entrepot; expanded by lease in 1898; briefly occupied by Japan 1941-1945; HK transferred back to China in 1997 as a semi-autonomous 'special administrative region'	Celtic kingdoms invaded by the Vikings, Normans, Tudors and Cromwell followed by establishment sectarian rule in 1600s, the Union of Great Britain and Ireland in 1801 and the partitioning of Ireland in 1921	Partition of the Ottoman Empire and British Palestine Mandate 1918-1922; 1947 UN partition of Jewish and Arab Palestine; 1947-1948 Civil War, Arab-Israeli War; independent state of Israel established, 1948	Since 1948, Korean Peninsula divided into North and South Korea. Annexed by Japan, 1910-1945
Paradox culture component	Belgitude self-mockery and surrealism in art	A 'one country, two systems' arrangement allows HK degrees of legal, administrative and economic	'The desire of knowledge, like the thirst of riches, increases ever with the acquisition	Hasidic enlightenment is ratso v'shov, a 'running and returning', an oscillation	Wonhyo's (617-686) philosophy of a non-dichotomous mind, the 'one mind' (Il-shim) made up of opposites that are reconciled and united

Paradoxy seed-bed	Renaissance *paradoxia epidemica* and *coincidentia oppositorum*, 1300s to 1600s	autonomy within the 'one country' of China Philosophical Taoism; Chan Buddhism; Britain's 'people of paradox' culture	of it', Laurence Sterne, *Tristam Shandy* Two waves of exilic literary culture, Goldsmith, Sterne, and Burke; Wilde, Shaw, Joyce and Beckett	Kabbalah, Southern France and Spain, 1100s; root: Talmud, 600 BCE	Philosophical Taoism; Buddhism; Confucianism; Calvinism
Characteristic of paradoxy outlook	Renaissance Franco-Flemish School of polyphonic vocal music; Rene Magritte, *The Red Model*, 1934; *The Empire of Light*, 1950; 'Georges Simenon... has been faithful to the concept of detective fiction as a search for social equilibrium', Becker, 1993	'I do nothing, and people become good by themselves. I seek peace, and people take care of their own problems. I do not meddle in their personal lives, and the people become prosperous.' Lao Tzu, *Tao Te Ching* 57	'Well, the way of paradoxes is the way of truth. To test reality we must see it on the tight rope. When the verities become acrobats, we can judge them.' Oscar Wilde, *The Picture of Dorian Gray*, 1891	Presence through absence, or to create the world, God must withdraw from the world (*Tzimtzum*)	Wonhyo's 'two truths' that are not two and yet not one: conventional and ultimate truth, the conditioned and the unconditioned, etc.; dualisms (specific and general, fine and course) that are not two separate things; that which merges dualities and yet is not one

(Continued)

Table 3.2 (Continued)

	Luxembourg	Netherlands	Switzerland	Taiwan
Cluster	Cantonal/ partitioned/ torn states	Cantonal/ partitioned/ torn states	Cantonal/ partitioned/ torn states	Cantonal/ partitioned/ torn states
Greater than twice the world's GDP per capita, decades	1940s-1960s, 1980s-2000s	1810s, 1840s, 1860s, 1920s, 1940s-2000s	1850s-2000s	—
High-growth decades	1960s,1980s-1990s	1920s, 1940s-1960s,1990s	1880s, 1920s,1950s-1960s	1950s-2000s
Paradoxy social-historical context: partition-union, dualism-combination	Occupied by Burgundy, the Bourbons, Habsburgs, Hohenzollerns, France, Germany and the Netherlands until 1839 followed by semi-independence then full independence in 1890 and German occupation in World War I and II	Medieval dualisms (kingdoms vs towns, province vs province, Frisians vs Franks) replaced by unitary Burgundy, Habsburg and Spanish rule. A confederation of provinces achieved independence in 1581 followed by the birth of a global mercantile sea-power	Confederation of rural cantons and city states from 1200s, disrupted by the Napoleonic conquest and followed by the restoration of the old confederal system (1814) marked by city-country conflicts and its regeneration as a federal state (1848) with significant local self-government	Ruled by Qing dynasty from 17th-century till Japanese assimilationist-settler colonization in 1895 followed by retrocession to the Kuomintang Republic of China in 1945, separated from Communist Mainland China
Paradoxy culture component	A state that is simultaneously a nation and a national cross-roads	'The reciprocal action of the opposites, inward and outward (spirit and nature), can lead us to see life — and therefore art — as a constant recurrence	'Is there an upward or downward trend? These are problems of successive equilibria... how does an upward movement go beyond	Mainland China and Taiwan: 'political alienation and economic integration', 'unification and independence', 'Taiwanese and Chinese' syncretism

		(in different ways) of the same thing, as continual repetition.' Mondrian, 1917–1918	the equilibrium point and itself become a cause of the movement in the opposite direction?' Pareto, 1906	
Paradoxy seed-bed	Cf. French, German and Dutch seed-beds	Renaissance *paradoxia epidemica* and *coincidentia oppositorum*	Renaissance Heterodox Protestantism (Calvinism)	Mahāyāna Buddhist paradoxical metaphysics, often syncretized with Taoism
Characteristic of paradoxy outlook	A modern Tower of Babel where local speakers switch unconsciously between Luxembourgish, French, German, Dutch and English	Pieter Bruegel the Elder, *The Fight between Lent and Carnival*, 1559; M.C. Escher, *Bird/Fish No 34*, 1941; *Ascending and Descending*, 1960	'Prayer unaccompanied by perseverance leads to no result.' John Calvin; 'Every form of addiction is bad, no matter whether the narcotic be alcohol, morphine or idealism.' Jung, 1961	'Although you may spend your life killing, you will not exhaust all your foes. But if you quell your own anger, your real enemy will be slain.' Nagarjuna, circa 150–250 CE

(Continued)

Table 3.2 (Continued)

	Austria	Germany	France	Japan	Singapore
Cluster	Core Europe	Core Europe	Core Europe	Insular/peninsula state	Insular/peninsula state
Greater than twice the world's GDP per capita, decades	1950s–2000s	1930s–2000s	1940s–1960s, 1980s–2000s	1960s,1980s–2000s	1980s–2000s
High-growth decades	1920s, 1950s–1970s, 1990s	1920s–1930s, 1950s–1970s	1920s, 1940s–1970s	1910s,1930s,1950s–1980s	1920s,1960s–2000s
Paradoxy social-historical context: partition–union, dualism–combination	The disintegration of the Austro–Hungarian Empire (1848–1922) into nation states with illiberal ethno-national and totalitarian world-views as capitalism, industrialism and urbanism generate militant reactions	An ungainly transition from feudalism to liberalism to statism and the consolidation of German principalities into the German Empire (1871–1918) with ongoing unresolved tensions between rural and urban, status and contract, personal and industrial, cosmopolitan and ethno-national, regional and national, Catholic and Protestant, liberal and illiberal world-views	Deeply-conflicted never-resolved transition from rural to urban society, status to contract, provinces to metropolises, absolutism to statism, liberalism to statism, notable for periodic waves of militancy and religious-secular tensions	Pre-feudal Japan: Decentralized government overtaken by Chinese-style centralized government; Feudal Japan: Centralized government declines in era of the 'warring states'; Western contact precipitates unification of the nation, isolationism, 'study of the nation'; Western contact (Perry) triggers recentralization of the state and modernization	Singapore federated with Malaysia in 1963 and was expelled from the Federation in 1965; the nominal union failed to bridge economic, political and ethnic divisions between the two nations

Paradoxy culture component	'Ornament is a crime against the national economy.' Adolf Loos, 1908; 'An aphorism can never be the whole truth; it is either a half-truth or a truth-and-a-half', Karl Kraus, 1909; 'There are women who are not beautiful but only look that way', Kraus, 1909; 'The making of a journalist: no ideas and the ability to express them', Kraus, 1909	'There are people who possess not so much genius as a certain talent for perceiving the desires of the century, or even of the decade, before it has done so itself.' Georg Christoph Lichtenberg, 1773-1775; 'You believe that I run after the strange because I do not know the beautiful; no, it is because you do not know the beautiful that I seek the strange.' Lichtenberg, 1776-1779	'But, is it possible for princes and ministers to be enlightened, when private individuals are not so?', 'Demand and supply are the opposite extremes of the beam, whence depend the scales of dearness and cheapness; the price is the point of equilibrium, where the momentum of the one ceases, and that of the other begins.' J.B. Say, *A Treatise On Political Economy* (4th edition, 1832)	Zen 'not two'/non-dualism: two are one and one is two; language discriminates, non-duality is beyond language	'had the mix in Singapore been different, had it been 75% Chinese, 15% Malays and the rest Indians, 15% Chinese, it would not have worked. Because they believe in the politics of contention, of opposition. But because the culture was such that the populace sought a practical way out of their difficulties, therefore it has worked.' Lee Kuan Yew, 1985
Paradoxy seed-bed	The Austrian Catholic Enlightenment; Viennese Modernist Classicism	Kant's antinomies, Hegel's dialectic, Modernist Classicism	Renaissance paradoxia epidemica and coincidentia oppositorum; Renaissance Burgundian polyphony and the contrapuntal chanson; Enlightenment skepticism and Pyrrhonism	Zen Buddhism; Higashiyama culture	Migratory Hakka Han 'guest people' 'outsider-insider' culture; South-east China coast diaspora culture impregnated with latent strains of philosophical Taoism, Zen Buddhism; Britain's 'people of paradox' culture

(Continued)

Table 3.2 (Continued)

	Austria	Germany	France	Japan	Singapore
Cluster	Core Europe	Core Europe	Core Europe	Insular/peninsula state	Insular/peninsula state
Characteristic of paradoxy outlook	'This process of Creative Destruction is the essential fact about capitalism.' Schumpeter, 1942; 'civilization begins when the individual in the pursuit of his ends can make use of more knowledge than he has himself acquired and when he can transcend the boundaries of his ignorance by profiting from knowledge he does not himself possess', Hayek, 1960	'It is not impossible that both of the contradictory statements may be true in different relations', Kant, 1781; 'If discord has arisen between intellectual insight and religion, and is not overcome in knowledge, it leads to despair, which comes in the place of reconciliation.' Hegel, 1832; 'Art is almost always a question of proportions', Mies van der Rohe, 1966	Equilibrium is 'the sole protector of general opulence', Boisguilbert, 1707; 'The perfect is the enemy of the good', Voltaire, 1772	'Motion in stillness', 'body's learning', 'seeing God in a place where there is no God', bitter-sweet sense of the transience of all things; Sesshū Tōyō, Splashed-ink Landscape, 1495	Hakka, a 'people of paradox' symbolized by the dandelion, the flower that thrives under the most trying conditions

	Denmark	Norway	Sweden	Iceland	Finland
Cluster	Nordic; insular/peninsula state	Nordic; insular/peninsula state	Nordic; insular/peninsula state	Nordic; insular/peninsula state	Nordic
Greater than twice the world's GDP per capita, decades	1920s, 1940s-2000s	1860s, 1910s-2000s	1940s-2000s	1940s-1950s, 1990s-2000s	1950s-1960s, 1980s-2000s
High-growth decades	1840s, 1920s, 1940s-1960s,1990s	1910s,1940s-1970s,1990s	1890s,1920s,1940s-1960s	1950s-1970s	1920s,1940s-1980s
Paradoxy social-historical context: partition-union, dualism-combination	Kalmar Union of Danish, Norwegian and Swedish kingdoms, 1397-1523; Union of Danish and Swedish kingdoms, 1524-1814; United Kingdoms of Sweden and Norway, 1814-1905	Kalmar Union of Danish, Norwegian and Swedish kingdoms, 1397-1523; Union of Danish and Swedish kingdoms, 1524-1814; United Kingdoms of Sweden and Norway, 1814-1905	Kalmar Union of Danish, Norwegian and Swedish kingdoms, 1397-1523; Union of Danish and Swedish kingdoms, 1524-1814; United Kingdoms of Sweden and Norway, 1814-1905	Norwegian settlers, Danish dependency (1523), home rule (1874), Union with Denmark (1918), independent republic (1944)	Swedish rule (1600s-1809), autonomous Duchy of Russian Empire (1809-1917); national independence (1917)
Paradoxy culture component	Intellectual irony: Niels Bohr chose as his motto Contraria Sunt Complementa, Opposites are complementary, 1947. A culture of irony, sarcasm, and dry humor	Political irony: inside and outside the European Union, sovereign state and rule-taker simultaneously, self-determination-subordination paradox	Social irony: nominal high egalitarianism generates low actual gender equality, the paradox of rhetoric and reality, goal and pattern	A society immersed in pagan-Christian, technology-landscape, industry-nature, urban-country parallaxes	The paradox of being squeezed between two empires, expressed in dark, dry, sarcastic, and self-deprecating humor

(Continued)

Table 3.2 (Continued)

Paradoxy seed-bed	Heterodox Protestantism (Pietism); Baltic philosophical paradoxia: Immanuel Kant and Soren Kierkegaard; Niels Bohr's philosophical physics of complementarity; Nordic Modernist Classicism	Heterodox Protestantism (Pietism); Baltic philosophical paradoxia: Immanuel Kant and Soren Kierkegaard; Nordic Modernist Classicism	Heterodox Protestantism (Pietism); Emanuel Swedenborg's science mysticism; Baltic philosophical paradoxia: Immanuel Kant and Soren Kierkegaard; Nordic Modernist Classicism	Culture-nature, landscape-memory symbiosis forged by twentieth-century urbanization and modernization	Nordic Modernist Classicism '…the best designs should comply with classical norms… Human life is a combination of tragedy and comedy. The shapes and designs which surround us are the music accompanying this tragedy and this comedy.' Alvar Aalto, 1957
Characteristic of paradoxy outlook	'Just as philosophy begins with doubt, so also a life that may be called human begins with irony.' 'Irony limits, finitizes, and circumscribes and thereby yields truth, actuality, content; it disciplines and punishes and thereby yields balance and consistency.' Kierkegaard, *The Concept of Irony*, 1841	'A voice cries: "Now shalt thou create and be created"'; 'To be wholly oneself! But how, with the weight of one's inheritance of sin?' Henrik Ibsen, *Brand*, 1865	Swedish design: chaste balance of powers signifying frugality, humility, restraint, sense of duty and order; 'And if others have done it before me, then it pleases me that I have not been alone in my "paradoxes," as all discoveries are called.' August Strindberg, Preface to *Miss Julie*, 1888	Landscape redolent with memories; high national regard for independence and self-reliance combined with high levels of social friendship	Sam Vanni, *Contrapunctus* (Counter-point) mural, Adult Education Institute, 1959–1960, an abstract painterly representation of musical counter-point, the combining of two or more melodies in a musical composition, and the contrasting of chaos and order, abstraction and figuration

Source: James Jupp, The Australian People: An Encyclopedia of the Nation, Its People and Their Origins, Cambridge, Cambridge University Press, 2001, 293–297; Linda Hutcheon, Splitting Images: Contemporary Canadian Ironies, Oxford University Press, 1991; J.K. Galbraith, The Affluent Society, New York, Houghton Mifflin, 1998 [1958], 1; Patrick White, The Aunt's Story, London, Vintage, 1998 [1948]; DovBer Pinson, The Garden of Paradox: The Essence of Non Dual Kabbalah, IYYN Publishing, Brooklyn NY, 2012; C.G. Jung, Memories, Dreams, Reflections, New York, Vintage, 1989 [1961], 329; John Calvin, Institutes of the Christian Religion; Oscar Wilde, The Picture of Dorian Gray; Katherine Mansfield, 'Taking the Veil', The Doves' Nest and Other Stories, 1923; Alvar Aalto quote: lecture, November 15, 1957, given at the 'Schöner wohnen' ('To live more beautifully') design forum in Munich; James M. Buchanan, The Collected Works of James M. Buchanan, vol. 7 (The Limits of Liberty: Between Anarchy and Leviathan), 1975; J.A. Schumpeter, Capitalism, Socialism and Democracy, 1942, Part II, Chapter VII; F.A. Hayek, The Constitution of Liberty, 1961, part 1, chapter 2; Immanuel Kant, Critique of Pure Reason, 1781; G.W.F. Hegel, Lectures on the Philosophy of Religion, 1832; Mies van der Rohe in conversation with Bayerischer Rundfunk (Bavarian Broadcasting) in Der Architekt, 1966, 324; Piet Mondrian, Neoplasticism in Painting, 1917–1918; Vilfredo Pareto, Manual of Political Economy, 1906; Becker quote: 'Georges Simenon . . . has been faithful to the concept of detective fiction as a search for social equilibrium, an attempt to support and bolster the civilization and institutions created by human intelligence that assure us a certain order and tranquility', Lucille Frackman Becker, 'Science and Detective Fiction: Complementary Genres on the margins of French Literature' in Freeman G Henry (ed) On the Margins, Amsterdam, Rodopi, 1993; Boisguilbert quote: Gilbert Faccarello, The Foundations of 'Laissez-Faire': The Economics of Pierre de Boisguilbert, London, Routledge, 1999, 167; Hakka dandelion metaphor: Asia Society Northern California, Defining Hakka Identity: From History to Culture and Cuisine; Adolf Loos, Ornament and Crime, 1908; Lee Kuan Yew, President's Address, Debate on President's Address, Parliament of Singapore, March 1, 1985; Karl Kraus, Die Fackel no. 270/71, 19 January 1909; Sprüche und Widersprüche (Dicta and Contradictions), 1909; Half-truths & One-and-a-half Truths, 1986 [1909]; G.C. Lichtenberg, Notebooks E and F

Background: Modernist classicism: Peter Murphy and David Roberts, Dialectic of Romanticism, London, Continuum, 2004; Kenneth E. Silver, Chaos and Classicism, Art in France, Italy and Germany 1918–1936, New York, Guggenheim Museum Publications, 2010; Theodore Ziolkowski, Classicism of the Twenties: Art, Music and Literature, Chicago, University of Chicago Press, 2015; John Stewart, Nordic Classicism: Scandinavian Architecture 1910–1930, London, Bloomsbury, 2018; Austrian Catholic Enlightenment: Nicholas Till, Mozart and the Enlightenment, London, Faber and Faber, 1992; French skeptical Enlightenment: Peter Gay, The Enlightenment: An Interpretation Volume 1 The Rise of Modern Paganism, London, Weidenfeld and Nicolson, 1966; Richard Henry Popkin, The History of Scepticism: From Savonarola to Bayle, Oxford, Oxford University Press, 2003; Sébastien Charles, Plíni J. Smith (eds) Scepticism in the Eighteenth Century: Enlightenment, Lumières, Aufklärung, Dordrecht, Springer, 2013; Renaissance paradoxia epidemica and coincidentia oppositorum: Robert Grudin, Mighty Opposites: Shakespeare and Renaissance Contrariety, Berkeley, University of California Press, 1979; Rosalie Colie, Paradoxia Epidemica: The Renaissance Tradition of Paradox, Princeton, Princeton University Press, 1966; Iceland: Karl Benediktsson and Katrín Anna Lund (eds) Conversations With Landscape, Farnham, Ashgate, 2010.

*After the Seven Years War, New France came under British rule in 1763. The Quebec Act of 1774 established Quebec's autonomy on the basis of the French language, Catholic religion, and French civil law.

The most succinct cultural expression of a non-dualistic frame of mind is the joke: in humor, irony, satire, and parody we find the least self-conscious yet deepest idioms for expressing unions of opposites. The joke though is a none-too-easy phenomenon to measure and track in a quantitative sense. Easier to do, as a proxy for wit and humor in general, is the epigram, intellectual humor in its most concentrated form. The pattern of the epigram – the distribution of its origins worldwide – follows closely the location and pattern of axial moder-nity (Table 3.3). That said, a proxy is still only a substitute for the real thing. Using words as the proxy for the operation of the mind tends to screen out the role of visual, auditory, sculptural, kinetic, musical, and mathematical forms of the imagination. There are also many kinds of enigma. Take the case of China (Table 3.4). The cultural correlate of the rise of the coastal rim of China – from Guangdong to Shanghai and the Yellow River Basin onward to Tianjin and Beijing – is the paradox-laced philosophical-religious legacy of China's first Axial Age as well as the country's rich history of jokes, satire, humor, parody, and satire. A propensity for irony, parody, and satire or a knack for skeptical, enig-matic, or paradoxical world views is the mental counter-part of the quantum-like swing-shifts, waves, and oscillations characteristic of dynamic and creative economies.

I suppose we don't normally consider Calvinism to be a barrel of laughs. Yet it had a deep impulse to enantiodromia. This is the impulse to turn things into their opposites in the course of time. The sense that life is a mix of what is *enantios* (opposite) and *dromos* (that which runs its course) is the basis of the modern economic cycles. The deep root of this way of thinking, like that of the enigmatic union of freedom and necessity in the Calvinist work ethic, lies in the late Renaissance. It was part of a wellspring of paradoxical worldviews that bubbled up in that era. Whether the outlook is religious or secular, whether it pivots to John Calvin, Francis Bacon, William Shakespeare, or John Donne, or somewhere in between them is less important than the ability of this way of thinking to condense opposites into paradoxical unions.

The move towards generalized prosperity starts in the late nineteenth cen-tury when economic growth begins to spread across the world. But the model for growth economies is older. Prosperity is an historical phenomenon that starts at a specific point in time. A handful of states pioneer economic growth from the late Renaissance onwards. Indeed, in the case of these seedbed socie-ties, much of their economic success in the nineteenth and twentieth centuries is a case of building steadily on the already significant levels of GDP per capita that they had achieved by the end of the eighteenth century (Table 1.1).

The seedbed societies are the exception that prove the rule that almost no economic growth in real terms occurred between the beginning of the Roman Empire and the start of the nineteenth century. What occurs after 1800 sharply differentiates modern societies from their predecessors. No premodern socie-ties enjoyed anything comparable either in terms of broad prosperity or in terms of increasing standards of living. The period between 1500 and 1800 is an intermediate stage. In this intermediate phase, an 'axis' of countries, or more

Table 3.3 Epigrams per million population

	Take-off half century		Take-off: GDP per capita is 150 percent or more of documented world GDP in most decades of the half century								Militant era		
Nation	1500–1549	1550–1599	1600–1649	1650–1699	1700–1749	1750–1799	1800–1849	1850–1899	1900–1949	1950–2000	1990–
Australia									0.4	1.6	
Austria								1.2	13.7	3.6	
Belgium						1.8					
Canada								4	2.3	1.3	
Czech									1.9	2.9	
Denmark								10.6	2.4		
France	0.1	2.8	0.3	5.1	2.6	5.8	3	3.2	6.1	1	
Germany	0.2					6.7	1.2	1.7	1.9	0.1	
Hungary					7.7	11.9	0.1		1.1	1.6	
Ireland	1.1			0.7				50	12.1	3.1	
Italy	3				0.5		0.2		1	0.4	
Netherlands			2.5						0.1	0.1	
Romania										2.8	
Spain	0.2		1.5						1.5		
Sweden		1.7			0.5	23.3			1.2		
Switzerland								5.4	4.1	0.2	
United Kingdom		19.3	28.8	8.3	22	6.5	14.1	9	11.8	6.1	
United States					11	0.5	6.9	4.8	2.6	1.2	

Source: M.J. Cohen, The Penguin Dictionary of Epigrams, London, England, 2001; population data: Angus Maddison, Growth of World Population GDP and GDP Per Capita before 1820, Table B – 10, World Population, 20 Countries and Regional Totals, AD 0–1998; www.populstat.info/; www.tacitus.nu/historical-atlas/population/; http://geography.cz/geograficke-rozhledy/wp-content/uploads/2007/10/str26-27.pdf

Note: Table 3.3 includes only countries in which the count for at least one period is 1 or higher. For the purpose of this table, the epigram authors are classified by their country of birth rather than their country of residence. The table sets out the incidence per capita of the epigrams listed in Cohen, 2001, for each period and by nation. The per capita figure is arrived at using the size of each national population at the midpoint of each half-century. The principal aim of the table is to show the relative incidence of prominent epigram creation as this occurs between different nations and periods. The body of work of each epigram creator is dated to 40 years after their birth.

Table 3.4 Heterodox religion: Chan, Seon, Zen Buddhism, number of major figures (masters) per 10 million population average, 600s–1900s

	600s	700s	800s	900s	1000s	1100s	1200s
China	0.2	**4.6**	**7.5**	**2.9**	1.6	1	0.7
Korea							
Japan						1.4	**10**
	1300s	1400s	1500s	1600s	1700s	1800s	1900s
China			0.1	0.1			
Korea	**6**		0.9			1.3	**9.1**
Japan	**10**	2		2.3	1.1	0.3	0.9

Source: Ingrid Fischer-Schreiber, Franz-Karl Ehrhard, Kurt Friedrichs, Michael S. Diener, The Encyclopedia of Eastern Philosophy and Religion: Buddhism, Hinduism, Taoism, Zen – A Complete Survey of the Teachers, Traditions, and Literature of Asian Wisdom, Boston, Shambhala, 1989; Korean Buddhism Net, Korean Seon Masters

Source for historic population estimates: Ko Dong Hwan, 'When did Joseon's population reach ten million?' in Everyday Life in Joseon-era Korea: Economy and Society, edited by Michael D. Shin, Leiden, Brill, 2014; Population Statistics, Korea www.populstat.info/; Angus Maddison, Growth of World Population GDP and GDP Per Capita before 1820, Table B – 10, World Population, 20 Countries and Regional Totals, AD 0–1998; Jean-Noël Biraben, 'The History of the Human Population From the First Beginnings to the Present' in Demography: Analysis and Synthesis (eds) Graziella Caselli, Jacques Vallin, Guillaume J. Wunsch Vol 3, Chapter 66, 5–18, Academic Press, San Diego, 2005, Table 66–1; William Wayne Farris, Japan's Medieval Population: Famine, Fertility, and Warfare in a Transformative Age, University of Hawaii Press, Honolulu, 2006; Judith Banister, 'A Brief History of China's Population' in Dudley L. Poston and David Yaukey (eds) The Population of Modern China, Boston, Springer, 1992, 52, Table 3.1 Historical Population Estimates AD 2–1953; *Years 700–1000:* Hu Huanyong, ed, The population geography of China, Shanghai, East China Normal University Press, 1984, 10 cited in www.china-profile.com, Analyses: Tables, Figures and Maps, China's population: AD 0–2050, 18 December 2011 www.china-profile.com/data/fig_pop_0-2050.htm

Note: The table includes all Chan, Seon, and Zen Buddhist masters listed in Fischer-Schreiber et. al. and Koran Buddhism Net: 30 for Korea, 144 for China, and 30 for Japan. A high incidence of masters per capita is indicated in boldface.

specifically cities, ranging from the city-states of Northern Italy through Switzerland to the Netherlands and Belgium to England, began to seed and pioneer a distinctive kind of modernity – an axiomodernity. That model eventually spreads elsewhere. But it began, in the late Renaissance era, with a distinctive heterodox ethos.

The past of the past

That said, nothing is completely unprecedented, for the Renaissance, itself, was a cultural rebirth. In part what was reborn was a prior, much older, wellspring of paradoxical cultures and seedbed societies in the Axial Age, the period between the eighth century BCE and the third century of the Common Era. This period gave rise to a series of energetic societies with richly paradoxical worldviews. This period is notable for the development of coinage, money economies, and the expansion of long-distance trading networks. Innovative non-tribal political forms developed, including the citizen-city, city federations, republics, and 'civilizational' empires. The Maurya Empire era was the seedbed of Buddhism and Jainism; the Zhou Dynasty of Han China intersected with the development in the Yellow River Basin of multiple contending philosophies, Taoism, the *yin-yang* Naturalists, and (what we can guess about) the School of Forms and Names among them; while Greco-Roman antiquity saw a long procession of philosophies and theories that speculated about the 'union of opposites' and the 'mean between extremes'. These ranged from the Pre-Socratics through Plato and Aristotle to the Epicureans, Stoics, and Sceptics.

The Renaissance witnessed a re-birth of one of these clusters, the Greco-Roman constellation. The model of the modern prosperous society and economy grew out of this almost unconsciously. The philosophers, dramatists, and theologians of the Renaissance did not write systematic treatises on financial management or political economy. Any more than a handful of their contemporaries read what they wrote. The first treatise on what is, in sketch, an outline of a modern economy arguably appears in the work of the French thinker and Jansenist Pierre Boisguilbert in the late 1600s and early 1700s. Jansenism was a theological movement, originating with the Dutch Catholic bishop Cornelius Jansen (1585–1638), who emphasized Augustinian, which is also to say Calvinist style, ideas of grace and predestination. Jansenism was in effect a paradoxical Catholic-Calvinist hybrid.[7] Among those attracted to it were Jean Racine and Alexis de Tocqueville.

Jansenism was also the intellectual basis for the 'Austrian Enlightenment'. For a period from the 1740s to the 1780s the Austro-Hungarian Empire was influenced by the Jansenist form of Catholicism.[8] Jansenism is one of those heterodox intellectual milieus whose influence far exceed their size. In the Austro-Hungarian case, Jansenism spread as a consequence of the Habsburg monarchy's control of the Austrian Netherlands between 1714 and 1797. The Austrian Empire controlled the 'Southern Netherlands' made up in essence of Belgium and Luxembourg. The structure of thought of the Jansenist 'Catholic Puritans' bridged the acutest abyss in European religious thought. The traces they left behind provided the deep context for the remarkable series of economic thinkers that Austria produced between the 1870s and the 1920s. This was also the context from which the anti-Baroque spirit of Viennese intellectual modernism sprang as well as the satire of Karl Krauss. Two of three of the most influential economic thinkers of the twentieth century, Joseph Schumpeter and Friedrich Hayek, were Austrians. Their views, though different in many respects and almost entirely secular in nature, share a common way of seeing the world in comic Pascalian terms, where paradox rather than reason explains the most important aspects of human experience.

As Blaise Pascal, the philosopher, mathematician, and seventeenth-century French Jansenist, put it, human beings know that they know and on the other hand they know that they cannot know fully. Their limited knowledge is a sign of their wretchedness. Their knowledge of their limited knowledge is a sign of their grandeur.[9] In short, human beings live in a state of 'two equally constant truths'.[10] At first glance, this metaphysics of paradox may appear to be distant from everyday practical experience. And for many purposes that is true.

Nonetheless a subtle bond between the two exists. Among the many things he did, Pascal invented the first scheduled public bus service in 1661, in Paris, then a city of over half a million residents, merging the idea of a fixed schedule and route with the multi-passenger horse-drawn carriage.

Many of the most ingenious forms of economic behavior require a balance to be struck between two equally constant truths. Such a union of opposites tacitly expressed itself in the adoption of double-entry bookkeeping by Genoa's merchants in the 1300s. Double-entry bookkeeping was the principle that in maintaining financial records, every transaction has an equal and opposite effect in at least two different accounts (debit and credit, liabilities and assets, inventory and cash, etc.). A merchant's business is trade not metaphysics. Yet metaphysics – whether it is religious, secular, or syncretic – percolates in the background. Korea's Kaesong merchants developed a four-sided ledger method – recording the receiver's name, the giver's name, the commodity or cash received, and the commodity or cash disbursed – in the mid-Goryeo period during the eleventh to thirteenth centuries. That parallels the adoption of Seon Buddhism as the state religion in the same Goryeo era.[11] Seon was Korea's version of Chinese Chan or Japanese Zen Buddhism. All of these derived ultimately from the merger of Taoist quasi-philosophical paradox with Mahāyāna Buddhist metaphysics.[12]

In their financial accounts, eleventh- and twelfth-century Jewish bankers and merchants in Cairo would record cash receipts in one column and cash payments in another column. These would be 'footed' to give final balances.[13] The bankers would also make countervailing bilateral account entries for credits and debits. The same period – the eleventh and twelfth centuries – saw the development of mystical strands in medieval Jewish philosophy. Mysticism and business might seem worlds apart. But in fact mystics are often highly practical people. The twentieth-century French Jewish-Catholic philosopher and mystic Simone Weil is a good example. While she was starving herself to death as an identification with human suffering during World War II, she was writing letters to Charles de Gaulle about how to organize the French government after the end of the war.[14]

What emerged in the late Renaissance was axiomodernity. There are many kinds of modernity, many different paths in, through, and out of modernity. Axiomodernity is one of these. Its core is paradox. It builds on 'unions of opposites' in business, society, and culture. In doing so, it generates high levels of creative energy. It is dynamic. It is also subject to regular push-back from social and economic forces that dislike its typical features. Old, ascetic, and gnostic worldviews that disdain materialism are common in modernity. The dislike of what might be called 'axial bilateral symmetry' thinking – be it economic or cultural – is also not new. The fertile ancient Chinese Axial Era of the One Hundred Contending schools is a case in point. Axial ambidexterity was well exemplified during this period by the schools of Taoism, *yin-yang* naturalism, and the School of Forms and Names. Yet they faced many familiar agonistic and antagonistic opponents. Agon or battle is a kind of opposition without union.

It is opposition without irony or paradox and without the benefit of enantio-dromia, cyclical resolution, or eternal return. It is opposition to the union of opposites.

The era of the One Hundred Contending Schools at times feels like a trial-run (intellectually) for modernity. As well as the Taoists and the Naturalists and the School of Names, there were the Confucians who worked out a hierarchical model of society and an ethical justification for state intervention but with a cosmology that united opposites. The Yangists criticized state intervention on the grounds that individuals can only rationally look after their own well-being but not that of others. The Mohists argued for a philosophy of impartial caring, that is, caring equally for all, the view that all persons are equally deserving. The Legalists regarded *fa* (administrative methods, standards and impersonal regulations) as the preferred methods of running the state. These methods ignored the differences between kin and strangers or between noble and base persons in favor of impersonal bureaucratic standards. Then there were the Agriculturalists who proposed that the ideal society was agrarian. They argued against the division of labor and for a state that was egalitarian and self-sufficient and a closed commercial economy in which the prices of goods were fixed and unchanging.

All these positions have been repeated in the past two centuries. Some things do not change. That includes the discomfort with 'axial bilateral symmetry' thinking. Its enigmatic core – what one might call its 'mysticism' – is often detested. Its critics complain that it doesn't 'make sense'. In a way, that is true. If I broaden my horizon and look at the economics of axiomodernity across the economic *differend*, I can see that it is annoying and frustrating to say with Joseph Schumpeter that economic creation is based on destruction – or alternatively that social stability is based on mobility or that portable earphone listening devices (the Walkman, the iPod, etc.) were successful because these allowed consumers to be 'at home' in the public world. To posit propulsive conundrums as the basis of economic or social life strikes many persons, movements, and institutions, especially those lacking a sense of humor, as infuriating. Ambidextrous cognition, a kind of intellectual double-entry bookkeeping, is regarded with suspicion, even if, as it turns out, the path to a modern prosperous society is impossible without the paradoxes that axiomodernity rests on.

Notes

1 For accounts of the Axial Age and its world-views, see Jaspers, 2010 and Voegelin, 1999.
2 Schmitt, 2015; Murphy, 2017.
3 The Hanseatic League developed in the 1100s. The 'Hansa' (originally a 'convoy' of merchants travelling between cities) developed into a confederation of 40 merchant cities that linked the Baltic, the North Sea, and North-West Europe. A web of cities eventually connected Tallinn, Riga, and Königsberg with Gdansk, Hamburg, and Bremen and ranged from Stockholm to Frankfurt, Cologne, Berlin, and Krakow with 'offices' in London, King's Lynne, Bergen, Bruges, Antwerp, Malmo, and elsewhere. The League declined sharply in the 1500s, as European territorial states began to consolidate themselves.

4 Unlike most migrants to America who have typically been young and single, the Puritan settlement of Massachusetts was dominated by nuclear families commonly composed of older adults and dependent children.
5 Conversely, the merchant in China historically was socially defined as a stranger and an outsider (Hamilton, 2006, 59; Chirot and Reid, 1997).
6 Murphy, 2001.
7 Jansenism parallels what John Carroll (2004) calls 'the alternative reformation', represented most notably by the painter Nicolas Poussin (1594–1665).
8 Klueting, 2010.
9 Pascal, *Pensées*, 31, 34.
10 Pascal, *Pensées*, 36.
11 Jun and Lewis, 2006.
12 On Chan (Zen) Buddhist paradox, see Ho, 2016.
13 On the four-sided ledger method, see Scorgie, 1994.
14 Winch, 1989, 185–186; McLellan, 1989, 213, 237–238.

Bibliography

Carroll, J. 2004. *The Wreck of Western Culture*. Melbourne: Scribe.

Chirot, D. and Reid, A. (eds). 1997. *Essential Outsiders: Chinese and Jews in the Modern Transformation of Southeast Asia and Central Europe*. Seattle: University of Washington Press.

Hamilton, G.G. 2006. *Commerce and Capitalism in Chinese Societies*. New York: Routledge.

Ho, Chien-Hsing. 2016. "Interdependence and Nonduality: On the Linguistic Strategy of the Platform Sūtra". *Philosophy East and West* 66, no. 4: 1231–1250.

Jaspers, K. 2010 [1949]. *The Origin and Goal of History*. Abingdon: Routledge.

Jun, S.H. and Lewis, J.B. 2006. "Accounting Techniques in Korea: 18th Century Archival Samples from a Non-Profit Association in the Sinitic World". *The Accounting Historians Journal* 33, no. 1: 53–87.

Klueting, H. 2010. "The Catholic Enlightenment in Austria or the Habsburg Lands". In U.L. Lehner and M. Printy (eds), *A Companion to the Catholic Enlightenment in Europe*, 127–164. Leiden: Brill.

McLellan, D. 1989. *Utopian Pessimist: The Life and Thought of Simone Weil*. London: Palgrave Macmillan.

Murphy, P. 2017. "Land versus Sea". *Thesis Eleven: Critical Theory and Historical Sociology* 142: 130–145.

Murphy, P. 2001. "Marine Reason". *Thesis Eleven: Critical Theory and Historical Sociology* 67: 11–38.

Schmitt, C. 2015. 1942. *Land and Sea: A World-Historical Meditation*. Candor, NY: Telos Press.

Scorgie, M. 1994. "Medieval Traders as International Change Agents: A Comment". *The Accounting Historians Journal* 21, no. 1: 137–143.

Voegelin, E. 1999. *Collected Works* Volume 5 *In Search of Order* and Volume 18 *Order and History*. Columbia: University of Missouri Press.

Winch, P. 1989. *Simone Weil: The Just Balance*. Cambridge: Cambridge University Press.

4 Systems

The possibility of generalized prosperity has been with us for the past two centuries only. It is the result of a new kind of functional society. A functional society substitutes outcomes for eminence. What matters less is social standing and more accomplishment. The distinction is not absolute. Functional societies rank higher and lower achievement. That said, so much of that achievement is due to the nameless and anonymous working of mass-scale systems rather than to socially recognized 'persons of quality'. The distinction is also not absolute because modern societies tend to be bifurcated. They have a functional side. But this is partly offset by hierarchies that have been reconfigured for the modern context. Procedural bureaucracies are commonplace in these societies. The modern state and the modern firm typically have hierarchical structures organized around rules. Many modern societies exhibit powerful neo-patrimonial, familial, religious-ethnic, militant, party, party-class, and military hierarchies. The militant warrior-like impulses of traditional societies periodically find a sublimated outlet in modern societies in the form of militant ideologies and belief systems (Table 4.1).

The sublimation and transmogrification of old social principles into new modern forms causes quandaries. A classic example of such a quandary is contemporary China. It is torn between two poles. One is the party-state rank-ordered society. It is integrated into a single hierarchy that pivots around China's Communist Party and incorporates the wider state and society through rules and directions. The second pole is the systems of markets and industries. These generate prosperity. To be prosperous and to grow is the major legitimating factor in contemporary politics. But growth depends on self-organization. It requires millions of persons to participate in mass systems, largely anonymously, contributing micro-decisions that cumulatively express themselves in macro patterns, not least of all in patterns of growth and cycles of investment and innovation. In the decades since the 1980s, China has experimented with ways of reconciling state and markets, status order and industrial order.

The irony of modern prosperity is that socialism depends on capitalism.[1] The socialist model of administrative allocation, regulation, and organization can only avoid making a society miserable if it permits the Promethean (that is, capitalist) development of productive forces. This points to a larger conundrum.

Table 4.1 Militant eras

Nation	1500–1549	1550–1599	1600–1649	1650–1699	1700–1749	1750–1799	1800–1849	1850–1899	1900–1949	1950–1999
Australia										
Austria			Thirty Years War/War of Religion				1848 Revolution		1940s, Nazism	
Belgium							1830 Revolution			
Britain/United Kingdom			1640s, Civil War							
Canada							1830s, French Canadian Rebellions			1960s–1990s, Quebec separatism
China								1850s, Taiping Rebellion; 1890s, Boxer Rebellion	1920s, 1930s, 1940s, Civil Wars; 1910s–1920s, Warlordism	1950s–1980s, Maoism
Czech			Thirty Years War/War of Religion							
Denmark	War of Religion/ Succession									
Finland									1918 Civil War	
France		1560s–1590s, Wars of Religion	1620s, Huguenot rebellions			1790s, French Revolution	1830 and 1848 Revolutions			May 1968 revolt

Germany	Thirty Years War/War of Religion		1848 Revolution	1918–19 Civil War; 1930s–1940s Nazism
Hungary	Thirty Years War/War of Religion			
India				Partition
Ireland		1798, Irish Rebellion	1848 Revolution	1920s, Irish Civil War
Italy			1820s, Revolution	1930s–1940s Fascism
Japan				1920s–1940s, Militarism
Netherlands			1830 Revolution	
New Zealand				
Norway				
Poland			1830 Revolution	
Portugal			1820s Revolution	
Russia				1917–1922 Civil War; Leninism; Stalinism
Spain			1820s, Revolution	1930s Civil War
Sweden				
Switzerland				
United States		1770s, American Revolution		1861–1865, Civil War

What drives prosperity? Prosperity has a long and somewhat checkered history. It began with a handful of countries or city-regions that instituted a series of systems in place of social statuses from the end of the European Renaissance (Table 3.1). From the 1820s onwards, an increasing number of countries joined the process of accelerating growth, leading to dramatically improving standards of living. The growth process is not uniform. Some countries experience lengthy periods of super-growth; others have grown more steadily rather than spectacularly across two centuries. Others have moved vertiginously up and down between high and low growth.

Modern economic growth is historically unprecedented. Nothing in human history is comparable to it. So we are then faced with the question: what explains it? In the broadest terms, it is the outcome of a social switch that occurs in the modern age. This switch has roots in the Renaissance. It is evident to a degree through the 1600s and 1700s. It gains momentum in the 1800s and is challenged by contrary currents in the twentieth century. During the 1800s, we find various astute descriptions of what was happening then. A number of social theories described a tectonic shift that was taking place in a number of societies in the northwest segment of Europe. Social philosophies and political economies of the time talked about the shift from militant to industrial society (Comte and Spencer), status to contract (Maine), feudal to capitalist society (Marx), metaphysical to positive knowledge (Comte), and consumer to producer society (Comte). Later theories emphasized the shift from community to society (Tönnies), mechanical to organic solidarity (Durkheim), producer to consumer society (Veblen), the engineering to the price system (Veblen), ascription to achievement (Parsons), anarchic local power to pacified territorial power (Elias), and so on.[2]

All these theories had individual merit. Collectively what they represented was the shift from hierarchical to functional society. That is, a shift from a predominately heteronomous to an increasingly autonomous society.[3] The swing from one societal type to another was not black and white. Autonomous-type societies invariably preserve significant elements of heteronomy. Nonetheless, what drove the shift from mostly heteronomy to increasing autonomy was the expansion of self-organizing social systems. When the term 'self-organizing' is used, it often refers to markets. It is true that the market is a self-organizing system. However, it is not the only one. Functional modern societies pivot not just on one but on several self-organizing social systems. These typically don't replace the hierarchical principle of social organization. But they do displace it. The degree to which they displace the hierarchic principle varies from nation to nation, as does the manner in which this displacement takes place. Most modern societies are bifurcated. There are 'two Americas', 'two Britains', 'two Chinas', 'two Europes' – part self-organizing, part hierarchically or bureaucratically (legal rationally) organized. Each social principle vies for dominance.

To the degree that economic and social prosperity is the primary criterion, the greater is the dominance of self-organizing systems. Yet prosperity is also often a contested value. Many people in modern societies rage against prosperity. This does not mean they don't enjoy its fruits. But they dislike its processes and presuppositions. They prefer modernized, updated forms of social hierarchy. Personal hierarchies have largely disappeared in modern societies, whether in the family or in the broader society. But procedural hierarchies have flourished. In these cases, feudalism has been replaced by statism, or what sometimes is called a 'new feudalism'. In any event, at least a third of modern personalities prefer to live in societies that have a strong statist character. There are a variety of reasons for this. Partly, statism recreates status rankings. A distinct segment of modern personalities prefers status to function. Rank, title, recognition, reputation, and pecking order are much more attractive to them than functional achievement. They don't want to be like the anonymous American Shaker, making beautiful furniture without regard for name or fame. Some moderns become addicted to the promise, even if only by proxy, of renown, celebrity, or even notoriety. Others find rungs on a bureaucratic hierarchy equally satisfying. Even the most minor title coveys much sought-after status.

Then there is the question of security. Hierarchical society generates the illusion of security. The promise of security is powerful. People often fiercely commit themselves to hierarchies because these come with an implicit quid pro quo. Hierarchical authority expects to direct or regulate human behavior. Persons are happy to be directed and regulated in return for notional benefits – guarantees of protection, employment, and pensions. There is a limit to hierarchical authority, though. The limit is prosperity, for prosperity is a function of self-organization. To the extent that procedural hierarchies exist in the modern world, they only exist to the extent that prosperity funds them. The large bureaucratic firm only survives with all the benefits it pays and its promise of continuing employment if it is successful in the market place, technologically innovative, and able to locate its operations satisfactorily, that is, if it negotiates the large self-organizing systems of markets, industries, and cities sufficiently well that it generates profitable revenue. Likewise, states can only deliver benefits, such as welfare transfer payments, hospital beds, or school places, if the economy grows.

In turn, growth derives not from directions and procedures, grants and norms, allocations and regulations, or hierarchies and rules but rather from a combination of self-organizing systems. This does not mean a single system – the market. It means a number of functional systems that interact. These include industries, cities, lean governments, reading publics, and households as well as markets. All of these are mass entities. In the most extensively modernized societies, everyone participates in these systems. They are democratic in the broadest sense of that word. Millions everyday buy and sell goods and services; adopt technologies; congregate and commute; vote for or against cost-effective government; acquire functional reading, writing, and calculation capacities; and provide one another with mutual aid and emotional support.

Functional systems, at their best and most proficient, are systems of symmetrical reciprocity.[4] Relying on pattern media, they combine lender and borrower, buyer and seller, leasee and leasor, inventor and technology licensee, home owner and neighbor, public and private space, and so on. The parts of any society are integrated in three ways (see Table 4.2) – by hierarchies, rules,

Table 4.2 Social relations

Horizontal

Pattern	Union of opposites	Contract	Function	Fit	Observance	Political economy	
Shape	Contraries	Covenant	Purpose	Equilibrium	Wit	Satisfaction focused	Competition
Form	Contrasts	Vow	Task	Balance	Humor	Limited state	Minimize (optimize) costs
Arrangement	Symmetries	Promise	Work	Polarity	Irony	Broad legal principles	Maximize (optimize) profits
Configuration	Proportions	Agreement	Undertaking	Harmonization	Enigma	Anonymous operation	Technology/innovation
Model	Ideal ratios	Pact	Enterprise	Adaptation	Tragedy	Marginal utility	Entrepreneurial behavior
Archetype	Cycles	Treaty	Venture	Adjustment	Paradox	Supply and demand	Self-organizing
Design	Undulations	Transaction	Operation	Modification	Satire	Equilibrium	Aggregated knowledge
Rhythm	Analogies	Commitment	Industry	Assembly	Contrarianism	Factors of production	Ratios
Periodicity	Metaphors	Guarantee	Result	Poise	Sardonicism	Capital	Cycles
Principles	Webs	Pledge	Outcome	Ingenuity	Raillery	Labor/work	Waves
Limit	Lattices	Understanding	Achievement	Grace	Incongruity	Prices, profits, rents	Transaction patterns
Outline	Spirals	Bargain	Success	Elegance	Repartee	Productivity	Decentralized economy
System	Waves	Affirmation	Attainment	Beauty	Mystery	Efficiency	Spontaneous order

Vertical

Hierarchy	Status	Resemblance	Command	Observance	Political economy	
Rank	Honor	Identity	Instruction	Ritual	Allocation focused	Subventions
Title	Eminence	Continuity	Direction	Rite	Distributive state	Welfare state
Grade	Prestige	Likeness	Control	Routine	Taxation state	Social security
Layer	Stature	Sameness	Guidance	Liturgy	Grants	Appropriation
Level	Merit	Similarity	Order	Sacrament	Quotas	Nationalization

Stratification	Quality	Imitation	Domination	Custom	Allowances	State-owned enterprises
Title	Distinction	Sympathy	Prescription	Tradition	Subsidies	State capitalism
Echelon	Worth	Copying	Obedience	Mores	Stipends	Monopoly economies
Position	Standing	Uniformity	Superintendence	Mythology	Tariffs	Command economies
Ordering	Esteem	Permanence	Supervision	Practice	Benefits	Planned economies
Station	Reputation	Repetition	Oversight	Habit	Donations	Patrimonial economies
Social Pyramid	Fame	Replication	Prerogative	Cult	Assistance	Neo-patrimonial economies
Social Ladder	Respect	Reproduction	Fiat	Inheritance	Admissions	Patron–client relationships

Orthogonal

Law	*Rulings*	*Process*	*Authority*	*Observance*	*Political economy*	
Rules	Decrees	Method	Expert	Trend	Rule focused	Governance
Codes	Edicts	Procedure	Specialist	Style	Regulatory state	Reduce transaction costs
Regulations	Injunctions	Agency	Collegial	Fashion	Administrative state	Tax social costs
Legislation	Decisions	Organization	Professional	Movement	Interventionism	Pressure groups
Ordinances	Cases	Corporation	Managerial	Progression	Dirigisme	Procedural rational
Protocols	Judgements	Firm	Technical	Mode	Licensing	Legal-rational
Precepts	Writs	Office	Warrant	Tone	Rule-based behavior	Goal-rational
Standards	Remedies	Bureaucracy	Influence	Manner	Policy	Organizational order
Constitutions	Settlements	Administration	Permission	Trait	Managerialism	Institutionalized economies
Charters	Appeals	Calculation	License	Momentum	Organization-driven	Oligopoly economies
Principles	Tribunals	Plan	Mandate	Atmosphere	Large institutional actors	Knowledge economies
Sovereignty	Courts	Program	Document	Dynamism	Rule compliance	Control
Canon	Jurisdiction	Sequence	Advice	Charisma	Auditing and reporting	Guidelines

or patterns. All societies have three dimensions: the vertical, orthogonal, and horizontal. All social relations including modern functional or systemic ones involve degrees of all three. What distinguishes functional systems is that they rely heavily on horizontal or pattern media to integrate the complementary parts that they are composed of. That is, functional systems rely to a high degree on relationships of symmetry, proportion, and ratio and on branching, forking, network, lattice, slalom, osculating, knotty, and topological (etc.) pattern-ties.[5] Symmetrical reciprocity is a shorthand term for these kinds of relationships. In each of these relationships the condition of one party gaining something is that another party also gains something. Each party tacitly evaluates the respective gain from the relationship. Satisfaction – that is happiness – is measured intuitively by parties in terms of pleasing ratios or 'ideal' ratios that are expressed (or not) in and through these relationships. Ratio rather than equality is the principle of systems of symmetrical reciprocity.[6]

Self-organizing systems

The following is a typology of modern self-organizing systems. Different typologies are conceivable. No typology captures the entirety of what it represents. A typology is an idealized description of a social situation. It abstracts key or essential features from that situation. So it is with the typology of modern systems. Each system is a subcomponent of the social whole. Each system represents a principal functional dimension of a mature modern society. Prosperity is a result of the successful operation and interaction of these systems. How this works varies from nation to nation. No nation is the same. Each has strengths and weaknesses. Some achieve higher levels of market performance than others. Some are better at technology, others at the quality of cities. Others still excel in literacies and others in the quality of personal bonds.

Looking at the performance of the contemporary top-25 nations system by system (Tables 4.3 and 4.4), no nation excels in every system. All nations have systemic weaknesses. Yet they tend to perform at least adequately across the entire palette of systems. It is rare for any of the overall top-25 to drop out of the top-25 rank for any of the identified systems. That is to say, it is not enough for a nation to do well in one or two self-organizing systems. Rather, performance across the board is also important. Society is a multifactor entity. Its successful operation rests on the simultaneous performance of several key systems.

Markets

Economies combine factors of production, primarily land, labor, and capital. That said, why was it, across nearly two millennia from the opening centuries of the Roman Empire to the nineteenth century, there was little or no change in the wealth of nations? What was the difference that finally made the difference? The answer: efficiency and productivity. A key to this was markets, though not

Table 4.3 National economic and social performance (excluding resource-dependent states)

Rank	GDP per capita 2016	Life expectancy at birth, 2014	Life satisfaction OECD+ countries, 2017	Disposable income distribution Gini coefficient after taxes and transfers, more equal to less equal, OECD+ countries 2014–2016	Market income distribution Gini coefficient before taxes and transfers, more equal to less equal, OECD+ countries 2014–2016
1	Norway	Japan	Denmark	Slovak Republic	Korea
2	Singapore	Hong Kong	Finland	Slovenia	Iceland
3	Switzerland	Switzerland	Iceland	Czech Republic	Switzerland
4	Luxembourg	Spain	Norway	Iceland	Slovak Republic
5	Ireland	Italy	Switzerland	Finland	Norway
6	United States	Iceland	Netherlands	Norway	Turkey
7	Australia	France	Australia	Denmark	Canada
8	Hong Kong	Singapore	Canada	Belgium	Sweden
9	Netherlands	Australia	New Zealand	Sweden	Israel
10	Denmark	Luxembourg	Sweden	Austria	Netherlands
11	Germany	Sweden	Israel	Poland	Czech Republic
12	Sweden	Norway	Austria	Netherlands	Denmark
13	Canada	Israel	Germany	Hungary	Slovenia
14	Iceland	Korea, South	Ireland	France	Hungary
15	Taiwan	Netherlands	Belgium	Germany	Estonia
16	Austria	Austria	Luxembourg	Korea	Poland
17	Belgium	New Zealand	United States	Switzerland	New Zealand
18	Japan	Canada	United Kingdom	Ireland	Australia
19	United Kingdom	Greece	Czech Republic	Luxembourg	Latvia
20	Finland	Ireland	Mexico	Canada	Mexico
21	France	Belgium	Brazil	Estonia	Luxembourg
22	Korea	United Kingdom	France	Italy	Belgium
23	New Zealand	Finland	Spain	Australia	Austria
24	Italy	Germany	Slovak Republic	Portugal	Germany
25	Israel	Slovenia	Poland	Greece	Japan

(Continued)

Table 4.3 (Continued)

Rank	Property Rights, Judicial Effectiveness, Government Integrity 2018	Good Value HDI [public spending input to very high human development index outcome]**	Cost effectiveness of government, OECD countries, 2001–2011
1	Singapore	Singapore	South Korea
2	New Zealand	Hong Kong	Luxembourg
3	Sweden	Ireland	Switzerland
4	Norway	South Korea	Australia
5	United Kingdom	Switzerland	Norway
6	Finland	Australia	Mexico
7	Hong Kong	United States	Canada
8	Denmark	Japan	United States
9	Australia	Israel	Japan
10	Switzerland	Canada	New Zealand
11	Netherlands	Iceland	Ireland
12	Ireland	United Kingdom	United Kingdom
13	Canada	Luxembourg	Estonia
14	Estonia	Germany	Iceland
15	Luxembourg	New Zealand	Netherlands
16	Japan	Netherlands	Finland
17	Austria	Spain*	Germany
18	Iceland	Norway	Sweden
19	Germany	Sweden	Spain
20	United States	Austria	Belgium
21	Taiwan	Italy*	Austria
22	Israel	Denmark	Czech Republic
23	France	Belgium	Slovenia
24	Belgium	Finland	Denmark
25	Rwanda	France	France

Note: The United Nations Human Development Index measures life expectancy, literacy, education, standards of living, and quality of life. The United Nations HDI excludes Taiwan entirely from its rankings; Liechtenstein ranked 18 in the HDI listing has been removed from the rank order for the purposes of this table as other data for the country is too limited to make meaningful comparisons.

* Spain and Italy rank just under the 0.900 very high HDI threshold.

Rank	Market Freedom 2018 Business, Trade, Monetary, Labor, Investment Freedom	Economic Freedom 2016	Global Competitiveness Index (CGI) 2018	Services Trade Restrictiveness 2017, least to most	Ease of doing business 2017
1	Hong Kong	Hong Kong	United States	Latvia	New Zealand
2	Singapore	Singapore	Singapore	Germany	Singapore
3	Denmark	New Zealand	Germany	Ireland	Denmark
4	New Zealand	Switzerland	Switzerland	Netherlands	South Korea
5	Australia	Ireland	Japan	Australia	Hong Kong
6	United Kingdom	United States	Netherlands	Denmark	United States
7	United States	Georgia	Hong Kong	Lithuania	United Kingdom
8	Switzerland	Mauritius	United Kingdom	United Kingdom	Norway
9	Ireland	United Kingdom	Sweden	Czech Republic	Georgia
10	Netherlands	Canada	Denmark	New Zealand	Sweden
11	Czech Republic	Australia	Finland	Japan	Macedonia
12	Sweden	Taiwan	Canada	Canada	Estonia
13	Canada	Estonia	Taiwan	Spain	Finland
14	Finland	Lithuania	Australia	Sweden	Australia
15	Iceland	Chile	South Korea	Estonia	Lithuania
16	Georgia	Denmark	Norway	United States	Ireland
17	Austria	Malta	France	Slovenia	Canada
18	Estonia	Netherlands	New Zealand	Luxembourg	Latvia
19	Latvia	Cyprus	Luxembourg	Portugal	Germany
20	Bahrain	Germany	Israel	France	Austria
21	Mauritius	Romania	Belgium	Slovak Republic	Iceland
22	Luxembourg	Finland	Austria	Finland	Malaysia
23	Lithuania	Latvia	Ireland	Italy	Mauritius
24	Belgium	Guatemala	Iceland	Greece	Thailand
25	Germany	Luxembourg	Malaysia	South Africa	Poland

Note 1: *Market Freedom underlying data and terms*: Business, Trade, Labor, Monetary, Financial and Investment Freedom, *Wall Street Journal* and the Heritage Foundation Index of Economic Freedom 2018: Business Freedom (the extent to which the regulatory and infrastructure environments constrain the efficient operation of businesses including for starting and closing businesses, obtaining business licenses and utility services) is scored on the basis of World Bank, Doing Business; Economist Intelligence Unit,

(Continued)

Table 4.3 (Continued)

Country Commerce; US Department of Commerce, Country Commercial Guide; and official government publications of each country. <u>Trade Freedom</u> (the extent of tariff and nontariff barriers that affect imports and exports of goods and services) is scored on the basis of World Bank, World Development Indicators; World Trade Organization, Trade Policy Review; Office of the US Trade Representative, National Trade Estimate Report on Foreign Trade Barriers; World Bank, Doing Business; US Department of Commerce, Country Commercial Guide; Economist Intelligence Unit, Country Commerce; World Economic Forum, The Global Enabling Trade Report; and official government publications of each country. <u>Monetary Freedom</u> (the relative absence of inflation and price controls) is scored on the basis of International Monetary Fund, International Financial Statistics Online; International Monetary Fund, World Economic Outlook and Staff Country Report; 'Article IV Consultation'; Economist Intelligence Unit, ViewsWire and Data Tool; various World Bank country reports; various news and magazine articles; and official government publications of each country. <u>Labor Freedom</u> (a measure of regulatory restraints on hiring and firing employees, hours worked, severance payments, minimum wages plus labor force participation as a measure of labor opportunity) is scored using World Bank, Doing Business; International Labour Organization, Statistics and Databases; World Bank, World Development Indicators; Economist Intelligence Unit, Country Commerce; US Department of Commerce, Country Commercial Guide; and official government publications of each country. <u>Investment Freedom</u> measures regulatory restrictions imposed on investment including foreign investment restrictions, land ownership restrictions, foreign investment code burdens, sector restrictions, expropriations without compensation, foreign exchange, and capital controls. It is scored on the basis of official government publications of each country; US Department of State, Investment Climate Statements; Economist Intelligence Unit, Country Commerce; Office of the US Trade Representative, National Trade Estimate Report on Foreign Trade Barriers; World Bank, Investing Across Borders; Organization for Economic Co-operation and Development, Services Trade Restrictiveness Index; and US Department of Commerce, Country Commercial Guide.

Note 2: Economic Freedom underlying data and terms: Fraser Institute's Joshua Hall and Ryan Murphy, James Gwartney, Robert Lawson, Economic Freedom of the World, 2018 Annual Report scores countries on five areas: size of government, legal system and property rights, sound money, freedom to trade internationally, and regulation. <u>Size of Government</u> includes measures of the size of government consumption, government enterprise and investment, and the scale of high marginal taxation. Sources: World Bank, World Development Indicators; International Monetary Fund, International Financial Statistics; United Nations National Accounts; International Monetary Fund, Government Finance Statistics Yearbook; World Economic Forum, Global Competitiveness Report; European Bank for Reconstruction and Development, Transition Indicators; PricewaterhouseCoopers, Worldwide Tax Summaries Online; PricewaterhouseCoopers, Individual Taxes: A Worldwide Summary. <u>Legal System and Property Rights</u> are scored on judicial independence, impartiality of courts, property rights, military interference in the rule of law, legal enforcement of contracts, regulatory restrictions on the sale of real property, reliability of police and the business costs of crime. Sources: World Economic Forum, Global Competitiveness Report; PRS Group, International Country Risk Guide; World Bank, Governance Indicators; World Bank, Doing Business. <u>Sound Money</u> includes measures of money growth, inflation and freedom to own foreign bank accounts. Sources: World Bank, World Development Indicators; International Monetary Fund, International Financial Statistics; United Nations National Accounts; International Monetary Fund, Annual Report on Exchange Arrangements and Exchange Restrictions. <u>Freedom to Trade Internationally</u> is scored on revenue from trade taxes, mean tariff rates, tariffs, non-tariff trade barriers, compliance costs of importing and exporting, foreign investment restrictions, controls on visitors and controls on the movement of capital and people. Sources: International Monetary Fund, Government Finance Statistics Yearbook; International Monetary Fund, International Financial Statistics; World Trade Organization, World Tariff Profiles; World Economic Forum, Global Competitiveness Report; World Bank, Doing Business; International Monetary Fund, Annual Report on Exchange Arrangements and Exchange Restrictions; Robert Lawson and Jayne Lemke, "TravelVisas", Public Choice 154: 1–2, 17–36, 2012. <u>Regulation</u> is scored on the degree of onerousness of regulations controlling the ownership of banks, private sector credit, interest rates, the credit market, hiring and firing, hours of employment, employee dismissals, conscription, centralized collective bargaining, labor markets, starting a business, obtaining license requirements, and the costs of administration, bureaucracy, corruption, and compliance. Sources: World Bank, Doing Business; World Economic Forum, Global Competitiveness Report; and additionally World Bank, Bank Regulation and Supervision Survey; James R. Barth, Gerard Caprio, and Ross Levine, Rethinking Bank Regulation: Till Angels Govern, Cambridge University Press, 2006; World Bank, World Development Indicators; International Monetary Fund, International Financial Statistics; CIA, The World Factbook; International Institute for Strategic Studies, The Military Balance; War Resisters International, World Survey of Conscription and Conscientious Objection to Military Service.

Note 3: Ease of doing business underlying data and terms: A high ranking economy means that the regulatory environment is conducive to business operation. The index averages the country's percentile rankings on 10 topics covered in the World Bank's Doing Business. The ranking on each topic is the simple average of the percentile rankings on its component indicators. Topics: Starting a Business, Dealing with Construction Permits, Getting Electricity, Registering Property, Getting Credit, Protecting Minority Investors, Paying Taxes, Trading Across Borders, Enforcing Contract, and Resolving Insolvency.

Rank	International Innovation Index (Manufacturing) 2009	Industrial robots per 10,000 employees 2018	Mobile broadband internet subscriptions per capita 2017	Technological sophistication [complexity] of goods exported 2016	Creative outputs goods and services 2018	Multifactor (capital + labor) productivity OECD 1985–2016	Multifactor (capital + labor) Productivity OECD 2008–2016
1	Singapore	South Korea	Finland	Japan	Latvia	South Korea	South Korea
2	Korea	Singapore	Singapore	Switzerland	United Kingdom	Ireland	Ireland
3	Switzerland	Germany	Japan	Germany	Estonia	Finland	Australia
4	Iceland	Japan	Australia	South Korea	Switzerland	Austria	Japan
5	Ireland	Sweden	Sweden	Sweden	United States	Germany	United States
6	Hong Kong	Denmark	Denmark	Singapore	Croatia	Japan	Germany
7	Finland	United States	United States	Austria	Malta	United Kingdom	Canada
8	United States	Italy	Korea	United Kingdom	Hong Kong	United States	New Zealand
9	Japan	Belgium	Hong Kong	United States	Netherlands	Portugal	Denmark
10	Sweden	Taiwan	Iceland	Czech Republic	Belgium	France	Sweden
11	Denmark	Spain	Switzerland	Finland	Czech Republic	Sweden	Austria
12	Netherlands	Netherlands	Norway	Slovenia	Luxembourg	Netherlands	France
13	Luxembourg	Canada	New Zealand	Ireland	Malaysia	Australia	Spain
14	Canada	Austria	Ireland	France	Denmark	Denmark	Switzerland
15	United Kingdom	Finland	Israel	Hungary	Israel	Canada	Netherlands
16	Israel	Slovenia	United Kingdom	Slovakia	Japan	Belgium	United Kingdom
17	Austria	Slovakia	Luxembourg	Denmark	Slovakia	New Zealand	Belgium
18	Norway	France	Austria	Belgium	Sweden	Switzerland	Portugal
19	Germany	Switzerland	Netherlands	Italy	Singapore	Spain	Italy
20	France	Czech Republic	France	Israel	Panama	Italy	Finland
21	Malaysia	Australia	Germany	Poland	Austria	–	–
22	Australia	United Kingdom	Belgium	Netherlands	Slovenia	–	–
23	Estonia	China	Canada	Norway	Thailand	–	–
24	Spain	Portugal	–	Estonia	France	–	–
25	Belgium	Hungary	–	Mexico	Poland	–	–

Note: Creative Outputs Goods and Services are calculated on the basis of cultural and creative services exports as a percentage of total trade, national feature films per capita, entertainment and media markets per capita, printing and other media as a percentage of manufacturing, creative goods exports as a percentage of total trade, Global Innovation Index 2018.

(*Continued*)

Table 4.3 (Continued)

Rank	Highest number of couple households (with and without children) as a percentage of all households	Percentage of adults reporting that most people can be trusted, 2014, 2009*	Percentage of adults reporting they have one or more close friends outside workplace, 2001
1	Israel	Norway	Finland
2	Portugal	Netherlands	Norway
3	Singapore	Sweden	Denmark
4	Spain	China	Australia
5	Mexico	Finland	New Zealand
6	Greece	New Zealand	Israel
7	Ireland	Australia	United States
8	New Zealand	Vietnam	Canada
9	Australia	Switzerland	Brazil
10	Netherlands	Hong Kong	Switzerland
11	Canada	Germany	Japan
12	Switzerland	Canada	France
13	Italy	Indonesia	Cyprus
14	France	Singapore	Slovenia
15	Belgium	Estonia	Czech Republic
16	Poland	Yemen	Italy
17	Hong Kong	United States	Austria
18	South Korea	Japan	Germany
19	Sweden	Bahrain	United Kingdom
20	Germany	India	Latvia
21	Hungary	Montenegro	Poland
22	United Kingdom	Belarus	Spain
23	Denmark	Thailand	Philippines
24	Austria	United Kingdom	South Africa
25	Luxembourg	South Korea	Hungary

*2014 except for Norway 2009, Finland 2009, Vietnam 2009, Switzerland 2009, Canada 2009, Indonesia 2009, United Kingdom 2004, Montenegro 2004. Denmark was never included in any of the ISSP surveys.

Rank	Most productive cities (average GDP per capita of the nation/territory's major metropolitan areas) 2012	Most livable cities 2015, 2018	Most visited cities, 2016	Most beautiful cities, 2018	Gap between largest city and national GDP per capita, least to most	Percentage of the total population living in urban areas, as defined by the nation/territory	Gap between the largest city and national GDP per capita, least to most
1	Luxembourg	Austria, Vienna	Thailand, Bangkok	United Kingdom, London	Hong Kong, Hong Kong	Singapore	Hong Kong, Hong Kong
2	Singapore	Switzerland, Zurich	United Kingdom, London	Czech Republic, Prague	Singapore, Singapore	Hong Kong	Singapore, Singapore
3	Norway	Canada, Vancouver	France, Paris	France, Paris	Norway, Oslo	Belgium	Norway, Oslo
4	Switzerland	Australia, Melbourne	United States, New York	United States, Chicago	Canada, Toronto	Iceland	Canada, Toronto
5	Slovak Republic	Japan, Tokyo	Singapore, Singapore	United States, Washington DC	Korea, Seoul	Israel	Korea, Seoul
6	Ireland	Australia, Sydney	Malaysia, Kuala Lumpur	Turkey, Istanbul	Australia, Sydney	Japan	Australia, Sydney
7	United States	Canada, Toronto	Turkey, Istanbul	Japan, Kyoto	Germany, Berlin	Netherlands	Germany, Berlin
8	Finland	Germany, Frankfurt	Japan, Tokyo	United States, San Francisco	Austria, Vienna	Luxembourg	Austria, Vienna
9	Denmark	Germany, Munich	Korea, Seoul	Argentina, Buenos Aires	Japan, Tokyo	Denmark	Japan, Tokyo
10	Hong Kong	New Zealand, Auckland	Hong Kong, Hong Kong	Korea, Seoul	Mexico, Mexico City	Sweden	Mexico, Mexico City
11	Sweden	Denmark, Copenhagen	Spain, Barcelona	Netherlands, Amsterdam	Netherlands, Amsterdam	New Zealand	Netherlands, Amsterdam
12	Netherlands	Germany, Berlin	Netherlands, Amsterdam	Italy, Rome	Belgium, Antwerp	Australia	Belgium, Antwerp

(Continued)

Table 4.3 (Continued)

Rank	Most productive cities (average GDP per capita of the nation/territory's major metropolitan areas) 2012	Most livable cities 2015, 2018	Most visited cities, 2016	Most beautiful cities, 2018	Gap between largest city and national GDP per capita, least to most	Percentage of the total population living in urban areas, as defined by the nation/territory	Gap between the largest city and national GDP per capita, least to most
13	Austria	Germany, Hamburg	Italy, Milan	Spain, Barcelona	Denmark, Copenhagen	Finland	Denmark, Copenhagen
14	Australia	Australia, Perth	Taiwan, Taipei	Greece, Athens	Portugal, Lisbon	United Kingdom	Portugal, Lisbon
15	Canada	Australia, Adelaide	Italy, Rome	Hungary, Budapest	Spain, Madrid	United States	Spain, Madrid
16	Germany	Finland, Helsinki	Japan, Osaka	South Africa, Cape Town	Slovenia, Ljubljana	Norway	Slovenia, Ljubljana
17	Belgium	Canada, Montreal	Austria, Vienna	Hong Kong, Hong Kong	Greece, Athens	South Korea	Greece, Athens
18	Slovenia	Netherlands, Amsterdam	China, Shanghai	Canada, Vancouver	Switzerland, Zurich	Canada	Switzerland, Zurich
19	France	New Zealand, Wellington	Czech Republic, Prague	Australia, Melbourne	Ireland, Dublin	France	Ireland, Dublin
20	Estonia	Germany, Dusseldorf	United States, Los Angeles	Brazil, Rio de Janeiro	Italy, Rome	Taiwan	Italy, Rome
21	Italy	Sweden, Stockholm	Spain, Madid	Australia, Sydney	Estonia, Tallinn	Germany	Estonia, Tallinn
22	Hungary	Canada, Calgary	Germany, Munich	India, Jaipur	Finland, Helsinki	Switzerland	Finland, Helsinki
23	United Kingdom	Australia, Brisbane	United States, Miami	Israel, Jerusalem	Hungary, Budapest	Italy	Hungary, Budapest
24	Japan	Luxembourg, Luxembourg	Ireland, Dublin	Morocco, Fez	United Kingdom, London	Ireland	United Kingdom, London
25	South Korea	Oslo, Norway	Germany, Berlin	–	Czech Republic	Austria	Czech Republic

Table 4.3 (Continued)

Rank	OECD PISA 15-year-olds reading performance 2015	OECD PISA 15-year-olds mathematics performance 2015	OECD PISA 15-year-olds science performance 2016	OECD skills outlook tertiary graduate literacy performance 2013	OECD skills outlook tertiary graduate numeracy performance 2013
1	Singapore	Singapore	Singapore	Japan	Czech Republic
2	Hong Kong	Hong Kong	Japan	Netherlands	Belgium (Flanders)
3	Canada	Macao	Estonia	Finland	Netherlands
4	Finland	Taiwan	Taiwan	Sweden	Sweden
5	Ireland	Japan	Finland	Belgium (Flanders)	Japan
6	Estonia	B-S-J-G (Coastal China)	Macao	Australia	Austria
7	South Korea	South Korea	Canada	Czech Republic	Slovak Republic
8	Japan	Switzerland	Viet Nam	Norway	Finland
9	Norway	Estonia	Hong Kong	United States	Norway
10	New Zealand	Canada	B-S-J-G (Coastal China)	Poland	Denmark
11	Germany	Netherlands	South Korea	Austria	Germany
12	Macao	Denmark	New Zealand	Slovak Republic	France
13	Poland	Finland	Slovenia	United Kingdom★	Australia
14	Slovenia	Slovenia	Australia	France	Estonia
15	Netherlands	Belgium	United Kingdom	Germany	Poland
16	Australia	Germany	Germany	Denmark	United States
17	Sweden	Poland	Netherlands	Ireland	United Kingdom★
18	Denmark	Ireland	Switzerland	South Korea	South Korea
19	France	Norway	Ireland	Canada	Ireland
20	Belgium	Austria	Belgium	Estonia	Canada
21	Portugal	New Zealand	Denmark	Cyprus	Cyprus
22	United Kingdom	Viet Nam	Poland	Spain	Italy
23	Taiwan	Sweden	Portugal	Italy	Spain
24	United States	Australia	Norway	–	–
25	Spain	France	United States	–	–

Source: Real GDP per capita in 2011 US$, Maddison Historical Statistics, Groningen Growth and Development Centre, University of Groningen; Peter Murphy, Limited Government, Routledge, 2018, Table 14 Heath spending vs. health outcomes; OECD Better Life Index, 2017; OECD Statistics, Income Distribution and Poverty Data, 2014–2016; Property Rights, Judicial Effectiveness and Government Integrity, Wall Street Journal and the Heritage Foundation Index of Economic Freedom 2018; UN Human Development Index 2018; 2018 United Nations Human Development Index; OECD Data, General government spending Total, % of GDP, 2015; WSJ/Heritage Foundation, Economic Freedom Index 2015; Livio Di Matteo, Measuring Government in the Twenty-first Century, Fraser Institute, 2013, Table 5.7; Business, Labor, Monetary, Trade, Investment and Financial Freedom, Wall Street Journal and the Heritage Foundation Index of Economic Freedom 2018; Fraser Institute, Joshua Hall, Ryan Murphy, James Gwartney, Robert Lawson, Economic Freedom of the World, 2018 Annual Report; Boston Consulting Group and the US National Association of Manufacturers, International Innovation Index 2009; International Federation of Robotics 2018 Report; World Economic Forum, Global Competitiveness Index 2017–2018 based on International Telecommunication Union, ITU World; MIT Observatory of Economic Complexity, Economic Complexity Rankings (ECI) 2016; OECD Stats, Multifactor Productivity, Annual Growth/Change, 1985–2016; OCED Family Database, Table SF1.1.A. Types of household, 2011a; Family Council of Hong Kong, Family Survey 2015, Chart 3.1.4: Household Composition (%); Self-reported trust in others, Longitudinal Data World Values Survey, 2014, 2009; Number of other close friends, International Social Survey Programme ISSP, Social Networks II, 2001; OECD Stats, Metropolitan areas: GDP from cities, 2012 GDP per capita (US$ 2010), 2018; The Economist Intelligence Unit, 2015; The Mercer Quality of Living Survey 2018; Monocle Quality of Life Survey 2018; Global Top 20 Destination Cities by International Overnight Visitors (2016), Mastercard Global Destination Cities Index 2016; Cities Beautiful Index (2018), citiesbeautiful.org; CIA Factbook, The percentage of the total population living in urban areas, as defined by the country, 2018; OECD, PISA 2015 Results (Volume I): Excellence and Equity in Education, 2016, Figure I.1.1; World Values Survey, 2005–2009 and 2010–2014; OECD Skills Outlook 2013: First results from the Survey of Adults Skills, chapter 3, Figure 3.9 (L) and 3.9 (N).

Note: Table 4.3 excludes the following resource-dependent states: Chile ranks 18 in Life Satisfaction, 6 in Cost Effective Government, 10 in Services Trade, 9 in the gap between largest city and national GDP, 25 in market income equality; Russia ranks 23 in Friends, 23 in Higher Education, literacy and numeracy, 24 in market income equality; United Arab Emirates ranks 4 in most visited cities; Saudi Arabia ranks 21 in most visited cities. B-S-J-G (China) is Beijing-Shanghai-Jiangsu-Guangdong (China).

England/Northern Ireland.

Table 4.4 Index of indexes

Nation/territory	GDP	Life satisfaction	Life expectancy	Disposable Income	Market Income	Rule of law	Good value HDI spending	Cost-effective government	Market Freedom	Economic Freedom	Globally competitive	Services trade openness	Ease of doing business	Manufacturing Innovation	Industrial Robots	Mobile Broadband	Technology Sophistication	Creative Outputs	Productivity Long-run
Australia	7	7	9	23	18	9	6	4	5	11	14	5	14	22	21	4	69	27	13
Austria	16	12	16	10	23	17	20	21	18	27	22	28	20	17	4	18	7	21	4
Belgium	17	15	21	8	22	24	23	20	25	52	21	33	52	25	9	22	18	10	16
Canada	13	8	18	20	7	13	10	7	14	10	12	12	17	14	13	23	31	66	15
Denmark	10	1	27	7	12	8	22	24	3	16	10	6	3	11	6	6	17	14	14
Finland	20	2	23	5	28	6	24	16	15	22	11	22	13	7	15	1	11	34	3
France	21	22	7	14	32	23	25	25	47	57	17	20	31	20	18	20	14	24	10
Germany	11	13	24	15	24	19	14	17	26	20	3	2	19	19	3	21	3	32	5
Hong Kong	8	–	2	–	–	7	2	–	1	1	7	–	5	6	–	9	33	8	–
Iceland	14	3	6	4	2	18	11	14	16	59	24	–	21	4	–	10	–	33	–
Ireland	5	14	20	18	37	12	3	11	10	5	23	3	16	5	–	14	13	48	2
Israel	25	11	13	28	9	22	9	26	33	35	20	37	46	16	32	15	20	15	–
Italy	24	28	5	22	34	43	21	27	50	54	31	23	54	38	8	–	19	44	20
Japan	18	28	1	26	25	16	8	9	30	41	5	11	34	9	4	3	1	16	6
Luxembourg	4	16	10	19	21	15	13	2	23	25	19	18	63	13	–	17	–	12	–
Netherlands	9	6	15	12	10	11	16	15	11	18	6	4	32	12	12	19	22	9	12
New Zealand	23	9	17	30	17	2	15	10	4	3	18	10	1	26	27	13	47	43	17
Norway	1	4	12	6	5	4	18	5	39	25	16	34	8	18	26	12	23	64	–
Singapore	2	–	8	–	–	1	1	–	2	2	2	–	2	1	2	2	6	19	–
Slovenia	39	32	–	2	–	38	26	23	46	71	35	17	37	33	16	–	12	22	–
South Korea	22	29	14	16	1	30	4	1	32	38	15	26	4	2	1	8	4	37	1
Sweden	12	10	11	9	8	3	19	18	13	43	9	14	10	10	5	5	5	18	11
Switzerland	3	5	3	17	3	10	5	3	9	4	4	34	33	3	19	11	2	4	18
UK	19	18	22	31	29	5	12	12	7	9	8	8	7	15	22	16	8	2	7
United States	6	17	29	34	30	20	7	8	8	6	1	16	6	8	7	7	9	5	8

Table 4.4 (Continued)

Nation/territory	Productivity Near-term	Nuclear Households	Trust	Friends	Productive Cities	Livable Cities	Visited Cities	Beautiful Cities	City::Nation Parity	PISA Reading	PISA Mathematics	PISA Science	Graduate Literacy	Graduate Numeracy	Median of index rankings	Overall Ranking		GDP per capita ranking
Australia	3	9	7	4	14	4	25	19	6	16	25	14	6	14	11.00	1	Singapore	Norway
Austria	11	24	–	17	13	1	15	–	8	20	20	26	11	6	17.00	2	Hong Kong	Singapore
Belgium	17	15	–	–	17	28	32	–	12	20	15	20	5	2	20.00	3	United States	Switzerland
Canada	7	11	12	8	15	3	23	18	4	3	10	7	19	21	13.00	4	Japan	Luxembourg
Denmark	9	23	–	3	9	11	39	–	13	18	12	21	16	10	11.00	5	Switzerland	Ireland
Finland	20	26	5	1	8	16	–	–	22	4	13	5	3	8	13.00	6	Australia	United States
France	12	14	54	12	19	27	3	3	28	19	26	27	14	13	20.00	7	Denmark	Australia
Germany	6	20	11	18	16	8	20	–	7	11	16	16	15	11	15.50	8	Sweden	Hong Kong
Hong Kong	–	17	10	–	10	46	11	17	1	2	2	9	–	–	7.50	9	Netherlands	Netherlands
Iceland	–	29	–	–	–	52	–	–	–	35	31	39	–	–	17.00	10	New Zealand	Denmark
Ireland	2	7	–	–	6	38	21	–	19	5	18	19	17	20	14.00	11	Norway	Germany
Israel	–	1	40	6	–	76	51	23	–	37	39	40	–		25.00	12	South Korea	Sweden
Italy	19	13	29	16	21	42	14	12	20	34	30	34	23	23	23.50	13	Canada	Canada
Japan	4	31	18	11	24	5	9	7	9	8	5	2	1	5	9.00	14	Finland	Iceland
Luxembourg	–	25	–	–	1	24	–	–	–	36	33	33	–	–	18.50	15	Ireland	Austria
Netherlands	15	10	2	–	12	18	13	11	11	15	11	17	2	3	12.00	16	Germany	Belgium
New Zealand	8	8	6	5	–	10	–	–	–	10	21	12	–	–	12.00	17	UK	Japan
Norway	–	27	1	2	3	25	–	–	3	9	19	24	8	9	12.00	18	Austria	UK
Singapore	–	3	14	–	2	49	6	–	2	1	1	1	–	–	2.00	19	Iceland	Finland
Slovenia	–	32	50	14	18	–	–			14	14	13			24.50	20	Luxembourg	France
South Korea	1	18	25	–	25	58	10	10	5	7	7	11	18	19	12.50	21	Belgium	South Korea
Sweden	10	19	3	–	11	21	36		27	17	24	28	4	4	11.00	22	France	New Zealand
Switzerland	14	12	9	10	4	2	35	–	18	28	8	18	–	–	9.00	23	Italy	Italy
UK	16	22	24	19	23	47	2	1	24	22	27	15	13	17	16.00	24	Slovenia	Israel
United States	5	28	17	7	7	28	5	4	30	23	40	25	9	18	8.00	25	Israel	Slovenia

Note: The ranking in the columns for city beauty, visits, and livability varies from the ranking in the source cities tables. Where a nation has more than one city that is ranked in the tables for city beauty, livability, and visits, only the highest performing city per nation is ranked for the purpose of this table. This is to allow a comparison between cities and other aspects of a nation's performance.

just markets, for markets are an ancient phenomenon. It was not 'markets' but 'the market' that made the difference.

In modernity we see the rise of 'the market' compared with 'markets'. 'The market' is a mass phenomenon. It involves millions of persons who mostly are strangers to each other. 'The market' is an anonymous system. It is also a paradoxical one, for it presupposes the paradox of efficiency or productivity. This is the idea that the market can produce higher quality goods and services for lower prices. 'The market' does this through competition. Competitors seek to outdo each other by finding ways of maintaining or increasing the quality of their products while reducing the costs of producing those goods.

Table 4.5 Exports of goods and services as a percentage of GDP

World, 1960–2010						
1960	1970	1980	1990	2000	2010	
11.9%	13.3%	18.8%	19.2%	26.0%	28.7%	

Nations, 2017				International, 2017	
Australia	21.3%	Japan	17.7%	World	29.4%
Austria	53.7%	Luxembourg	223.1%	European Union	44.4%
Belgium	85.8%	Netherlands	83.0%	Least-developed countries	21.2%
Canada	31.0%	New Zealand	26.9%	OECD countries	28.8%
Denmark	54.5%	Norway	36.2%	High-income countries	31.2%
Finland	38.5%	Singapore	173.3%		
France	30.9%	South Korea	43.1%		
Germany	47.0%	Sweden	45.3%		
Hong Kong	188.0%	Switzerland	64.9%		
Iceland	46.1%	United Kingdom	30.1%		
Ireland	119.9%	United States	12.1%		
Israel	29.2%	China	19.8%		

Source: World Bank, Exports of goods and services (% of GDP).

The 'market' is a long-distance phenomenon. Most goods are not produced locally but rather imported across space. Many competitors and many producers in the modern large-scale 'market' are foreign. The relative weight of national and international markets in a modern economy varies from country to country (Table 4.5). But in either case, goods are routinely transported from distant locations. After the 1500s, as major economies were gradually globalized over centuries due to advances in oceanic shipping, and national economies were consolidated around train and telegraph networks, long-distance trade became a mass phenomenon. This was a repeat – yet on a much larger scale – of the earlier Roman-Indo-Chinese global trade in luxury goods. In the modern global economy, most goods are tradable across long distances.

Lean governments

An essential aspect of 'the market' and its paradoxical efficiency is lean government.[7] Lean government or limited government does not mean 'no government'. Governments properly provide laws and rules that underpin what is essential to a well-functioning market: honesty. Fraud and corruption impede and destroy markets. Corruption is ultimately a product of premodern patrimonial and feudal societies: it represents a personal client-like relation to government, rather than an impersonal one. To a degree, if imperfectly, we can measure levels of government corruption. There is a strong propensity of successful modern societies to minimize government corruption.

Fraud, dishonesty, cheating, deceit, lying, and duplicity of many different kinds likewise are destructive of the market. The virtue of honesty builds trust between strangers. 'The market' is filled with strangers. How do they know they can rely on each other? Because what they say is true, transparent, and frank. What they commit to, they will honestly do their best to deliver.

Good government helps enforce honesty. It also works to reduce violence in society. Like deceit, criminal and civil violence destroys markets. 'The market' is a spontaneous entity. Strangers voluntarily and readily exchange goods and services and produce goods and services to be exchanged. They do so because of mutual self-interest, itself another paradox of 'the market'. Pressure, intimidation, coercion, bullying, terror, threats, and extortion cripple this spontaneous interaction, replacing its horizontal reciprocity with a hierarchy of violence that is dominated by the physically strong and aggressive.

Not all government is good. There are gangster governments that intimidate their own citizens or that are corrupt. Expecting tributes and pay-offs for favored treatment is a form of asymmetrical reciprocity. That said, there is also a deeper problem with government, namely its capacity to crowd out 'the market'. It does this, often unwittingly, using techniques that are common to both premodern and modern states. These are techniques of licensing and subsidies, allocations and grants, regulation and industry protection. It is not that these techniques are in all instances bad or inappropriate. Nonetheless the 'logic' of the state and the 'logic' of the market are different. One is inescapably hierarchical. The other is self-organizing. The tendency of modern states is to replace personal hierarchy and personal service with impersonal hierarchies (organizations) and impersonal rules (regulations and procedures). The propensity, if not checked, to crowd out 'the market' remains.

That is why the obverse of the freedom of the market is limits on government. Markets do not operate free of rules and laws. Yet it can be so arranged that they operate free of onerous burdens imposed by such rules and laws. This is one of the conditions of a well-functioning and flourishing market. Rules can be efficient or inefficient. They can provide a terse effective focused minimal frame for responsible action. Alternatively, they can be a drag on action. Just as we can measure how much or how little governments behave like gangsters, so also we can measure the degree of onerous burden or conversely light touch that governments impose on markets. The optimal arrangement is for government to legally sanction market honesty and reliability with simple rules and procedures. These are framed so they do not consume large amounts of time and energy while at the same time expecting and requiring market participants to behave in ways that are transparent, trustworthy, and free from coercion in all its forms.

Cities

From the early modern age onwards, markets expanded around the world and across continents. The efficiency of transport grew. So did the size of states. The number of petty kingdoms and city-states declined, replaced by empires and nations. The politics and law of small states were consolidated into a range of larger nations, federations, and multinational unions. The territory administered by these latter political forms on the whole was significant and often large in physical size. The creation of wealth, though, moved in the opposite direction. It became increasingly concentrated in smaller city-regions that are located mostly in littoral and fluvial geographical places on the maritime rim of the Eurasian continental landmass and scattered across a limited number of continental riverine geographies (Table 2.2).

Both between nations and within nations, the pattern of wealth and prosperity is pointillist in character. A small number of littoral-fluvial city-regions dominate the world's wealth creation (Table 2.2). The degree of political harmony in a country often echoes the relative disparities between rich city-nodes and less wealthy regions and rural or ex-urban populations (Table 2.3). The existence of disparities is the lesser key question compared to that of the degrees of disparity. Successful modern societies tend be able to combine large and small entities in pleasing ways. Problems arise when the sense of proportion between large and small is disrupted.

Overall, the modern city entails a paradox. Modern transport, communication, and commerce disperse human activity and energy across space. Activity and energies spread, disseminate, and circulate. Production, creation, and location do the opposite. These cluster. They tend to be increasingly condensed in big cities that grow. This happens because cities tend to increase their productivity as their population expands and as their density increases.[8] Cities focus human energy. They concentrate, cluster, and mass that energy in ways that measurably increase productivity per capita and do so to a greater degree than do smaller towns and dispersed populations. Productivity is the single most important factor in generating economic growth. As population size and density and the interactive intensity of big cities increase, so the productivity of big cities tends to grow more rapidly than does the productivity of small towns or rural and rural-industrial regions.[9] This is true when we compare contemporary metro areas (Table 2.4).

Before the industrial revolution – and what it bequeathed, namely highly productive technology along with methods of transport and communication that multiplied the scale and reach of markets – the primary means of amplifying human productivity was the city (Table 4.6). It remains key to that endeavor today. What we call 'civilization' is a play on the city. It is where the spiritual, intellectual, and material meet in an uncanny fashion. The civilization of the city is not simply a belief system such as a religion or a political ideology. Unalloyed beliefs are mostly weak progenitors of high standards of living and quality of life. As Hegel rightly observed, opinion is a mix of truth and endless error. Opinions correlate little with successful societies. Civilization in contrast amalgamates intellect and matter, frames of mind and measurable social facts, the spiritual and the quantifiable, the invisible and the visible. In doing so, it reaches between the mystical or transcendent and the quotidian. At its peak, it

Table 4.6 Cities in history, percentage of population urbanized, 1500–1890

Year	1500	1600	1700	1800	1890
Belgium	21.1	18.8	23.9	18.9	34.5
France	4.2	5.9	9.2	8.8	25.9
Germany	3.2	4.1	4.8	5.5	28.2
Italy	14.9	16.8	14.7	18.3	21.2
Netherlands	15.8	24.3	33.6	28.8	33.4
Scandinavia	0.9	1.4	4	4.6	13.2
Switzerland	1.5	2.5	3.3	3.7	16
England and Wales	3.1	5.8	13.3	20.3	61.9
Scotland	1.6	3	5.3	17.3	50.3
Ireland	0	0	3.4	7	17.6
Western Europe	6.1	7.8	9.9	10.6	31.3
Portugal	3	14.1	11.5	8.7	12.7
Spain	6.1	11.4	9	11.1	26.8
China	3.8	4.0a[a]	n.a.	3.8	4.4
Japan	2.9	4.4	n.a.	12.3	16

Source: Angus Maddison, The World Economy: A Millennial Perspective, OECD, 2001, Table B.14.

[a] 1650.

achieves this in lucid and powerful ways. The uncanny bridge of civilization – and the tensions that it binds and balances – is one of the prime conditions of successful modernity.[10]

Industries

Modern prosperity is a function of productivity, which is a measure of the ability to produce more with less. As an economy grows each year greater wealth is produced per capita. Karl Marx lived from 1818 to 1883. In those 65 years, Britain's GDP per capita in constant 2011 dollars grew from US$3,241 per capita to US$5,879, a 180 percent increase (Table 1.1). The inflation-adjusted average wage and salary of British employees grew from £2,500 in 1855 to £25,000 in 2015, a tenfold real increase.[11] Marx assumed that capitalism would immiserate the population. It did the opposite. In part this was because of something that Marx himself observed, namely, the application of science to production.[12] When people talk about 'capitalism' what they imply without necessarily saying so is the system of industrial capitalism, a mix of markets and technologies. Technology has vastly increased the productivity of modern labor. The combination of capital and labor in the modern era has meant the combination of machines and human beings. Machines replaced premodern hand tools. The productive power of the machine is vastly greater than that of the hand tool.

Why did the machine, and its combination with the human workforce, emerge in the late eighteenth and early nineteenth centuries and from then on accelerate? We see the resulting rise of industrial societies for which there is no historical precedent. One reason among many for this was that the power of guilds declined. For centuries these had insulated skilled and semi-skilled craft-workers from competition. Both the cause and the effect of this protection was to constrain technological innovation. When machines replaced hand tools, the nature of labor changed. Underlying this was the paradoxical impulse of successful modern societies. In this case it was the paradox of creative destruction. The economist and sociologist Joseph Schumpeter used the term to describe how the creative power of modern capitalism, its capacity to radically drive up productivity over time, was rooted in destruction.[13] To create, one must destroy old techniques and methods of production, shrink old industries, and shift the locus of production from one town, region, or nation to another.

Schumpeter was not the first to observe the process of creative destruction. In 1832, in the second part of his drama *Faust*, Goethe explored the antonymic pair.[14] His work implied that destruction is built into modern acts of creation. In this version creation has a demonic character. After Goethe, a similar view echoes through the various currents of nineteenth-century political romanticism. The idea of creation-as-destruction culminates in Nietzsche. For him, the breaker *is* the creator.[15] Affirmation entails annihilation.[16] Schumpeter reversed this emphasis. For him, creation is not a break or a breach. Rather it is a cycle or rotation.[17] The destructive component of creation is expressed not in fractures, ruptures, and splits but rather in cyclical phases, in up-and-down turns, and in the endless recurrence of these.

In the case of successful economies, the increased use of machines means less use of labor. Labor is shed. There are negative – on occasions agonizing – social and human consequences of that process. But there are also greater positives. As less labor is used, the remaining labor force becomes much more productive. Increased productivity means higher real wages and a more affluent workforce. But what of those who exit an industry because of the greater use of machines? Increased productivity in an existing industry means that part of the capital that was once deployed to the old established industry can be invested in a new industry that employs, along with capital, labor. As one industry shrinks, another grows. Overall, the size of the economy measured in value produced per capita expands. Growth depends on shrinkage just as creation relies on destruction.

A further paradox is implied by this. A byword for the application of science to industry, and the development of technologies, is innovation. This shorthand makes sense colloquially. Whether it is a technology breakthrough or simply the adapting of an existing technology – both involve degrees of newness. No newness though is ever a ground-zero kind of newness. Even the most startling technologies, when looked at closely, have a long prehistory. There is also a misleading tendency to think of newness (to the extent that it characterizes a technology) as a kind of fashion that, like all fashion, will soon fall out of fashion. Like most areas of modern human endeavor, there are technology fads and crazes. Technology is no more immune to vogues, cults, manias, and trends than any other aspect of modern society. That said, the most powerful technologies (machine production, electricity, the car, the railway, the computer) endure. In the end, it is their durability and persistence over the long run that impresses more than their initial newness. Their long-lasting nature deeply impacts the shape of modern societies. Creation, in this case technological creation, in the long run is more a conservative phenomenon than it is a radical one, though this is so in the paradoxical way of successful societies. Because even the conservative and durable nature of major technologies entails a radical moment or succession of radical moments. But, equally, the converse is true, for little in the way of technology innovation is sui generis. Rather it accumulates in steps. It tends to build on what has come before. That is so even if some of those technological adaptations are so powerful that for a time they amaze, surprise, startle, and shock.

Modern political romanticism is a determined foe of productive modernity. Its impulse is to protest against the powers of inertia and to disdain whatever is established. The 'anti-establishment' bent is deeply rooted in modern life as much as the productive bent is. The two frequently war with each other, not least about whether creation is the ecstatic destroyer of the status quo or whether it is cyclical rather than progressive – meaning that technology change, like change in general, endlessly repeats and in so doing periodically refreshes economy and society. In this latter interpretation, change, including the deepest kinds of economic change, is a form of continuity. Through cyclical change, the underlying continuity of industrial capitalist societies is maintained and reinforced.

Such changes may periodically disconcert and alarm populations. Waves of scare follow waves of innovation. Just as technologies delight and enthuse moderns so mass technology change upsets and disquiets them. The result is an irony. The political romantics who decry whatever is established turn and decry this technological disestablishment. The tension is palpable. The romantic deifies originality, the pursuit of the new and deifies originality, the holding onto the original and the preceding. Initiative and the initial, the first-as-future and the first-as-past, coexist in the same mental universe. The impulse to tear down as a way of holding on to what exists is the result of this bivalent mentality. Holding on is nominally a type of conservative worldview but it is different in kind to the worldview of a Schumpeter. For the latter, it is not the origin that matters, and that represents the anchor of continuity. Rather it is the turning wheel, the rotation, by which a modern society and economy simultaneously refreshes and reaffirms itself.

Reading publics

Contemporary societies pride themselves on education. They eagerly tell anyone who will listen how much they spend on education. Quantitative rankings of national performance often treat education resource inputs as a prime criterion of social success. Yet when we look at the *results* of education (Table 4.7) – that is, the capacity of a country's 15-year-olds to read, write, and calculate – we find that spending per capita on education means little. There is no correlation

Table 4.7 Good value education spending

Rank	Primary + secondary education spending per FTE student OECD countries 2014 (2016 constant PPP US$) highest to lowest	PISA 15-year-olds Combined Reading, Mathematics, Science Performance Average Ranking 2015	Nation/territory	Plus or minus rank difference between education spending and education outcome	Nation/territory	PISA points average 2015	Cost per PISA point of a FTE student 2014 (2016 constant PPP US$)
1	Luxembourg	Singapore	Australia	−3	Australia	502	19
2	Norway	Hong Kong (China)	Austria	−23	Austria	492	28
3	Switzerland	Japan	Belgium	−14	Belgium	503	24
4	Austria	Macao (China)	B-S-J-G (China)	N/A	B-S-J-G (Coastal China)	514	N/A
5	United States	Estonia	**Canada**	**6**	Canada	523	20
6	Belgium	Taiwan	Czech Republic	−4	Czech Republic	491	14
7	United Kingdom	Canada	Denmark	−10	Denmark	504	23
8	Denmark	Finland	**Estonia**	**21**	Estonia	524	13
9	Sweden	Korea	**Finland**	**9**	Finland	523	19
10	Iceland	B-S-J-G (China)	France	−10	France	496	20
11	Germany	Slovenia	Germany	−2	Germany	508	21
12	Netherlands	Ireland	Hong Kong	N/A	Hong Kong	533	N/A
13	Canada	Germany	Hungary	−6	Hungary	474	12
14	Korea	Netherlands	Iceland	−24	Iceland	481	23
15	Japan	Switzerland	**Ireland**	**7**	Ireland	509	18
16	France	New Zealand	Israel	−10	Israel	472	14
17	Finland	Norway	Italy	−10	Italy	485	18
18	Australia	Denmark	**Japan**	**12**	Japan	529	19
19	Ireland	Poland	**Korea**	**5**	Korea	519	20
20	New Zealand	Belgium	Latvia	−4	Latvia	487	14
21	Slovenia	Australia	Luxembourg	−32	Luxembourg	483	44
22	Italy	Viet Nam	Macao	N/A	Macao	527	N/A

#							
23	Portugal	United Kingdom	Mexico	−18	Netherlands	508	21
24	Spain	Portugal	Netherlands	−2	Mexico	416	8
25	Czech Republic	Sweden	**New Zealand**	**4**	New Zealand	506	18
26	Estonia	France	Norway	−15	Norway	504	30
27	Latvia	Austria	**Poland**	**10**	Poland	504	13
28	Israel	Spain	Portugal	−1	Portugal	497	16
29	Poland	Czech Republic	Singapore	N/A	Singapore	552	N/A
30	Slovak Republic	United States	Slovak Republic	−11	Slovak Republic	463	14
31	—	—	**Slovenia**	**10**	Slovenia	509	18
32	—	—	Spain	−4	Spain	491	16
33	—	—	Sweden	−16	Sweden	496	22
34	—	—	Switzerland	−12	Switzerland	506	29
35	—	—	Taiwan	N/A	Taiwan	524	N/A
36	—	—	United Kingdom	−16	Turkey	421	9
37	—	—	United States	−25	United Kingdom	500	24
38	—	—	—	—	United States	488	25

Source: PISA 2015 Results (Volume I): Excellence and Equity in Education, OECD 2016; United States National Centre for Education Statistics, Digest of Education Statistics, Table 605.10. Gross domestic product per capita and expenditures by public and private education institutions per full-time-equivalent (FTE) student, by level of education and country: Selected years, 2005 through 2014 based on OECD data. B-S-J-G (China) is Beijing-Shanghai-Jiangsu-Guangdong (China).

Note: N/A, not available. Spending per student data available only for OECD countries. Canada's spending includes pre-primary education; Japan's spending includes postsecond-ary non-higher education. Figures in bold indicate good-value high performance.

between levels of spending and levels of student performance. The key literacies – the ability to read and comprehend proficiently, write and reason fluently, and grasp commonplace mathematical concepts and operations – are essential to a well-functioning society. They are the foundation of the reading public. The reading public in turn is the plinth on which all other publics – be they political, media, professional, or intellectual – rest. A person's ability to participate in public life of any kind is profoundly conditioned by their literate capacity, in particular their capacity for *sola scriptura*, their ability to read and understand a text and judge it for themselves.

One of the worst twentieth-century social theories was that of Marshall McLuhan, who advocated the oral word in place of the printed word.[18] This was a terrible idea. The handful of prosperous societies that emerged in the early modern period all enjoyed exceptional levels of literacy compared with other nations. They achieved that without public education acts. Beyond a modest level, the investment of increasing public and private resources in the standard modern teaching medium – the classroom – yields ever-decreasing results. Serious learning requires extensive and intensive book reading. It has a significant autodidactic component that classroom teaching cannot and does not replace (Table 4.7).

The historical models for this were small highly literate groups (such as the Zoroastrians, Jains, Jews, Huguenots, and Copts) that had a history of outsized social success in spite of various oppressions. The Gutenberg print revolution made possible the mass reproduction of books. Because of this societies rather than just small heterodox religious groups could aspire to literate autodidacticism. A handful of societies moved in this direction, though most did not because from the mid-nineteenth century onwards the focus of education shifted toward spending money on classrooms.[19] Beyond a certain point, every additional amount spent per head on classrooms had a diminishing value while high-performing states, cities, and regions retained various autodidactic ways of learning. These are typically home centered or library based rather than classroom focused.

A commonplace way of conceiving an economy is to assume it starts with a number of factors of production. This model supposes that these factors of production can be made more efficient and thus more productive. The model also assumes investment in public infrastructure and public services. The odd thing about this paradigm is that the second aspect of the model focuses on outputs while the third aspect concentrates on inputs. Education usually ends up being treated under the third aspect. This presumes that education is principally an input not an output. So what matters in education is the resourcing of schools and teachers, not the output, which is the student's measurable ability to perform intellectual tasks. This standard model of treating education means that education systems can be declared a success because they are allocated large resources by the state while their actual output – student cognitive performance – declines. The allocation model of education is premodern in spirit. It is essentially 'feudal' in character even if it is dressed up in ultra-modern procedural and legal-rational terms.

Systems are properly measured by their outcomes not their allocated inputs. The difference in the two assumptions is the difference between a hierarchical conception of society and a functional conception. The input versus output notion of education is not simply a matter of economic behavior. The input-output distinction characterizes two competing models of cognition. One supposes that cognition is driven principally by inputs – in the case of education, by instruction. This points to an underlying paradox of modern education: instruction is not learning, yet it is frequently mistaken for learning. The consequence of this is a tension. Modern societies value learning, yet they invest heavily in instruction. The latter, beyond a limited point, negates the former. Learning is primarily a form of self-education. It is a type of autopoietics. It is an act carried out, with discipline, concentration, and perseverance, by the learner. Instruction has some value in pointing the learner in the right direction. But that value is inherently limited compared with the fruits of disciplined self-formation and focused autodidactic behaviors underpinning capacious self-learning. Literate development is mostly an act that motivated persons perform on themselves.

Households

Successful modern societies bring large numbers of strangers together. These strangers interact through markets, technologies, reading publics, and big cities. Yet this is only possible because an opposite trend occurs simultaneously. This is the expansion of the importance of the nuclear family. Detached from the extended family typical of hierarchical societies, the nuclear family pivots on pair-bonded dual-headed households, with and without children. Successful societies maintain a high per capita number of these households compared with either extended households or sole-headed households. The nuclear family type offers flexibility in responding to the dynamic nature of modern systems. At the same time, it provides the necessary emotional intensity and closeness that the larger public world of strangers cannot provide.

The nuclear family is distinctly different from the extended family. The latter has patriarchal and patrimonial characteristics. The former has shed those traits. Relationships in the classic nuclear family are organized via pattern forms of complementarity and proportionality rather than hierarchy. Kinship relations and networks lose their importance. Among adults, protection and obedience relationships are replaced by models of mutual aid. The maturation of children involves ever-increasing autonomy and interaction with the public world of strangers. Between the world of strangers and the households lies the world of friends. Successful societies rely on the ability of adults to form stable long-lasting dual-headed households and for the members of those households to form friendships outside the household. Last but not least household members have to be able to draw on the emotional certainties of household members and friends but at the same time be able to trust the wider world of strangers and be comfortable and at ease in interacting with those strangers. They have to be able paradoxically to lean simultaneously on the strength of strong ties and

Table 4.8 Printed books and printed books per million persons (BMP), 1450–1800

150% or more of the Western European rate of BMP.

Periods	Western Europe printed books	Western Europe BMP	United Kingdom printed books	UK BMP compared to Western Europe	France printed books	France BMP compared to Western Europe	Belgium printed books	Belgium BMP compared to Western Europe	Netherlands printed books	Netherlands BMP compared to Western Europe	Germany printed books	Germany BMP compared to Western Europe
1450–1499	12,589	220	53	24%	191	87%	281	128%	498	226%	2,689	1223%
1500–1549	79,017	1,317	712	54%	2,229	169%	1,370	104%	1,004	76%	12,319	936%
1550–1599	138,427	2,048	1,855	91%	2,274	111%	3,751	183%	2,198	107%	2,215	108%
1600–1649	200,906	2,677	5,010	187%	3,225	120%	2,601	97%	9,584	358%	2,561	96%
1650–1699	331,035	4,213	11,825	281%	4,184	99%	3,894	92%	17,228	409%	3,753	89%
1700–1749	355,073	3,998	9,433	236%	3,220	81%	1,368	34%	20,840	521%	4,764	119%
1750–1799	628,801	5,768	10,162	176%	5,884	102%	1,740	30%	24,761	429%	5,753	100%

Periods	Western Europe printed books	Western Europe BMP	Switzerland printed books	Switzerland BMP compared to Western Europe	Italy printed books	Italy BMP compared to Western Europe	Spain printed books	Spain BMP compared to Western Europe	Sweden printed books	Sweden BMP compared to Western Europe
1450–1499	12,589	220	615	280%	432	196%	68	31%	11	5%
1500–1549	79,017	1,317	4,678	355%	1,529	116%	313	24%	58	4%
1550–1599	138,427	2,048	6,666	325%	3,434	168%	299	15%	72	4%
1600–1649	200,906	2,677	1,924	72%	2,670	100%	556	21%	2,467	92%
1650–1699	331,035	4,213	1,472	35%	3,274	78%	827	20%	3,504	83%
1700–1749	355,073	3,998	991	25%	2,656	66%	985	25%	4,592	115%
1750–1799	628,801	5,768	3,005	52%	4,446	77%	1,537	27%	10,820	188%

Sources: Angus Maddison, Growth of World Population GDP and GDP Per Capita before 1820, Table B – 10, World Population, 20 Countries and Regional Totals, AD 0–1998; Eltjo Buringh and Jan Luiten van Zanden, 'Charting the "Rise of the West": Manuscripts and Printed Books in Europe, A Long-Term Perspective from the Sixth through Eighteenth Centuries', *The Journal of Economic History* 69:2, 2009, 409–445, Table 2.

BMP, books per million persons.

weak ties. This requires a considerable ambidextrous ability to switch rapidly backwards and forwards between those who are close and those who are distant, those who are intimate and those who are alien. The necessary union of private and public, warmth and coolness, dearness and disinterest is not easy to attain but is richly productive when it is.

Strengths and weaknesses

Today, 193 countries are members of the United Nations. Twenty-two of those, plus the de facto city-state of Hong Kong – twenty-three altogether, or about 10 percent of the total – are classified here as successful societies. This means simply enough that across some 30 different performance criteria, those 23 states or territories routinely end up being placed somewhere in the top-performing cohort, that is, ranked 25th or above in the world (Table 4.4). The bottom two overall in the top-25 are examples of a country that is entering the top-25 (Slovenia) and a country that is exiting the top-25 (Italy). In the case of the latter, its historic success is unraveling while the former nation appears to be on its way to achieving a high level of economic and social success.

What is currently the case may change in the future. On the other hand, the relative achievement of nations compared to the global social mean is for the most part a long-term phenomenon. This in turn is an indicator of just how difficult it is for countries to reach the peak of successful modernity. It is not enough, say, to have an energetic free market economy without also performing well across the spectrum of innovative industries, attractive cities, lean governments, bookish literacies, and strong emotional ties. What matters is not one criterion but rather the mix or mosaic of criteria. What this underlines is that 'success' is a multi-dimensional pattern rather than a single-dimensional goal. Multi-dimensional pattern performance means that countries are successful (or not) in their own ways. There is not a single recipe for success. What there is though is a series of dimensions across which successful modern states have to perform well though not necessarily in each case outstandingly.

This brings us back to the nature of patterns. A pattern is a composition of different shapes, forces, and qualities. Patterns may resemble each other yet weigh and integrate those shapes, forces, and qualities in different ways. That's the strength of pattern thinking. We can recognize that A and Z are not the same yet are still alike. There are an infinite array of different examples of branching, nets, waves, bubbles, spirals, lattices, and so on. Yet we have relatively little difficulty recognizing each of these patterns in the numerous contexts in which they appear. Patterns are a cognitive shorthand. They are also a practical shorthand. They provide simple straightforward ways of putting together complex and disparate forms, materials, and qualities. The weight given to those disparate forms, materials, or qualities may vary significantly in each specific case but we still easily recognize the pattern that is common to each single instance of it.

The pattern of successful societies is a mix of free markets, lean governments, innovative industries, attractive large cities, nuclear households, and bookish literacies. How exactly those are achieved, and the degree to which they are achieved, varies from nation to nation. Prosperity depends on competitive dynamic markets and technology innovation. That is true. But several other factors are also important, including flexible self-help households, do-it-yourself literate behavior, and beautiful self-assembling cities.

Successful societies with (for example) high levels of market regulation may offset this deficit with iconic cities and a pervading sense of aesthetic order. Japan and Denmark are good examples of this. In short there is no identikit formula for each case of a prosperous society. Nonetheless, the same underlying pattern is repeated. It is a composite of six key elements. Because each of those elements are put together in different ways, the elements are present or weighted to larger or smaller degrees in each specific case. That means, as far as our 30 criteria and 6 key elements of performance are concerned, successful nations, even the most successful, have strengths and weaknesses (Table 4.3 and 4.4).

Take the example of Sweden. It performs well on the basics of GDP per capita, social prosperity, life satisfaction, broad wealth distribution, and the rule of law. It does markedly less well in terms of lean government and market freedoms. It is technologically sophisticated but underperforms in creative industries. The attractiveness of its cities and the level of its literacies are on the weaker side. It's a very high-trust society but its nuclear household fabric is under pressure. Compare that with its neighbor Denmark. It has many of the same strengths and weaknesses as Sweden, but there are some notable differences. Its cities are more attractive and its literacies are stronger.

The United States on the other hand has strong GDP per capita but its social prosperity is significantly weaker. Life expectancy in America is poor for a generally high-performing nation and both its markets and the state are poor at producing a balanced distribution of wealth, the happy medium between equality and inequality. The United States does well on cost-effective government, market freedoms, and industry performance yet is notably weak on levels of trust and the strength of its nuclear households. Its delivery of the rule of law is low for a country that tends to turn social issues into legal issues. It has aesthetically pleasing cities but not especially livable ones. The prosperity gap between America's major cities and the rest of the country is large and its pedagogic literacies are poor. Its performance in high-school mathematics is abysmal.

America is a settler society. Other countries that belong to that cohort include Australia, Canada, New Zealand, and Israel. Like America, Australia tends to be strong on market freedoms and cost-effective government. It performs much better on the rule of law. It is more effective at achieving a balanced distribution of wealth, principally in its case through the market rather than through the state. It enjoys high levels of trust and strong nuclear households. So its social fabric is in good condition. Its Achilles heel is industry innovation. It is not a strong technology innovator and its exports tend to dominated by technologically unsophisticated goods. Its cities are exceptionally livable with degrees of aesthetic iconicity. But its geographic distance from the world's population centers limits its attractiveness to visitors. Its reading and science literacies are only average, its math literacy is weak, and its creative output is mediocre.

Like Australia, New Zealand does a lot better distributing wealth through the market rather than the state. Its market freedoms are strong while its industrial innovation is much weaker. Unlike Australia, New Zealand does not have especially cost-effective government. Both Australia and New Zealand have improved their level of productivity over the long run, bringing them closer to high-productivity nations like the United States, Japan, Germany, Korea, and Singapore. New Zealand's household and literacy profiles are much like those of Australia. The social fabric of Canada in contrast is a bit weaker than its antipodean cousins but its pedagogic literacy is considerably higher. Across the rule of law, lean government, markets, and industries, Canada performs solidly. The technology sophistication of its exports though is low and its creative output is notably weak. Its cities are livable but not aesthetically compelling. The most recent addition to the settler society cohort, Israel, has a mixed record in government spending, weaknesses in its rule of law, poor levels of market freedom, mid-range levels of technology performance and creative outputs, and high levels of nuclear household bonds and friendship bonds but low levels of trust in strangers.

France is one of the members of core Europe, *Kerneuropa*, the economic pivot of Continental Europe. It is globally competitive and sits in the mid-range for technology yet the cost effectiveness of its government and its degree of market freedom and economic freedom is terrible. Its household and friendship fabric is mid-range while its level of trust in strangers is low. It ranks very high in attractive cities but much lower in livable cities. The gap between its major metropolis and its rural regions is large and its literacy performance is weak. Germany in contrast is mid-range in government cost effectiveness and market and economic freedom. It sits in the technological mid-range but ranks high in global competitiveness, the technology sophistication of its exports, and the level of its productivity. Its nuclear household fabric is somewhat frayed, its social trust is in the higher range, and its friendship networking middling. The livability of its cities, like its literacies, is on higher end; the attractiveness of its cities is on the somewhat lower end.

The highest performing entities, Singapore and Hong Kong, are in maritime East Asia. Japan and South Korea are also prominent. Taiwan as well would be in the 'top-25' of nations except that data for it has become increasingly hard to find. It has been 'disappeared' from global databases, in most cases because of political pressure from mainland China.[20] Singapore ranks high on virtually all criteria except city livability (even so it's a highly visited city). On trust in strangers and creative outputs, it is mid-ranking. Hong Kong is broadly similar. It performs highly on most criteria. Its exceptions are the technological sophistication of its exports, the fabric of its nuclear households, and the livability of the city (though like Singapore it is a highly visited city). The reading, math, and science literacies of Hong Kong and Singapore are both at the top level. Japan's also is very good. The Japanese strength is technology. Its weakness is economic freedom. Its social bonds are frayed. The state of the nuclear household in Japan is under considerable pressure. Trust and friendship ties are mid-range. Its government spending is quite effective. Its cities rank high on livability, visitation, and beauty. South Korea also has a highly efficient government, though poor rule of law and a poor level of market freedom. The nation is technologically sophisticated with high levels of productivity. Its nuclear households also are under pressure and its level of trust in strangers is poor. Its cities are attractive but not particularly livable.

Notes

1 Ludwig Erhard (1958, 186) put it this way: 'It should not be denied that in modern industrial countries even a good economic policy will have to be complemented by social policy measures. On the other hand it is true to say that every effective social aid will have to be based on an adequate and growing national income, which means an efficient economy. Thus it must be in the interest of every organic social policy to secure an expanding and sound economy, and to take care that the principles guiding this economy are maintained and extended.' Erhard dubbed this paradox 'the social market economy'.
2 Comte, 1875; Durkheim, 2014 [1893]; Elias, 2000 [1939]; Maine, 2017 [1866]; Marx, 1992 [1867]; Parsons, 1951; Spencer, 1978 [1897]; Toennies, 1971; Veblen, 1914, 1963 [1921], 1994 [1899].
3 The terms heteronomy and autonomy are borrowed from Cornelius Castoriadis (1997a, 1997b) though the term autonomy is used here in a somewhat different way than Castoriadis used it. For him, autonomy implied not just the replacement of social hierarchies but the conscious direction by society of itself, involving the large-scale participation by social actors in collective decision-making as if the whole society was a giant participatory parliament or series of such. At the same time, and at odds with this, Castoriadis emphasizes the anonymous way that society operates. In fact that latter anonymous quality makes the most powerful aspects of modern society autonomous. Systems, as I call them here, are self-organizing and hence autonomous in their functioning but not on the model of the conscious collective legislator but rather on the model of pattern-driven self-assembling order.
4 The term 'symmetrical reciprocity' is drawn from the work of Agnes Heller. See Heller, 1987, 220–256, 1990, 145–159.
5 On topology and other pattern-ties, see Murphy, 2017.
6 As Agnes Heller observed (1990, 148), premodern societies were dominated by social hierarchies. Modern societies have at least partially defenestrated this arrangement. In doing so modernity 'embarked on a unique historical experiment'. This involved the renegotiation of human coexistence. 'In the prudent discussion of "the social contract" or a "new covenant", the early moderns found an apposite metaphor for this renegotiation. The term "contract" is awkward, yet it still grasps the most crucial aspect of modernity. *Symmetrical reciprocity* is the name of the new arrangement, at all levels – from the family to political decision-making through the relationships of cultures, peoples and states.'
7 Murphy, 2019.
8 Bettencourt et al., 2007, 2010.
9 Bouchet, Liu, and Parilla, 2018.
10 Murphy and Roberts, 2004.

11 Economic Research Council, Chart of the Week: Week 41, 2015: Historical Real Average Salary (Source: Bank of England).
12 For example, 'modern industry . . . makes science a productive force distinct from labor and presses it into the service of capital', Marx, 1992 [1867], 20.
13 Schumpeter, 2010 [1942].
14 Goethe, 2008 [1832].
15 Nietzsche, Zarathustra's Prologue, *Thus Spake Zarathustra*, 1961 [1883–1885].
16 'Denial and destruction are inseparable from an affirmative attitude towards life.' Nietzsche, Why I am a Destiny, *Ecce Homo*, 2007 [1888, 1908].
17 Schumpeter, 1939.
18 McLuhan, 1962.
19 As this occurred so did a trans-valuation of values, a reaction against literacy and in favor of orality, epitomized by McLuhan, 1962.
20 This is not merely a political and moral disgrace but it also distorts accounts of what is a powerful economic and social reality of China. Namely that there are 'two Chinas' – one maritime and riverine; the other territorial China. Taiwan should be regularly reported on as Singapore and Hong Kong are. So should the PRC sub-set of Beijing-Shanghai-Jiangsu-Guangdong, as the OECD's Programme for International Student Assessment (PISA) already does.

Bibliography

Ackroyd, P. 2004. *Albion: The Origins of the English Imagination*. London: Vintage.
Bettencourt, L.M.A., J. Lobo, D. Helbing, C. Kuhnert and G.B. West. 2007. "Growth, Innovation, Scaling, and the Pace of Life in Cities". *PNAS: Proceedings of the National Academy of Sciences of the United States* 104, no. 17: 7301–7306.
Bettencourt, L.M.A., J. Lobo, D. Strumsky and G.B. West. 2010. "Urban Scaling and Its Deviations: Revealing the Structure of Wealth, Innovation and Crime across Cities". *PLOS One* 5:11.
Bouchet, M., S. Liu and J. Parilla. 2018. *Global Metro Monitor 2018*. Washington, DC: Metro Policy Program, Brookings Institution.
Castoriadis, C. 1997a. *World in Fragments*. Stanford, CA: Stanford University Press.
Castoriadis, C. 1997b. *The Castoriadis Reader*. Oxford: Blackwell.
Comte, A. 1875. *System of Positive Polity*. London: Longmans, Green.
Durkheim, E. 2014 [1893]. *The Division of Labor in Society*. New York: Free Press.
Elias, N. 2000 [1939]. *The Civilizing Process*. Revised edition. Oxford: Blackwell.
Erhard, L. 1958. *Prosperity through Competition*. New York: Praeger.
Goethe, J.W. von. 2008 [1832]. *Faust Part 2*. Oxford: Oxford University Press.
Heller, A. 1990. "Rights, Modernity, Democracy". In *Can Modernity Survive?* 145–159. Blackwell: Polity.
Heller, A. 1987. *Beyond Justice*. Oxford: Blackwell.
Maine, H. S. 2017 [1866]. *Ancient Law*. Abingdon: Routledge.
Marx, K. 1992 [1867]. *Capital*, Volume 1. Harmondsworth: Penguin.
McLuhan, M. 1962. *The Guttenberg Galaxy: The Making of Typographic Man*. Toronto, ON: University of Toronto Press.
Murphy, P. 2019. *Limited Government*. Abingdon: Routledge.
Murphy, P. 2017. "Topological Creation and the Homoeomorphic Imagination". In C.R. Dinesen, M. Meldgaard, A. Michelsen, H. Oxvig and I. Berling (eds), *Architecture Drawing Topology*, 235–246. Baunach: AADR/Spurbuch Verlag.

Murphy, P. and D. Roberts. 2004. *Dialectic of Romanticism: A Critique of Modernism*. London: Continuum.

Nietzsche, F. 2007 [1888, 1908]. *Ecce Homo: How to Become What You Are*. Oxford: Oxford University Press.

Nietzsche, F. 1961 [1883–1885]. *Thus Spoke Zarathustra: A Book for Everyone and No One*. London: Penguin.

Parsons, T. 1951. *The Social System*. London: Routledge and Kegan Paul.

Schumpeter, J. 1939. *Business Cycles: A Theoretical, Historical and Statistical Analysis of the Capitalist Process*. New York: McGraw-Hill.

Schumpeter, J. 2010 [1942]. *Capitalism, Socialism and Democracy*. London: Routledge.

Spencer, H. 1978 [1897]. *The Principles of Ethics*, Volumes 1 and 2. Indianapolis, IN: Liberty Fund.

Toennies, F. 1971. *On Sociology: Pure, Applied and Empirical, Selected Writings*. Chicago, IL: University of Chicago Press.

Veblen, T. 1994 [1899]. *The Theory of the Leisure Class*. Mineola, NY: Dover.

Veblen, T. 1963 [1921]. *The Engineers and the Price System*. New York: Harcourt, Brace.

Veblen, T. 1914. *The Instinct of Workmanship and the State of the Industrial Arts*. New York: Macmillan.

5   Patterns and rules

The very, very long modernity

As one door closes another opens. Amidst the chaos of Rome's fall, the 400s saw the birth of two unprepossessing social formations. One was on the North-West rim of the disintegrating Western half of the Roman Empire. The other was on the South-East rim. Their existence barely registered at the time. Yet in the long run the Venetians and the North Sea Anglo-Saxons each offered a powerful alternative to the landed power and terrene mentality of the Continental states that followed in the footsteps of Charlemagne (742–814). The least prepossessing of these two rim societies was that of the Anglo-Saxons. In the long run, though, they proved to be the most influential. Such is the irony of history. Escapees from the Gothic invasions founded Venice on a sliver of Roman-Byzantine territory along an isolated lagoon-dominated stretch of coast. Venice would emerge as the last of the great sea powers before the onset of the modern oceanic age. Around the same time in the 400s, the Angles, Saxons, Jutes, and Frisians invaded, migrated to, and settled in post-Roman Britain. By 600 they had split Celtic Britain in half. They occupied the part that at its distant westward points stretches from present-day Edinburgh through Birmingham and Bristol to Plymouth.

These settlers came from a small arc-like strip of coastland that runs from the tip of the Jutland Peninsula, facing both the North Sea and the Baltic Sea, south to the tidal-prone lower reaches of the Elbe River and then westward along the Friesian coast. This narrow semicircular span today can be traversed by travelling from Danish Ålborg to Dutch Rotterdam through German Lübeck and Hamburg. The geographic midpoint of this bowing journey is the North Sea mouth of the Elbe. Here on the coastal rim of North-Western Europe was the seedbed of an eccentric series of influential societies. Among them were the Hanseatic League (whose founder-city was Lübeck), the Netherlands, and England.[1]

The diaspora of this littoral region carried with them, right up until today, a taste for long-distance activity. The Danes first appear in recorded history in the mid-500s straddling between Skane (southern Sweden) and the Jutland Peninsula. From 800 to 1100 the Danish-Norwegian 'Vikings' made extraordinary long-distance maritime trading, raiding, and colonizing voyages across oceans and seas and along rivers to Iceland, Newfoundland, the Black Sea, the Caspian Sea, Constantinople, and the Caliphate of Cordoba in Spain. They conquered much of the 'Danelaw' North of England in the 800s and Normandy in the 900s. The Norman descendants of those Norsemen then reconquered Britain in 1066. With them came the Frankish and Romano-Gallic ways they had assimilated. Norman castles and manors subjugated the English. But to a surprising degree old North Sea Germanic and Danish property, family, and venturing norms persisted beneath the surface of the vanquished society.

What the North Sea landers and later the Danes brought with them to the island home of the Britons were the rudiments of *gesellschaft*. That's what the nineteenth-century North Frisian German sociologist Ferdinand Tönnies called it.[2] He was a socialist and disliked *gesellschaft*. Yet he understood its significance, perhaps not least because Frisia from the 900s through the 1400s successfully resisted feudalism and a manorial economy. Neither a nobility nor obligatory feudal labor took root there. Frisian municipalities were self-governing with voting based on a property franchise. A *gesellschaft* is a society dominated by impersonal, contractual, and indirect relationships. Every society has a social glue that holds it together. Across most of human history that glue has been various kinds of personal hierarchy. The oldest are kin-based hierarchies. Later on, client-style patrimonial societies developed. The bonds of master and servant, lord and vassal, patron and client are among the many ways that cultures manage to bolt individuals together in ladder-like structures.

Even today most states, whatever their superficial modernity, are neo-patrimonial in nature. The need for *guanxi* or connections to navigate contemporary China's Communist state is a classic yet commonplace example. Patrimony was the Continental European norm from the days of Charlemagne until the mid-nineteenth century when impersonal procedural bureaucracies began to appear. These replaced fealty with rules, nobility with qualifications, patrons with supervisors, and connections with contacts. Socialists like Tönnies sentimentalized patrimony as a kind of *gemeinschaft* or community. Yet they were also instrumental in replacing the personalized status step-ladders of European patrimonial societies with an impersonal system of 'rule by rules' in which outward communitarianism was matched by inward officiousness.

In the beginning was the household

The Anglo-Saxons pursued a pathway that was atypical. By historical standards they had an unusual social structure. It was not based on elaborate kinship networks but rather on what anthropologists call the absolute nuclear family.[3] In the late 1970s the Cambridge historian Alan Macfarlane began to write about the importance of this.[4] This was a society that emphasized immediate close family rather than the larger kinship group of aunts, uncles, and cousins. Macfarlane suggested that by the 700s this unusual individualistic settler-family structure held sway over much of England.[5] Keep in mind that the original

Anglo-Saxon settlers numbered somewhere between 20,000 and 100,000. This is compared with an estimated Celtic population of several million.

The nuclear family model is economically and socially adept.[6] It presupposes monogamy, one married partner at a time. It focuses on couples rather than kin as the key social unit. It separates husband and wife from the households of relatives. These factors together encourage economic flexibility and mobility. They are the oil of mercantile and dynamic settler societies. In contrast with kinship, coupling turns households into units of economic growth. In this model children exit the parental household once they grow up. Offspring are brought up to be independent. There is no customary or legal expectation that children will inherit parental property or in what proportion or manner. Families can keep property intact if they want or break it up if they wish or give it away to a cat charity if so inclined. This allows tremendous adaptability in property matters. Owners do not have to check with anyone including blood heirs before selling their property.

The nuclear family model is historically atypical.[7] The way, for example, English family-inheritance norms developed contrasted sharply with those of Continental Europe. There the practice evolved of multiple generations living in the family house and the compulsory division of family property equally among children. The model of the absolute nuclear family was the historical norm only in the eastern part of the British Isles, Brittany (where British Celts migrated in the 450s–600s), the Netherlands, and Denmark and in the southern parts of Sweden and Norway.[8] Interestingly, Macfarlane notes that one of the few countries that developed a family structure similar to the Dutch and English was Japan.[9] We normally think of economic growth as a consequence of industrial technology. Yet even before industrialism, England and its East Asian littoral alter-ego Japan both observed Malthusian-busting late marriage and low-fertility practices.[10] In kin-based societies, this is tantamount to cultural suicide. In couple-based societies, though, the social dynamics are very different.

A people of paradox

Why did the English pursue what is – in the broad sweep of human history – an atypical path? In other words, what singled out the Anglo-Saxons as an unusual people?

Their atypical nature was in part a function of their distinctive social structure. Paralleling this was their culture. The Anglo-Saxons were a people of paradox. They were not a people of paradox in a high civilization sense. Their society did not teem with great buildings, artefacts, and large cities. Rather, they were a people of paradox in a more low-key demotic sense. Peter Ackroyd described this very well.[11] Theirs was a culture that developed an 'abiding interest in paradox and contrast', 'intricate patterns and puzzles', and intellectual games.[12] It begins with the sea and sea-like rhythms, music-like poetry, alliteration, rhymes, rhythms, and patterns of stresses that 'allow for a complete interrelation between parts in a series of oppositions and contrasts'.[13] The culture weaves, knots, intersects, and interlaces – and in doing so creates patterns of 'repetition and variation', 'parallel and antithesis', 'contrast and recapitulation'.[14] English writing replicates the rising and falling rhythms of speech and the plangent lamenting rhythms of the tolling bell and the crashing waves.[15]

One of the effects of this is on the perception of time. Patterns of contrast and recapitulation do not induce a sense of 'linear development' but rather a sense of the 'recurrence of human behavior and the circularity of time'.[16] This is a vision of a world that has 'no beginning and no end', 'no sequence and no progress'. This is summed up in the images of Edmund Spenser's 'euer-whirling wheele' and Robert Burton's 'we weave the same web still'. The recapitulation of patterns and the pattern of recapitulation – the English music so to speak – and its 'constant interplay of opposing forces' lent the English mind a ready capacity to blend comedy with tragedy, legend with history, and resolve with reticence.[17] The most potent of such blends are paradoxes. A paradox is a contradictory statement that is well-founded and true. It contains an antinomy of opposing parts each of which is true but that also make sense and are valid in unison. Paradox both fertilized and was fertilized by the interest of the English in mysteries, puzzles, and enigmas. This interest was partly an effect of the country's insular weather, its fogs and sea mists.[18] These mysterious effects of nature resonate in English gnomic verses and enigmata, in riddles and epigrams like Thomas Wyatt's 'A lady gave me a gift which she had not / And I received her gift which I took not'.[19]

The Anglo-Saxons had a strong sense of fate or destiny and 'what will be'.[20] This expressed itself in a culture of endurance and reticence.[21] Anglo-Saxon poetry had 'an impersonal force'. It eschewed 'place-names or personal names, guided by litotes and understatement toward a powerful compression of feeling'.[22] This solicited a brevity of expression, one that ultimately 'fades into silence'.[23] This – the sound of silence – had several effects on the character of the English voice. One was to encourage a voice that is succinct, crisp, and terse. What follows from this is that 'great debates are foreshortened and reduced to practical discussion of pragmatic import'.[24] In a more general sense the 'what will be' (necessity and destiny) encouraged a voice that was understated and that valued anonymity and reserve. Among modern literary cultures, the English have been exceptionally productive. Yet ironically the English voice tends to muteness, its discourses end in mystery, its rhetoric in puzzles and riddles. Its practical sense is underwritten by an Alice-in-Wonderland-like sense of the comic absurdity of things.

The English language lends itself to epigrams. It compounds contrasts. Night is bound tightly to daytime as tragedy is to comedy. This compression marries the parochial and the providential. The English genius is to be rooted and yet rove at the same time. The culture is rich in densely packed enigmas, riddles, puzzles, and paradoxes. This gives it an impersonal feel with an undertone of fate or destiny that extends from *Beowulf* to Tolkien via Augustinian Christianity and Puritan predestination. It percolates through the works of Shakespeare, Donne, Shaftesbury, Burke, and Smith.

Like all cultures, the culture of the Anglo-Saxons was not just evoked in sounds or written in words. It was also visual. Yet it was visual in a distinctive way. From the earliest times the English world has been evoked more by sparse subtle etched geometries than by courtly ritual or magic. Temperamentally, the culture was predisposed towards borders, edges, and limits. It was circumambient in spirit. This was a linear not a plastic culture, suggests Ackroyd. That meant a culture in which outline, 'pattern and border' predominated over figure and body.[25] Another way of putting this is that this was a flat rather than volumetric culture, one that derived ultimately from the 'abstract patterns inscribed on weapons and jewelry'.[26] Accordingly, it was preoccupied with 'spirals, whorls and lines rather than human figures'.[27] This corporeal absence mirrors the English tendency to understatement, as if the abstract tracery of words is more important than their volume or bulk.

Linear patterns do not necessarily mean straight lines but more commonly ones that curve and curl. They spiral up cones or are circular or wind around things.[28] But their quiet, almost unspoken abstractions hint at the providential sacrifices of citizenship and nationality and help make sense of the fact that we have obligations to people whom we do not know and will never meet.[29] These abstractions on the one hand foreshadow a society of strangers that is glued together not by personal connections but by impersonal patterns.[30] On the other hand they help make sense of a world bound together not by archaic ties of kinship but rather the deep emotional intimacy of spousal pairs knitted together as almost unfathomable pairings of opposites and contrasts, uncanny twos in ones.

Ending violence

Kin-based societies are prone to aggression, feuding, and bloodshed.[31] They breed pugnacity, cruelty, and brutality. The Anglo-Saxons, and the waves of Viking raiders and Danish conquerors that followed them, were similarly violent. A visitor to York today is struck by the vivid historical memory of the ferocious Viking conquests. Yet the Danes and Norwegians, who pillaged and rampaged, are also the stock from whom the Quakers descended.[32] How did the English manage to get from violent cruelty to Quaker pacifism?

Two steps were involved. The first, ironically, was due to chronic war. In *A History of the English-Speaking Peoples* Winston Churchill points out the cascading effects of this.[33] First the perpetual battles of the Anglo-Saxons elevated war chiefs above clan chiefs. Next the crews of the Viking long boats were allowed to keep their war booty as private property. Traditional communal claims by kin over the property of the deceased in Scandinavian law were set aside for the maritime raiders.[34] The warrior-farmer Danes, who conquered and settled England (in an apex that stretched from today's Whitby to Liverpool to London), did the same. In short, absolute private property emerged from the conditions of protracted English warring.

But we don't get to the Quakers unless that chronic violence is then abated (Table 5.1). The turning point was the Protestant Reformation. Medieval society continued to be riddled with violence. Among primates the rate of intra-species killing is 2 percent of deaths.[35] Humans killing other humans rose to an appalling rate of 12 percent of recorded deaths in the medieval period. By the twentieth century, the rate worldwide had fallen to 1.33 percent. One key to this change was provided by Calvinism. In the English case, John Carroll describes how the English Calvinists found ways in the 1600s to channel human aggression into vocational work and companionate marriage.[36] This was laid on top of the Anglo-Saxon development of absolute private property and the nuclear family.

The Calvinists had a dim view of domestic violence and reduced it markedly. Companionate marriage assumed that spouses were bound to each other in a 'bundle of love'.[37] John Calvin's view of marriage in the 1540s was founded on the idea of marriage as a covenantal relationship based on mutual consent, sacrifice, and faithfulness and on sincere, solemn, and public promises to each other, the joining of two opposites in mutual love and mutual protection.[38] Love in this sense was less the *caritas* of the weak and vulnerable and more the reciprocal mutual aid and comfort of interlocking pairs. The Catholic view of marriage, systemic from the 300s, had already had broken the nexus between property and kinship, tribal, clan, and caste groups.[39] Calvin's view of marriage doubled down on this.

Calvinism failed to produce a workable model of public authority. Its idea of official power tended to lurch from the severe and bizarre to the gloomy and despotic. Yet that belies its remarkable historical contribution. The modern world exists in no small part because the heterodox Calvinists pioneered ways of sublimating aggression in work, companionate marriage, and self-education. The latter had its roots in *sola scriptura*. This was the idea that believers had to read scripture for themselves.

Table 5.1 Annual homicide rate per 100,000 persons, 1300–2015

Nation/territory	1300	1550	1625	1675	1725	1775	1812	1837	1862
England	23	7	6	4	2	1	2	1.7	1.6
Germany and Switzerland	37	11	11	3	7	8	3	4	2
Italy	56	47	32	–	12	9	18	15	12
Netherlands and Belgium	47	25	6	9	7	4	2	0.9	1.7
Scandinavia	–	21	24	12	3	0.7	1	1.4	1.2
	1887	1912	1937	1962	1984	1990	2000	2010	2015
England	0.8	0.8	0.8	0.7	1.2	0.9	0.7	0.6	0.5
Germany and Switzerland	2.2	2	1.4	0.9	1.2	1.5	1.2	0.9	0.8
Italy	5.5	3.9	2.6	1.3	1.7	1.9	1.3	0.9	0.9
Netherlands and Belgium	1.3	1.7	1.3	0.6	1.2	1.7	1.7	1.2	1.1
Scandinavia	0.9	0.8	0.8	0.6	1.2	1.8	1.5	1.2	1

Source: M. Eisner, 'Long-Term Historical Trends in Violent Crime', *Crime and Justice* 30, 2003, 83–142, Table 1.

Success often is ironic and unintended. Calvinism is typical of this. It was driven by a paradox. The Calvinists did not seek this-worldly success but rather other-worldly salvation. Nevertheless the way they approached the latter led to the former. Hard work replaced good works; high (biblical) literacy led to high (scientific) literacy and the desideratum to think for oneself. Gradually softened and stripped of its forbidding style of authority, Calvinism's behavioral ethos and its intellectual paradoxes (such as the anchoring of human freedom in providential necessity) gradually seeped into the broader English Anglican culture as well as into secular English culture. A subtle almost imperceptible Anglicized 'cultural Calvinism' affected the English way of doing business by osmosis.

One influential example was the image of a predestining grace. The idea that human beings are subject to a larger destiny or necessity (the Anglo-Saxons' 'what will be') that is simultaneously liberating was a paradox that underpinned global discovery, trade, and settlement. At the same time it buttressed the idea of large-scale self-organizing markets and industries. It challenged interventionism and mercantilism and the notion that acts of deliberate choice or free will can readily change macro-economic outcomes affecting whole societies. It left in its wake an economics of grace. This view held that balance, ratio, and equilibrium – in short, the elements of grace – are more important in creating economic dynamism than are offices, rules, and regulations.

The individualistic property and family structures of the Anglo-Saxons, and their taste for paradoxes and puzzles, later on were overlaid by and interlaced with the views of the heterodox English Calvinists. The latter repeat, enrich, and extend the Anglo-Saxon model of the flexible mobile nuclear family and alienable property with a paradoxical soteriology, an ethic of hard work and thrift, an ideal of companionate marriage, an emphasis on reading for oneself, and an elective affinity with littoral societies. This combination was one of the seedbeds of much of modern capitalism and industrialism. It was not the only seedbed. We ought not to reduce modern capitalism to the Calvinist work ethic. What's key is the culture of paradox, of which Calvinism is a part but not a whole. It is but one element among a profusion, many of which are secular not religious.

Calvinist strongholds in Britain in the 1600s mirror almost exactly where the Anglo-Saxons settled in the 500s. The Puritans were concentrated in a geographic arc that runs from Kings Lynne through Tunbridge Wells to Portsmouth. Winston Churchill had a deep knowledge of his island nation. In 1922 he moved his home to Chartwell in Kent. Chartwell is located almost at the center point of this historic arc. Unlike central England, south-east England managed to sidestep much of the Norman manorial labor-service land-tenure system.[40] Macfarlane estimates that, in spite of the French conquest, by the 1200s freehold tenure covered a third of England. A large land market existed and cash played a significant role in local economies.[41]

A specific conclusion is sometimes drawn from this, namely, that individual property rights are the key to understanding the liberty and prosperity of Anglosphere societies.[42] This is England's version of Enlightenment philosophy.

It is epitomized by John Locke. Locke's philosophy hypothesized that individuals had inalienable natural rights. These preceded and were superior to government. This implied limits on the state. These limits were embodied in bills of rights, the rule of law, the separation of legislative, judicial and executive authority, and the constitutional balance of these powers. One of these natural rights was the right to property. Locke supposed that individuals had a right to the fruits of their own labor. This was a conceptual breakthrough. The dominant *gemeinschaft* ('community') social mentality across millennia had looked upon human output as a pool to be distributed. Naturally, this discouraged human productivity and encouraged forced labor, including slavery. States, landlords, patrimonial kings, and clerical and scholarly castes feasted on this pool.

Prosperous societies replace extended kinship structures with the flexible and effective nuclear family. Families, clans, and tribes lose their political influence. The pair-bonded nuclear family provides mutual aid, social purpose, and personal stability. Internally, it pools its resources. Externally, it encourages productive effort instead of pooling and sharing wealth among extended kin, clans, or tribes. In the larger society over time freehold property replaces the leasing of land from the Crown. Function supplants status. Learned achievement overtakes ascribed inheritance. Aristocracies, patricians, monarchies, principalities, and patrimonial empires gradually shrink in influence. Old metaphors die. The king is no longer the 'father' who 'feeds' the people. Government is no longer carried out by the royal 'household' and its 'servants'.

Locke's most influential contribution to this modern matrix was to attribute inalienable natural rights of life, liberty, and property to all individuals. This was reformulated in America's Declaration of Independence as the right of life, liberty, and the pursuit of happiness. The Bill of Rights in the American Constitution refined this further. The natural rights of individuals – to speak, assemble, and bear arms; get a fair jury trial; and not have their houses, papers, or property seized by the government – carved out a sphere of human life that was independent of government. Modern natural rights were not imputed to the state or corporate bodies (be they guilds, chartered companies, unions, or firms) but rather to individuals.

The natural rights view is important. Yet natural rights alone is an insufficient explanation of prosperous economies and their dynamism. Arguably, dynamism, unique in human history, arises because of the peculiar ambidexterity of these economies. One example of this is their tendency towards the antinomy of 'competition and cooperation'. Industries, as Alfred Marshall observed, cluster.[43] This means that very fierce competitors will co-locate so they can exchange information and learn from each other all the while engaging in intense rivalry. It is not a company being cooperative or being competitive that matters as much as its capacity to do both simultaneously. Modern natural rights in property are a precondition of this. Because such firms do not have to rely on the permissions, licenses, and grants of the state, individuals are free to cooperate and compete with each other. But it takes a 'people of paradox' to leverage secure rights in property in a way that sets in motion this uncanny productive

power. As entrepreneurs and firms cooperate and compete, contract and inno-
vate, the scope and scale of markets, industries, cities, and publics grows. In turn,
productivity and prosperity expands.

Peoples of paradox

The significance of Britain as an economic pioneer in the modern world is as
much metaphysical as it is material. In modern societies that enjoy high levels
of prosperity, the metaphysical and the material intersect and overlap. Take the
case of the Quakers, one of the four influential British cultures that seeded
America.[44] The most interesting religious precepts, like their secular counter-
parts, are paradoxical. In the case of the Quakers it was the merger of silence *and*
voice in church meetings and the image of God as immanent *and* transcendent.
From paradox arises invention and humor.

John and Henry Walker were two such enterprising Quakers. In 1746 they
apprenticed a young farm boy by the name of James Cook in their coastal merchant shipping business based on Yorkshire's North Sea coast. Cook learnt his
trade, including navigational mathematics and geometry, as he plied back and
forth between Whitby and London. Three years after his apprenticeship was
completed he was commissioned as a captain in the Walkers' Baltic fleet but
soon after resigned to join the British Navy. What followed was an extraordinary life of exploration and discovery. He mapped the coastlines of Newfoundland, New Zealand, East Australia, and North-West America. The names of
ships he commanded, *Endeavour*, *Resolution*, and *Adventure*, sum up the worldview of the handful of great productive modern societies. Cook's personality,
modest and bashful, was the other side of this coin: head down, hard at work,
grappling with the larger forces that determine human fate.

At a very deep level, modern prosperity is anchored in the ambidexterity of
freedom and nature, choice and destiny. To be able to navigate between these
without sacrificing one or the other is essential. This is why it is not sufficient to
trace the arc of modern prosperity either to natural rights in property or to the
Enlightenment, or to the specific case of John Locke. These roots extend much
deeper into the soil of history. Arguably more important than the Enlightenment was the contribution of the Renaissance.[45] In this respect the dates of the
American founding are revealing. The colony of Virginia was settled in 1607,
the Plymouth colony in 1620. Shakespeare died in 1616. Locke's *Two Treatises
on Government* was published in 1689. The settlement of America emerges out
of the world of Shakespeare, not Locke. The importance of the Renaissance
for modern prosperity is not just that key institutions develop in the period –
including banking, insurance, and joint-stock companies along with ocean-
going technology. Even more importantly the period produces a distinctive
kind of thinking. We cannot fully understand the modern kind of dynamic-yet-
stable economy separate from a metaphysics of paradox.

Martin Luther's *posteriora Dei* (what God reveals is concealed) and John
Calvin's liberal scolds share a common structure of thought with Baldassare

Castiglione and William Shakespeare.[46] Shakespeare's 'wicked meaning in a lawful deed' parallels the modern conservative precept that good intentions often produce unintended bad consequences.[47] In *The Book of the Courier* Castiglione observed that 'there is no contrary without a contrary'.[48] Society, he argued, is not a utopia. There is no good without evil, no health without infirmity, and no pleasure without pain.

Luther put it in these terms: faith 'has to do with things not seen'. Hence, he reasoned, in order that there may be room for faith, it is necessary that 'everything which is believed should be hidden'. But, he observed, a hidden thing 'cannot, however, be more deeply hidden than under an object, perception, or experience which is contrary to it'.[49] This is exactly the kind of paradox that underpins interesting societies and dynamic economies. This is not the fruit of the Enlightenment. Truth, as the Enlightenment understood it, is a function of logical consistency. Rational truth for many purposes is useful. But in other ways it falls short. The interesting truths are paradoxical not logical.

There are many nominally liberal societies around the world. However, the stalwarts of modern prosperity are a very specific subset of those societies. Let's call them the Shakespearean societies. There are a small number of them. Likewise it is no accident that the other great modern success stories are a handful of East Asian states and city-regions that have a Taoist and Zen Buddhist undertow. Characteristically, Zen tries to free the mind from being enslaved by words and constricted by logic. It elevates paradoxical intuitions above prolix reasoning. Likewise, Shakespeare is the master of words who avoids one-sided reason with dramatic parallax.

Modernity is home to several peoples of paradox. Each is different. None can match the British in literary paradox (Table 3.3). Their history of literary wit, from Shakespeare and Bacon to Johnson and Pope to Chesterton and Churchill, is unmatched. It is unsurprising that the early American emblem of the enterprising personality was Benjamin Franklin, an inveterate inventor and the originator of the modern tradition of the joking one liner.[50] There is a course that runs from humorous leaps to inventiveness to modern technological enterprise. But this sequence and its creative vaults, though related, are different in flavor and nature from the arch irony and wit of the English. America is many things but it is not an ironic nation, nor, unlike Canadians, do Americans have a taste for self-parody and self-deprecation.

Nevertheless in its own way, as Michael Kammen observes, America is a 'contrapuntal nation'. It is filled with contradictory tendencies that are half-truths rather than whole truths.[51] This means a number of different things. First, there are the simple contradictions that are not in any sense productive paradoxes. There is nothing uncanny about these. Common examples include middle-class welfare or when American farmers lobby to limit their own production and be paid by the government for not producing things. Contradictory America is expansive. It extends welfare to those capable of looking after themselves, plans obsolescence, promotes corporate socialism, and protects market-based industries with import quotas. These are contradictions that arise when a modern society seeks to fuse *gemeinschaft* and *gesellschaft*. Another kind of contradiction is the lawless streak in a society preoccupied by legalism and law.

America is a republic of laws that often has considerable difficulty applying laws to its own legislators and government agencies. To an unusual degree Americans tolerate the graft and misdemeanors of their political leaders. Americans in the same moment will embrace temperance and bootlegging. Along with the law-lawless streak in American life, you find Americans who advocate American singularity in the same breath as racial or ethnic separation. There are those who love their country, those who hate it, and those who love-hate it. The majority of Americans embrace the idea of a moderate republic of checks and balances. Yet a minority prefers militant politics. Some see themselves as belonging to a lonely crowd; others enjoy the company of familiar strangers. Americans design private institutions to serve the public good yet will aggressively lobby public bodies to serve private interests. The country nurtures secular religions and religious secularity and not always in a very coherent or illuminating way. America also exhibits many productive paradoxes. It aspires to classless inequality. It upholds majority rule and minority rights. It encourages a property-owning poor. Americans practice formal informality and enjoy mass-produced eccentricity. America is a place where business failure is often taken as a sign of success.

The picture that Kammen paints echoes Castiglione's maxim. America is an instantiation of the Renaissance principle that 'there is no contrary without a contrary'. Not every one of these contraries is productive. Some are destructive. But they do generate great energies. The passionless mind and mindless passion coexist in America along with nationalism and universalism, puritanism and hedonism, materialism and idealism, isolationism and interventionism, conformism and individualism, nobility and baseness, economic ingenuity and conspicuous wastefulness. America matches movement and change with nostalgia and inertia, tumult with stability, and respect for the law with violence. It exults both the Everyman and the Superman.

The first great modern upsurge of the principle of 'no contrary without a contrary' occurred during the late Renaissance (Table 3.3): Renaissance contrariety though has its own long prehistory. That back-story was well known to eighteenth-century Americans. Both the American political elite and the general population were well read – unlike today.[52] Locke was just one among a vast array of authorities and works consulted by the American colonists as they debated their own future. The histories and philosophies of the English constitution, the Dutch republic, the Genevan, Florentine and Venetian city-states, the Anglo-Saxon gothic commonwealth, the Roman republic, the ancient Greek city-states and federations, and much else were picked over with an eye to creating a workable modern commercial republic, one which today exists in a state of perpetual contradiction that works to a point yet without a resonant metaphysical self-understanding of its own contradictoriness. It is evident when we look at the history of American success and failure (Table 1.1) that its success as a modern prosperous society, while significant, is not as significant as might be assumed, nor is America's level of creation, impressive though it is, as great or as sustained or as deep going as one might casually suppose.[53]

An interesting point of comparison is Australia, another settler society and another fragment spun off from Britain. Its record of wealth creation in the nineteenth century far exceeds that of the United States. America did not match Australia until 1920 and overall on average has only modestly exceeded Australia's performance since then. Both Australia and America are peoples of paradox but in different ways. If America is an off-shoot of the Renaissance, then Australia is a late flowering of English skeptical eighteenth and early nineteenth-century neo-classical culture that ranged in representative personality from Johnson and Pope to Gibbon and Burke to Hazlitt and Austen. This culture was distinguished by the balanced sentence and the witty epigram. Its irony, wit, and innate comic sense bequeathed to Australia, more so than the case of America, a disposition to fuse opposites and generate pleasing congruities out of powerful incongruities.

That is to say, on the whole Australia was better at shaping its contraries into interesting and coherent wholes. This capability was not particularly expressed in or through literature. Australia did not develop as a literary culture like Britain (Table 3.3), nor for that matter did America. It did develop a demotic culture of satire and sardonic humor and a sense of the absurd that emerged in tandem with a rate of economic growth unmatched by any country in the nineteenth-century (Table 1.1). The explanation for the latter lies in Australia's era of foundation, the Macquarie period in the 1810s. Australia developed through a series of practical paradoxes. Its demotic culture mirrored this and made it entirely palatable. Australia was a garrison economy that Macquarie turned on its head into a free-market economy. It was a penal colony that rapidly transformed into a free society. Its greatest paradox was Macquarie's vision to create this on the basis of emancipists, prisoners who were given their freedom. This enigmatic class of incarcerated-turned-free persons forged a society that swiftly transitioned from a status society to a functional society. Recreating Old World status–class divisions proved practically impossible in Australia.

Paradoxes extended in other directions. Australia was the product of an empire that planted self-governing colonies. It was a continental country that was an island, a predominately agricultural economy where the majority of persons lived or worked in cities, and a circumambient society not so much in the Anglo-Saxon literary sense but rather reflected in the concentration of the Australian population on the country's coastal margins. Australia had an inland that was and has remained largely empty. It was a penal colony whose visionary governor Macquarie treated it as an experiment in city beautification, a reminder of how much important a role visual aesthetic order, not least beautiful cities, plays in intense and rapid economic development. As the British Georgian era understood it, beauty, not least material beauty, uses proportion and ratio, symmetries and similitudes to reconcile and merge contrasting qualities and forces into coherent and attractive unions. The result of this in Australia suggests that the practice of an urban aesthetic economy is among the most successful ways of creating prosperity along with markets and industries.

Notes

1 Common to the region was a North Sea species of German. James Bennett and Michael Lotus (*America 3.0*, 77) point to the work of Edward Augustus Freeman who, in 1870, concluded, on the basis of linguistic evidence, that the English language was derived from Germanic 'low Dutch'. This was the root language of the Danes and those of coastal Holland. The word 'low' (*neder*) is a reference to the Netherlands downriver location on the Rhine-Meuse-Scheldt delta. A more recent classification calls this root language North Sea Germanic.
2 Toennies, 1971.
3 Todd, 1985.
4 The evolution of his thinking is captured in the academic essays, papers, and talks from 1978 to 2005 collected in Macfarlane, 2013.
5 Macfarlane, 2013, 48.
6 Macfarlane, 2013, 48–59.
7 Bennett and Lotus, 2013, 26–49, 52, 71–79.
8 Todd (1985) distinguished between various historic family types: *absolute nuclear* (no inheritance rules), *egalitarian nuclear* (equal-division inheritance rules), *authoritarian* (cohabitation of married child-heir with parents), exogamous, endogamous, asymmetrical *community* (married sons cohabit with parents), and *anomic* (informal cohabitation of married children and parents) family types.
9 Macfarlane, 2013, 48–59, 60–81.
10 Macfarlane, 2013, 37, 79.
11 Ackroyd, 2002.
12 Ackroyd, 2002, 26–27.
13 Ackroyd, 2002, 23.
14 Ackroyd, 2002, 28.
15 Ackroyd, 2002, 85.
16 Ackroyd, 2002, 28.
17 Ackroyd, 2002, 29.
18 Ackroyd, 2002, 78–80.
19 Ackroyd, 2002, 27–28.
20 Ackroyd, 2002, 59.
21 Ackroyd, 2002, 60.
22 Ackroyd, 2002, 60.
23 Ackroyd, 2002, 117.
24 Ackroyd, 2002, 118.
25 Ackroyd, 2002, 90–91.
26 Ackroyd, 2002, 91.
27 Ackroyd, 2002, 91.
28 Ackroyd, 2002, 73.
29 Scruton, 2006, 10, 54–55, 83, 128, 136, 2019, 23–24, 54, 58, 68, 91, 181.
30 Related to this is J.R.R. Tolkien's point in his 1936 lecture 'Beowulf: The Monsters and the Critics'. Critics had complained that the epic dealt with battles against monsters rather than the more realistic ins-and-outs of internecine English tribal warfare. Tolkien responded that the subject of the poem was human destiny. It was not a documentary of war. Indeed, it was precisely a sense of destiny that helped the English clamber up out of the pit of tribal politics.
31 In the case of the Middle East, see Pryce-Jones, 2002.
32 Fischer, 1989, 446.

33 Churchill, 1974, 49–50, 69, 76.
34 A parallel can be drawn with the Puritans who ventured to New England. As Hannah Arendt noted in *On Revolution,* the Mayflower compact, the mutual agreement of the ship-borne Calvinist Separatists to bind themselves into a 'civil body politick' to frame laws and government, laid the foundation of the American political order. Arendt, 1973 [1963], 167, 173.
35 Engelhaupt, 2016. Engelhaupt's article summarizes research reported in Gómez et al., 2016.
36 Carroll, 1985, 97–122.
37 A puritan quoted in Fischer, 1989, 24.
38 John Witte, director of the Center for the Study of Law and Religion (CSLR), Emory University School of Law, provides an epitome of Calvin's views on marriage in 'John Calvin on Marriage and Family Life', www.johnwittejr.com/uploads/5/4/6/6/54662393/a140.pdf
39 'Adoption of Christianity as a state religion in AD 380 led to basic changes in the nature of European marriage, inheritance, and kinship. The Papacy imposed a pattern which was dramatically different from that prevailing earlier in Greece, Rome, and Egypt and later in the Islamic world. Marriage was to be strictly monogamous, with a ban on concubinage, adoption, divorce, remarriage of widows or widowers, consanguineous marriage with siblings, ascendants, descendants, including first, second, and third cousins, or relatives of siblings by marriage. A Papal decision in AD 385 imposed priestly celibacy. The primary intention of the new regime was to channel assets to the church which became a property owner on a huge scale, but it had much wider ramifications. Inheritance limited to close family members and widespread adoption of primogeniture broke down loyalties to clan, tribe, or caste, promoted individualism and accumulation, and reinforced the sense of belonging to a nation-state. . .' Angus Maddison, 'Measuring and Interpreting World Economic Performance 1500–2001', https://crawford.anu.edu.au/pdf/edges/Maddison.pdf
40 Homans, 1962, 147–156, 179–180; Doody, 2015, 265–266.
41 Macfarlane, 2013, 14. Freehold meant that no feudal conditions attached to the tenure, rather only conditions related to tax, compulsory purchase, the exercise of police powers, and the like.
42 Hannan, 2016, chapter 4. Hannan draws explicitly on Macfarlane's history in making his case.
43 Marshall, 2013 [1920], chapter 10, 'The Concentration of Specialised Industries in Particular Localities'.
44 Fischer, 1989.
45 For a birds-eye view of the Renaissance, see Heller, 1978.
46 Calvin: 'There are people who are known to be very liberal, yet they never give without scolding or pride or even insolence' (*Golden Booklet of the True Christian Life*, 1550).
47 Shakespeare, *All's Well that Ends Well*, III.VII.
48 Castiglione, 2003, 76.
49 Luther, *Bondage of the Will* (1525).
50 Johnson, 2019, 17–30.
51 Kammen, 1972. The following draws on chapter 9 of Kammen's work.
52 Murphy, 2001, 260, 2019, 155–181.
53 See chapter 9.

Bibliography

Ackroyd, P. 2002. *Albion: The Origins of the English Imagination*. New York: Anchor.
Arendt, H. 1973 [1963]. *On Revolution*. Harmondsworth: Penguin.
Bennett, J.C. and M.A. Lotus. 2013. *America 3.0*. New York: Encounter Books.

Carroll, J. 2004. *The Wreck of Western Culture*. Melbourne: Scribe.

Carroll, J. 1985. *Guilt: The Grey Eminence behind Character, History and Culture*. London: Routledge and Kegan Paul.

Castiglione, B. 2003 [1528]. *The Book of the Courtier*. New York: Dover.

Churchill, W. 1974 [1956]. *A History of the English-Speaking Peoples*, Volume 1. London: Cassell.

Doody, M. 2015. *Jane Austen's Names: Riddles, Persons, Places*. Chicago, IL: University of Chicago Press.

Engelhaupt, E. 2016. "How Human Violence Stacks Up Against Other Killer Animals". *National Geographic*, September 28. https://www.nationalgeographic.com/news/2016/09/human-violence-evolution-animals-nature-science/

Fischer, D. H. 1989. *Albion's Seed: Four British Folkways in America*. New York: Oxford University Press.

Gómez, J.M., M. Verdú, A. González-Megías and M. Méndez. 2016. "The Phylogenetic Roots of Human Lethal Violence". *Nature* 538, no. 13: 233–237.

Hannan, D. 2016. *How We Invented Freedom and Why It Matters*. London: Head of Zeus.

Heller, A. 1978. *Renaissance Man*. London: Routledge.

Homans, G.C. 1962. *Sentiments and Activities: Essays in Social Science*. London: Routledge.

Johnson, P. 2019. *Humorists: From Hogarth to Noel Coward*. New York: HarperCollins.

Kammen, M. 1972. *People of Paradox: An Inquiry Concerning the Origins of American Civilization*. New York: Knopf.

Macfarlane, A. 2013. *Individualism, Capitalism and the Modern World: Essays, Talks and Lectures*. Kindle.

Marshall, A. 2013 [1920]. *The Principles of Economics*. Eighth edition. London: Palgrave.

Murphy, P. 2019. *Limited Government: The Public Sector in the Auto-Industrial Age*. London: Routledge.

Murphy, P. 2001. *Civic Justice: From Ancient Greece to the Modern World*. Amherst, NY: Humanity Books.

Pryce-Jones, D. 2002 [1989]. *The Closed Circle: An Interpretation of the Arabs*. Chicago, IL: Ivan R. Dee.

Scruton, R. 2019 [2014]. *How to Be a Conservative*. London: Bloomsbury.

Scruton, R. 2006. *England: An Elegy*. London: Continuum.

Todd, E. 1985. *The Explanation of Ideology: Family Structures and Social Systems*. Oxford: Blackwell.

Toennies, F. 1971. *On Sociology: Pure, Applied and Empirical, Selected Writings*. Chicago, IL: University of Chicago Press.

6   Voice and exit

To whom do I turn?

All societies provide an answer to the question, *if I need something, to whom do I turn?* Historically and in many respects even today, the most common answer to this question is 'kin' or 'patrons'. Yet there are two other ways of answering the same question. Modern bureaucratic societies say, the state. In this case a person turns to mentors, managers, allocated benefits, and grant committees. The final answer to this question is, mutually beneficial contracts, exchanges, interactions between strangers, and intense relations between spouses.

One of the peculiarities of the medieval English was the extent to which they relied on the latter response to the question: *who can help us?* That historic reliance may often have been only tacit. Yet reliance on spouses and strangers was important. For example, instead of employing kinfolk to do farm work the English hired strangers for cash. By the 1300s a third or more of English households had non-family servants.[1] In East Anglia the figure was at least 50 and possibly as high as 70 percent. The Angles had settled there in the 500s. The same region in the 1600s had large numbers of Puritan dissenters and supporters of Parliament in the English Civil War. The consequence of this commercialized household economy was that adult children had to make their own way in the world. They went off to work for strangers. The economy was interwoven with mobility. Grants, favors, or monopolies between persons familiar to each other mattered less. Contracts, exchanges, and interactions between strangers mattered more. What emerged from this was a civil society.

In civil societies, horizontal associations of peers ranging from platoons to colleges form readily and easily. Along with companionate marriage they function as primary reference points for individuals. Couples and peers rather than superiors and kin lie at the core of how people in civil societies think about relationships. They embrace close intimacy and distant strangers. Aid is mutual while life is orientated to independence. Work, income, contributions, and savings are key. Property is non-communal.

In contrast, in uncivil societies, hierarchies matter most. These social ladders can be personal or organizational or a mix of both. From communal property flows benefits, grants, and allocations. Dependence is elicited in many, often subtle, forms, including intellectual ones. People see themselves as clients, beneficiaries, or recipients. Contemporary neo-tribal and neo-patrimonial societies are riddled with patron and client relationships. They operate on the basis of 'who you know' and pay offs to officials. Skills appear far down the list of what is important. Competency and independency is much less significant than cousins, kin, chiefs, hierarchs, brotherhoods, lineages, fraternities, cliques, cronies, and coteries. But just as common as the neo-patrimonies are the impersonal procedural management hierarchies that typify economies and societies with large goal-rational corporate firms and big governments subject to large volumes of micro regulations and procedural norms.

In *England: An Elegy* Roger Scruton observed that so many key English institutions involved finding ways of including strangers in common enterprises.[2] These ranged from the councils of the Anglo-Saxons to the great wave of modern finance-market institutions created in the coffee houses of the Augustan age. From maritime insurance underwriters to the stock exchanges, these institutions were neither familial nor patrimonial but rather collegial. They were clubs of strangers. Their members were inner-directed towards work and accumulation rather than outer-directed towards status and connections. Their glue was a mix of shy reserve and rock-like quiet industriousness. They encouraged persons who were well-spoken not boisterous, who were well-mannered not demonstrative, and who communicated a sense of stoic calm in the midst of storms. What resulted were institutions built on honest transparency rather insider connections.

When Margaret Thatcher's government in 1986 reformed UK financial markets, it forced the City, the hub of British finance, to replace face-to-face dealing with electronic trading. That became key to the great power it achieved by the early decades of the twenty-first century. Friedrich Hayek argued that transactions between strangers are the heart of self-organizing markets.[3] The interaction of strangers, though, shapes more than just markets.[4] It underwrites the shift from orality to literacy and country to city. Puritan literate self-education created the invisible congregation of readers. Adam Smith stressed the importance of strangers massing in cities, particularly in port and riverine cities.[5] High literacy and littoral city-life correlate strongly with economic well-being. So does technology. Tinkering functions a lot like publics, markets, and cities. Each involves a mix of pattern thinking, stranger interaction, do-it-yourself initiative, and alternatives to personal and managerial hierarchies. People participate in these worlds either anonymously (as buyers and sellers, voters or visitors) or else as members of clubs, associations, and parties. Either way, strangers are drawn together by spontaneous shared loves, whether it be of the beautiful city, the picturesque countryside, ingenious machinery, skilled work, or stories, real or imagined, of romance, adventure, drama, and mystery.

Two Englands

The German sociologist Max Weber observed something else atypical about the English. They often did away with paid administrators. From the 1100s the English gentry took on the role of justices of the peace and refused payment for service. The normally understated Weber almost shouts his astonishment that in England 'administration by justices of the peace reduced all local administration bodies outside the cities almost to insignificance'. Royal patrimonial bureaucracy and manorial administration were side-lined in 'one of the most radical types of an administration solely by notables ever carried through in a big country'.[6] The amateur administrator is the flip side of lean government, one of the key factors in modern prosperous societies. Lean government promises large outcomes for small economical inputs of public and social resources. It is the application of the paradoxical principle of efficiency to government, the notion that fewer inputs can produce a greater number of outputs.

The spirit of the amateur suffuses a kind of citizenship that exists among people who give back to society with their time, effort, and sacrifice. It is a characteristic of Anglophone civil society that, at decisive moments, the skilled amateur will replace the paid professional. The amateur in science and sport played a crucial role before the bureaucratization of the universities and the managerial takeover of sports in the second half of the twentieth century. The aim of managerialism is to replace the isomorphic associations of civil society with legal-rational bureaucracies. The shift from amateur to professional in the twentieth century echoed a much longer and deeper divide between England's civil society and its patrimonial hierarchies. In the twentieth century the latter were replaced in substantial measure by procedural hierarchies as the organizational age appeared.

In 1066, the Normans invaded England. As Alan MacFarlane observes, this involved varying degrees of colonization. In the North and the Midlands, the Normans successfully imposed a manorial economy, less so in the South-East of England. By the nineteenth century the English South-East was still a largely agrarian and relatively poor part of England. This contrasted with the industrializing Midlands and North. The South-East was the source of the wave of Puritan settlers (21,000), who sailed to New England in the 1630s, and the 162,000 convicts who were transported to Australia between 1788 and 1868.[7] The most Anglo-Saxon, least Norman, and least Celtic part of England laid a series of heterodox foundation-seeds in Australia and America. The influence of these kernels or spores far exceeded their initial scale or size.

David Hackett Fischer proposed that four distinct UK cultures (or folkways) seeded America.[8] There were the Cavaliers (and their indentured servants) from the South and West of England, where historically freeholding had been less common. They went to Virginia and then onto the Deep South, importing along with them the slave plantation model from the Caribbean. This culture was strongly hierarchical, oral, ritualistic, and violent. Next were the Puritans from South-East England, the Quakers from the Midlands, and the militant-clannish Presbyterian 'borderlanders' from Northern Ireland (Ulster), Scotland, and Northern England.[9] The Puritans settled New England and subsequently spread westwards. DNA studies show that their progeny ended up as the Mormons, today's most entrepreneurial Americans. The Quakers, many with a trades or crafts background, were the basis for the Midwest industrialism that grew out of Philadelphia.[10] The 'Borderers' entered America via Virginia and moved south-west from Appalachia to Texas. The Australian foundation is somewhat less fractured. Until 1880, most Australian immigration came from South-East England, where historically the Anglo-Saxons and later the Calvinists were concentrated and whose economy historically had been relatively free from the grip of a manorialism and largely based on independent property owning.

What the expatriates to Australia and America left behind was a country that echoed with layer upon layer of cultural geography. The British nation was divided between the overlapping cultural geographies of Danelaw and Saxon Essex, Anglo-Saxon and Celtic Britain, Norman and Anglo-Saxon England, Puritan and anti-Puritan Britain. Its Celtic part divided between Catholics and Protestants, as did the entire nation. Celtic Britain in its origins was a tribal society based on the common ownership of land and livestock, and communal labor tasks. The Danelaw areas mixed together a tenanted manorial economy with a social structure of independent landowners who simultaneously had a 'service' obligation to the manors.[11] The Normans had a manorial economy. The Anglo-Saxons and Puritans had a structure of independent landowning. These divisions reproduced themselves in the twentieth century, as divides between private ownership and the nationalization of property and between the employee who entered into a 'contract of service' (singular) to work under the direction of an employer and the independent contractor who 'supplied services' (plural) in the form of work necessary to complete a task or achieve an outcome.

The idea of a 'benefit' provided in return for 'service' had its roots in the Roman and medieval eras.[12] 'Service' was originally service to the state, later the church and the manor. Eventually, the concept was adapted to employees of the modern firm. In contrast to an employee, an independent contractor does not work for a 'benefit' – be it today a wage, salary, leave, retirement, or 'long service' benefit – but rather works to terms, outcomes, and standards of work agreed in a contract with a contractee. As a mental construct or outlook, 'service' supposes what Albert Hirschman called 'loyalty' in the sense that 'service' is a continuing relationship over decades.[13] The 'supply of services' entails the converse mentality of entry-and-exit into/out of relationships based on contractual terms, the delivery of those terms, and a competent performance in doing so. Service is tenurable; the supply of services is not.

Organizations such as business firms, government bureaucracies, and modern universities emphasize tenure and loyalty, long-term 'service', and allocated benefits. The suppliers of 'services' emphasize arrangements that they are able to enter and exit on the basis of time-specific promises and the competent performance of tasks. 'Entry-and-exit' and 'loyalty-service-and-benefit' are two fundamental images of society. They are competing and often incommensurable ways that persons think about the kind of social structure that they prefer and that they feel most comfortable in. Through the twentieth century, this division reproduced itself in many guises, most notably in the split between socialism and capitalism. It echoes through repeating schisms between economic intervention and self-reliance, allocation and production, distribution and creation, and regulation and self-organization.

History repeats

'Entry-and-exit' has many expressions. One is sea traffic and the portal city. The portal city is a Janus-like entity, a gateway constantly rotating as traffic arrives and departs. There are two great modern city types. One is the commercial entry-and-exit portal city. The other is the political capital city. One orientates to the sea, the other to the land ('the country'). One sequesters a large share of GDP in order to allocate it politically. The other produces the wealth represented by the gross product of the nation. Each one epitomizes a side in the divide between 'service' and 'services', allocation and production, land and sea. This divide constantly mutates. It takes on new guises. In the second decade of the twenty-first century it assumed the guise of a divide between the European Union (EU) and the United Kingdom. This was dramatized by the referendum vote by Britons in 2016 to exit the European Union.

The French President Charles de Gaulle understood that the swimmable 21-mile-wide gap of the English Channel belied a deep fault line that separates Britain from its Continental neighbors. Europe is a terrestrial world; Britain is a maritime society and an island nation. This is true whether one thinks of this literally or metaphorically. The fault line between the 'crescent' of Europe and the 'outer crescent' of the United Kingdom is traceable back to 400 CE.

Picture the following: the Roman Empire in the West is collapsing. The southward migration of German tribes is overrunning an ageing ailing imperium. From the early Frankish kingdoms will grow the Carolingian Empire. By 800 Charlemagne's domain, central to the foundation myth of the European Union, stretched from the Elbe River to the south of France and the south of Italy. On its back arose the Holy Roman Empire. As the architects of the Europe Union saw it, the Holy Roman Empire was the first European Union.[14] It had a territorial radius comparable with that of the EU. The spirit of the Holy Roman Empire was landed and parochial – and expansive. The Islamic conquest of Spain and Sicily in the 700s and 800s shuttered the Mediterranean, the bustling inland-sea heart of the old Roman world. Europe's long-distance maritime trade that once had stretched to India came to virtual standstill.

Like its peers on the European Continent, Britain through the twentieth century developed a big government with all the regulation and management and allocation-and-redistribution mechanisms that naturally accompanied it. In that respect Britain and the European Union were obvious bedfellows. Yet beneath the surface of the United Kingdom there remained a stubborn streak of liking for the economics of grace. The tension between the two grew over time and culminated in a slim majority of Britons voting in 2016 to leave the European Union, which it had joined in 1973. The UK's vote to exit from the EU promised a reorientation of the country away from the terrestrial Continent to the world's littoral-rim.

Why did the UK vote to leave the European Union? For one thing, the Union is ruled by an unaccountable bureaucracy. It is a facade democracy. Conceived during World War II by the Italian communist Altiero Spinelli, its elected parliament can neither propose nor repeal laws, only amend them.[15] EU legislation is crafted by the unelected European Commission. The European Parliament is designed not to limit government but rather rubberstamp its expansion. The Commission is a lawmaker and executive in one. EU insignia, citizenship, referenda, and elections in different degrees are all contrived. The European Union is contemptuous of opponents and disdainful of public opinion. It conducts itself by political stealth and subterfuge. Its ministers are anonymous appointees. It ignores referenda outcomes, overturns governments, and violates its own laws if it doesn't like them.[16] Its temperament is omniscient and authoritarian.

The EU is a self-appointed supranational power that operates by means of the capillary action of a million microscopic rules. Its officials enjoy Soviet-era *nomenclatura*-style private shopping malls, national-tax exemption, and low-tax privileges. From its inception as the European Steel and Coal Community in 1951 the Union was a political project. It was designed to create a technocratic-bureaucratic super-state that eventually would replace Europe's nation-states. In five decades it evolved from a customs union into a regulatory leviathan. The final step of evolution envisaged by its advocates is a mega-state with taxing and fiscal powers and an army. Every failure of the EU is met with one response: we need more power.

The European Union's founding notion was that nationalism, not goose-stepping militarism or totalitarianism, led to two world wars. From day one the EU's purpose has been to white-ant the sovereignty of its member states. The rulings of the European Court of Justice repeatedly invalidate national laws in favor of EU directives. This is underpinned by a long-lasting historical imaginary of Europe as a territorial empire. This self-conception of a supernational Europe began with the Carolingian Empire and was reproduced in the Holy Roman Empire, the Napoleonic Empire, the German Empire, the Nazi Empire, and finally in the European Union.

The EU sees itself as a super-state based on the free movement of labor, services, capital, and goods. In reality the 'eurocracy' oversees a parody of these principles. Sixty years on, the EU still has in place innumerable regulatory barriers to free trade in financial services. The EU Customs Union applies a modest overall rate of tariffs but combines this with high tariffs to protect French agriculture and German car manufacturing. Rather than the free movement of skilled labor, EU rules tacitly encourage benefit-seeking and kin-driven immigration. Any mass flow of people, whether it is legal or illegal, internal or external, that comes from kin-based low-growth societies or regions potentially places a drag on dynamic economies. High-growth societies replace kin with couples, dependence with independence, and low skills with high skills.

The long-term growth of migration both into and across the EU from Southern Europe, Eastern Europe, and Africa is understandable in terms of geographic proximity, push factors, and juridical possibility. Yet accompanying this has been a subtle trend to substitute dependency-prone extended family groups for self-reliant skill-based nuclear households. The tendency is evident when we consider the ratio of family to work migration and the level of unemployment among foreign-born compared with local-born persons (Table 6.1).[17] The tendency is also evident from the relatively high incidence of immigrant children from Southern and Eastern Europe and Africa who support parents.[18] This is a social indicator of a lack of degrees of separation between parental and marital households, a sign of the absence of an independence ethos. Independence is one of the few value markers that clearly demarcates between high and low performance economies.

The lower 'skill-independence' ethos is reflected in the degrees of neo-patrimonialism in a range of migration source countries. Just as kin-based societies distinguish poorly between extended family and individual property, so their counterpart – neo-patrimonial states – distinguish weakly between public office and private property. A clear indicator of the latter is high levels of corruption. The European Union is a hybrid. It contains states with low levels of corruption, notably the Nordic states. It combines these with states that exhibit high levels of corruption, notably states in Eastern and Southern Europe (Table 6.2). The latter is also reflected in the incidence of fraud in EU institutions. The EU is an assiduously procedurally rational and rule-governed body. Yet it is one with an undercurrent of neo-patrimonial behavior.

Observable in a lot of modern societies is the fluid relation between neo-patrimonialism and legal-rationalism. In its public rhetoric the EU epitomizes legal-rationalism. In this context 'legal' means rules and 'rationalism' means organizational interlocutors. The EU talks incessantly to big government, big companies, big science, and big global bodies. These share a common stilted language. They are organized in similar ways. Legal-rationalism tends to end in bureaucratic cronyism. It is a system where large organizations pressure official rule makers – and vice versa. It is a world of hushed behind-the-scenes polished-chrome meetings, networks, and chums. Its participants barter complex rules. Size matters. The big are favored. Small companies can't afford lobbyists or in-house regulatory experts. Only 6 percent of small businesses in the UK export to the EU. Yet all of them have to follow EU regulations. Lobbies exist to get regulators to make amenable rules. But influence also runs in the opposite direction. The European Union uses the lobbies that lobby it to lobby for it. This is the *quid pro quo* of bureaucratic politics.

During the 2016 referendum on whether the UK would remain in the EU or leave it, British university vice-chancellors willfully ignored the UK Charities Commission guidelines on political neutrality. They did so in order to

Table 6.1 Migration and employment, 2015–2017

EU Nations	Three largest sources of migrants, 2017	Unemployment rate of foreign-born > locally born persons, 2016	Rate of employment of low education locally born persons > low education foreign-born persons, 2015	Free movement migration, thousands, 2016	Family migration, thousands, 2016	Work migration, thousands, 2016	Family accompanying work immigrants, thousands, 2016
United Kingdom	Poland, Pakistan, India	0.7%	5.1%	215.4	53.2	27.6	17.2
France	Algeria, Morocco, Portugal	7.5%	5.6%	86.9	98.4	6.4	0
Germany	Poland, Turkey, Russia	3.2%	-0.2%	454.1	105.6	50.5	0
Sweden	Finland, Syria, Iraq	11.0%	18.9%	30.5	31.7	3.8	0.555
Ireland	United Kingdom, Poland, Lithuania	1.6%	1.9%	30.5	4.1	6.4	0.313
Netherlands	Turkey, Morocco, Suriname	5.2%	13.4%	78.1	24.8	14.8	0
Denmark	Germany, Turkey, Poland	5.9%	13.4%	27.9	7.7	8.2	4.3
Comparator nations							
Australia	New Zealand, China, United Kingdom	0.2%	N/A	19.7	57.4	60.7	67.9
Canada	China, United Kingdom, India	0.7%	-1.2%	0	78	69.7	86.3
United States	Mexico, China, India	0.9%	-19.2%	0	804.8	65.6	72.3

Source: OECD Data, Employment, unemployment and participation rates by place of birth and sex, 2016; OECD Data, Employment rates by place of birth and educational attainment (25–64); OECD Data, International Migration Statistics, Permanent immigrant inflows, 2016; Source migration countries data: United Nations, Population Division, International Migration, 2017.

Table 6.2 Perceived corruption and kinship tightness in European Union and comparator countries, 2017–2018

	CP	KTL		CP	KTL
Denmark	88	0–0.05	Finland	85	0–0.05
Sweden	85	0–0.05	Switzerland	85	0–0.05
Norway	84	0–0.05	Netherlands	82	0.05–0.25
Luxembourg	81	0–0.05	Germany	80	0–0.05
United Kingdom	80	0–0.05	Iceland	76	0.05–0.25
Poland	60	0.25–0.5	Slovenia	60	0.75–0.85
Portugal	64	0.25–0.5	Lithuania	59	0.25–0.5
Spain	58	0–0.05	Italy	52	0–0.05
Slovakia	50	0.25–0.5	Croatia	48	0.75–0.85
Romania	47	0–0.05	Hungary	46	0.25–0.5
Greece	45	0.25–0.5	Bulgaria	42	0.25–0.5
Comparator countries					
Morocco	43	0.5–0.75	Turkey	41	0.75–0.85
India	41	0.75–0.85	China	39	0.5–0.75
Albania	36	0.75–0.85	Algeria	35	0.75–0.85
Pakistan	33	0.75–0.85	Mexico	28	0.05–0.25
Russia	28	0.05–0.25	Iraq	18	0.25–0.5
Libya	17	0.75–0.85	Syria	13	0.5–0.75

Source: Transparency International, Corruption Perceptions Index, 2018; Benjamin Enke, Kinship Systems, Cooperation and the Evolution of Culture, NBER Working Paper Series, Working Paper 23499, National Bureau of Economic Research, Cambridge MA, June 2017, Figure 1. The Corruption Perceptions Index ranks 180 countries and territories by their perceived levels of public sector corruption based on multiple expert assessments and surveys of business persons.

Note: Enke's KTL is a measure of the historic (typically dating to 1898) level of kinship tightness or looseness of societies before the onset of industrialization and urbanization matched to contemporary populations. The measure begins with data collected in Murdock's Ethnographical Atlas, 1967, and matches this to contemporary societies based on data from the World Values Study and the European Social Survey. A society with a tight kinship structure is one whose common social behavior pivoted on shame rather than guilt, correct local norms rather than the nature of a transcendent God, extended rather than nuclear families, local compared to non-local post-marital residence, in-group loyalty rather than out-group trust, and in-group favoritism rather than impartiality in business behavior. Tight kinship structures lean toward group, tribal, and local values, and against trade with strangers, economic specialization, and geographic mobility. Societies and populations may urbanize and industrialize but historic social structures may mutate in ways that preserve the imaginary of a tight kinship society reconfigured in non-traditional ways ranging from statism, bureaucratic clientelism, protectionism, and neo-patrimonialism to expressions of ideological correctness, paranoia and fealty.

CP, corruption perception ranked out of 100: 0, highly corrupt; 100, very clean.

KTL, kinship tightness/looseness ranked 0–0.5 (loose) to 0.95–1 (very tight).

influence UK voters to stay in the EU.[19] Universities used to be successful collegial associations of strangers. Today they are bureaucratic organizations preoccupied with rent-seeking. To them the European Union is an irresistible pool of grant money. The *quid pro quo* is that they lobby on behalf of their funder. EU grant money ultimately is collected from long-suffering taxpayers in rundown places like Sunderland in the UK. It is recycled through many handsomely paid hands until it is returned in miniscule dribs to fund meaningless signature projects in down-at-heel places. Britain at the time of the referendum to stay or leave was sending £18 billion a year to the EU. It received only half of that (£9 billion) back in grants or rebates.[20]

The higher the income of the UK voter, the more likely they were to vote in 2016 for the United Kingdom to remain in the EU. The lower the income, the more likely a person was to vote to leave. The modern welfare state of grants and subsidies was built on the idea that the least well-off would receive the most welfare benefits. The Brexit vote was an ironic rejection of the failure of this idea. It is doubly ironic that London – the section of Britain that in the 2010s traded most extensively with the fastest growing economies in the world, which were in East Asia – voted to remain in the European Union's regulatory and customs union.

When voters in the working-class city of Sunderland opted in the 2016 referendum to leave the EU, they were voting in big numbers (61 percent to 39 percent) against the EU's grant system. That system had given them the Sunderland Aquatic Centre, the Sunderland Software City business center for software entrepreneurs, and Sunderland University. The principal beneficiaries of such grants are the professional and administrative classes, who run universities, centers, and the like. Their opposite numbers in various Brussels bureaucracies dole out the grant money. In this North-Sea-side former shipbuilding city, it is the Japanese Nissan car factory not the European Union that provides blue-collar jobs. In the end, only markets and industrial technologies, not state allocations, can offset economic decline.

Blue-collar jobs have shrunk across Britain's north for decades as manufacturing's share of employment worldwide has declined. The problem though has not just been de-industrialization. The UK's Atlantic trade contracted after Prime Minister Ted Heath, an admirer of Mao Tse-tung, led Britain into the EU. The ports of Glasgow and Liverpool once bustled.[21] Stories of The Beatles and their peers listening avidly to country and blues records brought into Liverpool by American sailors are still within living memory. Shifting the focus of trade policy from the Atlantic to the Continent had a stifling effect.[22] Scottish nationalists today would like to exit from the UK and live off EU subsidies. Yet the 2016 vote to leave the EU happened because disenchanted Labour voters in England's north had started to realize that subsidies ruin economies.

Rather than existing on grants extracted by unctuous political lobbying, Scotland today arguably would be much better off if it gave up its mendicant model and adopted a mutual-benefit model like the "Northern Union" concept. The Northern Union is the term used by the contrarian Bremen sociologist Gunnar Heinsohn. He argues for a commercial and military alliance of an independent Britain with Ireland, the Netherlands, Flanders, Denmark, Greenland, Iceland, Norway, Sweden, Finland, Estonia, and the German states of Schleswig-Holstein, and Hamburg.[23] This sea-girt region has a population of 120 million, most of whom, Heinsohn notes, speak English as a first or second language.

Britain today doesn't do much trade with its northern neighbors. Yet it did so in the past.[24] From time to time faint echoes of the old Hanseatic League are still audible.[25] That's what The Beatles unconsciously emulated when they exported themselves and their music to Hamburg in 1960. Theirs was a regime of get-up-and-go endeavor, hard work ('eight days a week'), self-education, peers, adventure, and the resolution to stick at it in Hamburg's grueling club land. The Beatles model is as good as any for the future of cities like Sunderland. Waiting like poor old Godot for the subsidies to work, whether they come from Brussels or London, is a recipe for economic and psychological depression.

Political arithmetic

Almost all highly prosperous societies are split between two bodies of opinion. One is organizational-loyalist opinion, which thinks that remaining in legal-rational organizations is the key to prosperity. This view holds that control is essential to prosperity. Control takes many forms. It can be rules, regulations, plans, procedures, state ownership, state budgeting, state spending, central banking, managerialism, and more generally the dominance of large organizations across the social landscape. The second body of opinion is that of the entry-exiteers. This body of opinion supposes that economic and social goods arise when persons, firms, and states freely enter and exit arrangements that they deem suitable or not. The media for doing this are not directions and plans but rather promises and agreements. The attitude of the entry-exit cohort is that a person or body of persons remains in an arrangement so long as it works and so long as it is consistent with any time-limited promises that have been made. However, no arrangement or organization is forever. Instead continuity is an expression of a ceaseless diaphragm-like activity of admission and leave-taking.

On the large social scale, the entry-exit model assumes the 'simultaneous existence of ways of life bound together by ties of symmetric reciprocity'.[26] In the economic setting, specifically, this means entry into and exit from a large variety of arrangements that are tied together by promises, contracts, commitments, assurances, undertakings, and guarantees and that are subject to the ambidextrous principle of high quality work and low cost pricing. The rationality of the entry-exiteer is one of reason-as-ratio. All human arrangements are composed of things that are good and bad, worthwhile and worthless. For every success there is a failure, for every gain, a loss. The relation between these contraries, and the way we reason about them, is a matter of ratio. That is, to what extent does the good outweigh the bad? Is the appropriate ratio 60:40 or 40:60? Depending on that, do we continue with the arrangement or do we end it?

The view of the organizational-loyalist is rationalistic in nature. The spirit of the ingress-egress group is skeptical. For the latter, all things sit in a balance. Over time, the balance tips one way or the other. The question that the entry-exiteer asks is, Does it work? The question the organizational-loyalist asks is, Is it right? Right, in this case, is defined by reason. Reason is anchored in discourse and argument that leads to consensus.[27] For the organization-loyalist there is one right answer – namely, what is 'rational' to do. For the skeptic, everything is a trade-off. Economy and society is a dynamic balance between goods and goods, goods and bads, goods and evils. Argument is only satisfying when we agree on basic assumptions. Left to support itself, argument is unfulfilling. Arguing with those who hold fundamentally different assumptions is pointless. It leads to shouting, rage, and affront. Untethered reason ends in unreason. It is neither charming nor enchanting. The way that contemporary political debate quickly descends into expressions of outrage and foot-stamping reminds us of the limits of reason. You can argue all you wish about 'equality', yet equality exists only in the company of inequality just as freedom does in the company of necessity.

The rationalist and the skeptic hold two different worldviews. In between the two is the matter of voice. Persons who are dissatisfied with organizations can either leave them or voice their dissatisfaction with them. Voice is ambivalent. It can signify that there is too much or too little organization. It can also lead to ironic outcomes. Often those who seek to reduce an organization implement reforms whose effect is to expand the organization. In the last century voice has tended to be rationalist rather than skeptical. The intelligentsia in most prosperous states have sided with the side of the organizational-loyalist. The critique of the state or other large procedural-rational organizations is usually at its root a demand for purposive-rationality and procedural-rationality on even a larger scale.

Exit, loyalty, and voice can all be understood as different kinds of political arithmetic. In the politics of prosperous societies, the simplest kind of voice is the popular vote. Most public opinion around the world divides into ratios in the range of 45:55. This is the same with voting. It doesn't matter what kind of society it is. No matter whether it is free-market Hong Kong or big-government Sweden, the split of voting and opinion is largely the same (Table 6.3). Asked whether a free market is good or big government is good, opinion normally divides in the 55:45 range. This appears to have nothing to do with any actual-existing social arrangement. In part this is because of the ambidextrous nature of voice. Much the same applies to values (Table 6.4). In most instances strongly held values are expressed in similar degrees in prosperous and significantly less prosperous societies. The exceptions to this are 'perseverance and determination' and 'independence'. These are more commonly avowed in prosperous societies just as 'obedience' is more commonly affirmed among the less prosperous cohort. Otherwise, there is not much difference in the spread of stated opinions and values between the two groups of nations.

Political debates, such as Britain's 2016 referendum on EU membership, are noisy affairs. They are conducted on the basis that reason determine outcomes. But what kind of reason? There is the reason of the rationalist and the reason-as-ratio of the sceptic. These are not commensurable. For one type of reason leads to better organization. The other kind leads to better balance. Britain's referendum on whether to stay or leave the European Union did not decisively resolve this tension. For like most big political votes, it ended up in the 55:45 range, in this case 52 percent opting to leave and 48 percent of voters choosing to stay in the European Union. This narrow political arithmetic was then convoluted by another political arithmetic created by the divide between politicians and voters.

Table 6.3 Opinion

On a 1 to 10 scale, the mean of the scores selected by those who were asked:	N = negative	Global mean	Australia	Germany	Hong Kong	Japan	Korea	Netherlands	New Zealand	Singapore	Sweden	United States
Should incomes be made more equal?	10 = N	5.3	4.77	4.08	5.97	5.2	6.45	5.47	5.16	5.74	4.88	5.58
Should government ownership of business and industry be increased?	1 = N	5.6	4.67	5.12	5.77	4.51	5.53	5.49	4.54	5.23	5.21	3.71
Should people take more responsibility to provide for themselves?	1 = N	4.45	5.66	4.75	6.09	3.72	3.55	5.81	6.3	5.29	5.52	6.22
Is competition good?	10 = N	3.85	3.36	4.11	3.96	4.14	3.88	4.81	3.45	4.41	3.69	3.45
Does hard work usually bring a better life?	1 = N	4.2	3.9	4.61	3.98	4.68	4.35	4.79	3.75	4.47	4.3	3.83
Do people only get rich at the expense of others?	10 = N	6.23	6.1	5.83	7.09	5.89	6.04	6.09	6.22	5.82	5.95	6.36
Governments tax the rich & subsidize the poor is an essential characteristic of democracy	1 = N	6.31	6.04	6.95	6.04	6.5	7.44	6.1	5.47	6.33	6.42	5.04

On a 1 to 10 scale, the mean of the scores selected by those who were asked:	N = negative	Global Mean	Argentina	Brazil	China	Estonia	Malaysia	Mexico	Nigeria	Philippines	Poland	Slovenia	South Africa	Spain	Egypt
Should incomes be made more equal?	10 = N	5.3	4.94	5.09	4.45	3.79	6.66	5.36	6.44	6.3	6.32	3.48	6.09	5.14	4.3
Should government ownership of business and industry be increased?	1 = N	5.6	6.14	5.15	5.7	5.88	6.09	6.05	5.46	6.31	6.45	4.84	6.24	5.37	6.69
Should people take more responsibility to provide for themselves?	1 = N	4.45	5.05	4.01	4.65	3.7	5.97	4.58	4.3	6.09	4.51	4.1	5.77	4.35	3.04
Is competition good?	10 = N	3.85	4.71	3.74	3.67	3.78	3.53	3.65	3.82	4.13	4.86	4.24	5.21	3.88	2.43
Does hard work usually bring a better life?	1 = N	4.2	4.29	4.19	3.69	5.13	3.64	3.32	4.29	3.73	5.67	4.61	4.77	4.27	2.68
Do people only get rich at the expense of others?	10 = N	6.23	5.81	7.56	6.96	5.5	6.86	7.71	5.85	6.02	6	5.19	6.14	5.62	7.18
Governments tax the rich & subsidize the poor is an essential characteristic of democracy	1 = N	6.31	5.58	4.51	7.29	7.15	6.68	5.06	5.26	6.62	5.7	6.29	6.69	7.02	7.27

Source: World Values Survey 2012.

Table 6.4 Values

Above global average

Here is a list of qualities that children can be encouraged to learn at home. Which, if any, do you consider to be especially important?

Nation/territory	Determination and perseverance	Thrift & saving	Independence	Hard work	Feelings of responsibility	Imagination	Obedience
	Percentage of survey interviewees who mentioned the listed value						
Australia	50.3	30.7	65	59.1	65.9	39.8	28.2
Germany	59.6	38.1	73.5	17.9	80.9	29.5	12.6
Hong Kong	43	43.7	72.6	58	79.3	18.8	17.7
Japan	67.8	47.8	67.6	35.1	87.3	31.6	5
Netherlands	37.1	47.5	60.7	31.3	90.8	20	25.6
New Zealand	48.5	33.4	53.5	50.2	56.1	36.3	24.1
Singapore	44.3	47.4	72.1	60.8	69.7	18.8	37.5
South Korea	54.5	65.1	57.8	64.3	87.8	14.5	8.7
Sweden	33.6	38.6	70.3	13.8	82.5	46.7	12.2
United States	35.7	31.6	53.6	66.4	65.2	30.5	27.9
Comparator countries							
Argentina	25.1	13.4	44.1	40.6	57.3	31.4	35.3
Brazil	28.2	26.6	37.6	64.1	77.9	24.4	51.5
China	26	50.7	69.7	75.3	65.9	17	7.5
Estonia	69.4	77	54.5	87.5	11.6	36.8	62.7
Egypt	17.8	22.5	80.2	50.4	59.2	6.2	42.1
Malaysia	40.1	60.4	71.7	43.6	64.9	24.4	24.9
Mexico	27	34.6	38.5	38	74.9	23.8	54.6
Nigeria	36.9	19.1	38.9	78	42.6	15.1	62.8
Philippines	29.9	41.9	65	69.5	67.2	14	40.8
Poland	19.3	49.5	43.4	17.9	81	16.8	34.1
Slovenia	65.2	54.6	88	50.9	83.1	26.2	41.2
South Africa	35.3	30.4	63.5	70.2	57.4	28.1	37.2
Spain	37.5	29.6	43.1	66.6	78.6	24.8	31.4
Global average	**39.5**	**39.4**	**51.5**	**60.5**	**70.9**	**22.9**	**41.7**

Source: WorldValues Survey 2012.

Politicians, by virtue of what they do and irrespective of whatever nominal beliefs they may have, tend in practice to be organizational-loyalists. This is because they create rules and allocate monies on behalf of the state. They thus find it almost impossible in practice to say that organizational rationality is the problem not the solution. It is structurally difficult for them to vote for ties of symmetrical reciprocity (agreements, contracts) when government by its nature is a progenitor of control-plan, service-benefit, allocation-recipient, and grant-grantee relationships. That is what government does. Politicians may notionally represent voters who habitually vote somewhere in the range of 55:45. But whenever they have a choice between rationalism and ratio, parliamentarians in practice do what British members of parliament did during the Referendum campaign and in Parliament after the campaign. They divided 65 percent to remain in the European Union and 35 percent to leave. Each of the major political parties committed to respect the Referendum result during the 2017 British elections – and then their parliamentarians promptly ignored those commitments and repeatedly voted in 2018 and 2019 to dodge any kind of lucid unambiguous exit from the European Union.[28]

Notes

1 Macfarlane, 2013, 55.
2 Scruton, 2006.
3 Hayek, 1973, 35–54.
4 Scruton, 2014, 19, 23–24, 42, 54, 58, 67–68, 91.
5 Smith, 1970, 502.
6 Weber, 1978, 1061. The system began to break down at the end of eighteenth century when there was a failure to translate rural voluntary administration into the new big industrial-age cities.
7 Jupp, 2001 [1988], 275–343.
8 Fischer, 1989.
9 The militancy was reflected in retribution, feuding, violent behavior, and a warrior ethos.
10 They believed in general literacy but were hostile to higher learning. That together with their craft rather than laboring background, their asceticism, and their opposition to slavery, needless courtesies, idleness, and violence naturally drew them to the industrial arts.
11 Hadley, 1996, 3–15.
12 Murphy, 2019, 183.
13 Hirschman, 1970.
14 'I would say wherever the name of Charlemagne carries weight, that is where Europe is,' remarked Jean-Claude Trichet, president of the European Central Bank in 2011. Lotharingia, the medieval successor to the Carolingian Empire, was another model invoked by EU founders.
15 The principal building of the EU Parliament is named after him.
16 The EU sidestepped inconvenient popular votes that rejected the Maastricht, Nice, and Lisbon treaties and the EU Constitution. They ignored voters or made them vote again till the right choice was made. The president of the European Commission Jean-Claude Junker stated the matter succinctly: 'If it is a yes we will say "on we go", if it's a no we will say "we continue".' Under the EU Treaty, EU bailouts for state debts are illegal. Following the 2008 Global Financial Crisis the law was ignored. When Greek and Italian prime ministers, Papandreou and Berlusconi, criticized EU policies they were

promptly replaced by pliant technocrats in parliamentary coups. The attitude of the EU's autocratic technocracy was spelled out again by Jean-Claude Junker: 'There can be no democratic choice against the European Treaties.'

17 Employment data: OECD stats, employment, unemployment, and participation rates by place of birth and sex, 2016.

18 Inter-generational support data: Bordone and de Valk, 2016, Table 3b. Southern European, Eastern European, and African cohorts exhibit relatively high levels of child-to-parent support typical of non-nucleated dependency family patterns.

19 Yorke, 2016.

20 This is made up of a member-state contribution less a rebate and public-sector receipts.

21 Hull, England's poorest city, once was a prosperous North Sea fishing port. When the UK entered the EU, Britain's territorial waters' fishing rights were reallocated to other EU states under the Common Fisheries Policy, devastating Hull's economy (Legatum Institute, 2016).

22 In contrast to the Continent, UK ports are smaller in volumes handled but relatively larger in number. In short they are more decentralized. This means that they also more readily expand or shrink as the country's trade orientation changes.

23 Heinsohn, 2016.

24 Abulafia, 2016.

25 On the Hanseatic League, see Parker (2004, 132–150).

26 Heller, 1987.

27 The classic twentieth-century statement of the idea that rational argument leads to consensus was made by Jürgen Habermas (1984).

28 At the time of writing the battle between the Remain and Exit (Leave) factions in British parliamentary politics was unresolved. Whosoever reads this knows the result.

Bibliography

Abulafia, D. 2016. *Lübeck and the Hanseatic League* Lecture. London: Legatum Institute, February 10.

Bordone, V. and H. A. G. de Valk. 2016. "Intergenerational Support among Migrant Families in Europe". *European Journal of Ageing* 13, no. 3: 259–270.

Fischer, D. H. 1989. *Albion's Seed: Four British Folkways in America*. New York: Oxford University Press.

Habermas, J. 1984 [1981]. *The Theory of Communicative Action* Volume 1 *Reason and the Rationalisation of Society*. Boston, MA: Beacon Press.

Hadley, D.M. 1996. "Multiple Estates and the Origins of the Manorial Structure of the Northern Danelaw". *Journal of Historical Geography* 22, no. 1: 3–15.

Hayek, F. 1973. *Law, Legislation and Liberty*, Volume 1. Chicago, IL: University of Chicago Press.

Heinsohn, G. 2016. "A Northern Alliance? How the U.K. Can Liberate Post-Brexit Europe from Brussels". *City Journal*, July 13.

Heller, A. 1987. *Beyond Justice*. Oxford: Blackwell.

Hirschman, A.O. 1970. *Exit, Voice and Loyalty: Responses to Decline in Firms, Organizations and States*. Cambridge, MA: Harvard University Press.

Jupp, J. (ed). 2001 [1988]. *The Australian People: An Encyclopedia of the Nation, Its People and Their Origins*. Cambridge: Cambridge University Press.

Legatum Institute. 2016. *Prosperity to Poverty – and Back? A Portrait of Hull, the UK's Least Prosperous City*. London: Legatum Institute.

Macfarlane, A. 2013. *Individualism, Capitalism and the Modern World: Essays, Talks and Lectures*. Kindle.

Murphy, P. 2019. *Limited Government: The Public Sector in the Auto-Industrial Age*. London: Routledge.

Parker, G. 2004. *Sovereign City: The City-State through History*. London: Reaktion.

Scruton, R. 2014. *How to Be a Conservative*. London: Bloomsbury.

Scruton, R. 2006. *England: An Elegy*. London: Continuum.

Smith, A. 1970 [1776]. *Wealth of Nations*, ed. A. Skinner. Harmondsworth: Penguin.

Weber, M. 1978 [1922]. *Economy and Society*, Volume 2. Berkeley: University of California Press.

Yorke, H. 2016. "Britain's Best-known Universities Have Urged Their Students to Vote to Stay". *The Telegraph*, May 28.

7   Ratio

Unit-ties

As prosperity in the past two centuries has expanded and at an accelerating pace, this has brought with it greater interaction with strangers combined with more intense interaction with a small number of intimates, immediate family members in the first place, but also crucially circles of friends and friendly acquaintances (Table 4.3). As modernity has matured, the world has become both more distant and closer at the same time.

This is a symptom of a larger phenomenon: the rise of unit-ties.[1] All societies have bonds or ties. If they don't, they fall apart. In premodern societies, ties were predominately hierarchical in nature. A second kind of tie was the collegiate bond: the ties of the citizens of a city, the aristocrats of a council, the members of a guild, the scholars of a university, and so on. The tendency of modern societies was to replace both of these kinds of ties with unit-ties. Unit-ties are units of ties of closeness and distance, strength and weakness, concreteness and abstraction. Modern personalities have to master these antipodal ties, while being careful not to sacrifice one polarity for the other. Such ties are also reversible. That is, some strong ties become weak, as the marriage tie does in divorce. Conversely, some ties to strangers, such as national feeling, that normally are low-key become intense in times of war.

The feeling of being part of a nation arises out of the patterns of a settled place that we share with others.[2] The nation though is not just a locality, for a nation is populated by strangers. It entails expectations of and obligations towards persons whom we do not know personally and most of whom we will never met. A nation is not an ethnic, tribal, or kin group, a princely hierarchy or patrimony. It usually has a predominant language but does not necessarily incorporate all the speakers of that language. England the nation for example is distinct from the English-speaking peoples. A nation typically is accompanied by a sovereign state yet the nation is not the same as the state. A sovereign state creates enforceable rules and laws, raises taxes, conducts defense, and provides public services. These are practical matters subject to pattern-like principles such as the checking and balancing of powers. A nation in contrast is a symbolic pattern. It combines contrasts and has an aesthetic-like feel but in this case for edifying rather than practical purposes, hence flags, stamps, insignia, anthems, landscape, townscape, and the indubitable national sense of wit, place, and taste.

Hierarchies scale from bottom to top. Unit-ties also scale, from small and intense to medium to large and diffuse. Unit-ties move across a spectrum from very strong household ties to milder but strong friendship ties to more abstract national loyalties to diffuse and much looser market and industry commitments. A marriage vow is an intense tie. It typically binds a small unit: the household and the nuclear family. Friendship is a more diffuse yet still personally intense tie. Nations, markets, and industries bind strangers together. Nation–states are the primary modern locus of law and government, complemented in some cases by federated states or city-states. In moments of crisis the ties to a nation may become intense. But mostly they are not intense simply because the nation is an impersonal abstraction. It is necessarily abstract because we don't and can't know most people who make up a nation, similar to markets and industries. They succeed because that they have ties but those ties are loose and diffuse. They demand things of us but not in an intense way. A tie is a bond. Unit-ties bond us in complementary but contrasting ways: we make vows to spouses, pledges to children, commitments to friends, allegiances to nations, promises to contract partners, undertakings to industry associates, guarantees to professional clients. Each implies a certain steadfastness and staunchness, a dedication and devotion to something, but not in each case to exactly the same thing and not with the same degree of intensity. Unit-ties imply a human capacity to move from one intensity to the other, from mild to strong, and all points in between.

What is often called 'modern capitalism' introduced a potent mix of large-scale markets, industries, and cities – along with publics.[3] The key to this is that systems and associations replace small-scale close-knit communities. Old status hierarchies shrink. Individuals interact with growing numbers of strangers. Our family, immediate neighbors, friends, and acquaintances total around 150 people. In a modern society, we add to that '150' the thousands of strangers we buy things from, listen to on the radio, pass by on our travels, and sit with in arenas and theatres. This social pattern is the exception not the rule in human history.

High-performing societies tend to exhibit an elevated incidence of relaxed interaction (trust) between strangers. Strangers populate modern markets, industries, cities, and publics on a large scale. This is true whether the system operates at a metropolitan, national, regional, or international level. For example, some nations engage in trade principally with themselves or their near neighbors. Others trade extensively around the world (Table 4.5). The ratio of export trade to GDP is low in Japan, the United States, the United Kingdom, New Zealand, and Australia; moderate in South Korea, Switzerland, and Sweden; and high in Singapore, Hong Kong, and the Netherlands. All of these nations and city-states though report either relatively high levels or high levels of trust when interacting with strangers (Table 4.3).

This is important because neither rules nor hierarchies work very well in integrating and coordinating buyers and sellers, investors and borrowers, or technologists and device adopters. The economics of grace works considerably better. Typical media of grace are abstract patterns, ratios, proportions, and the operations of balance and equilibrium. These, much more so than commands or rules, are effective in mediating systemic large-scale stranger interaction, be it domestic or global, national or continental. This is why societies with a strong aesthetic or design sensibility are often good economic performers. These are societies where large-scale aesthetic-like patterns (including cycles, ratios, proportionality, scaling, similitude, clustering, and branching) play as prominent a role in economic and social life as fiscal and monetary policy or law and regulation do.

This is echoed for example in the emphasis that Lee Kuan Yew and Goh Keng Swee's Singapore model of development placed on the city as a driver of economic growth. What accompanied this was a strong sense of urban aesthetics. In Lee's case, that meant a fastidious vision of Singapore as a 'garden city'.[4] Something similar can be observed in high-performing societies like Japan and Denmark, where aesthetics permeate society. That is also why city beauty and the related factor of city visitation are two of the measures of successful societies (Table 4.3). The highest forms of material achievement in part are reached via civic beauty. Important elements of aesthetic grace are built into the most propulsive market and industrial systems. Causality in this case does not just operate in one direction – from matter to grace. Rather, it is circular. Matter and grace are intertwined on a continuum.

Hierarchy, equality, proportionality

A classic objection to modern prosperity is that it is not 'equal'. The assumption underlying this is that modern functional societies replace hierarchy with equality as their organizing principle. This assumption mostly is false. Alexis de Tocqueville thought that modernity was the age of equality.[5] In a negative sense, it was, if we take equality to mean the dismantling of communal, feudal, and patrimonial hierarchies. But if we mean by equality, equal income, wealth, and assets, then, the answer is 'no'. Modernity is not the age of equality. Rather, equality is the great illusion of the epoch. Equality of sorts is only possible by immiserating a population, taking away their property, and reducing their income to a minimum by terrorizing them. Despots can do that. But despotism also means inequality. The despot and his apparatus has wealth and power and status that the terrorized population in their egalitarian misery don't and can't have. Equality produces the worst kind of inequality.

Modern functional societies replace hierarchy with proportionality or ratio, not equality.[6] The optimal outcome in a modern functional society is the golden ratio focal point between absolute equality and absolute inequality. This represents a moderate social regime. The model that was worked out by the Italian statistician and sociologist Corrado Gini illustrates the point. He developed what became known as the Gini coefficient. Gini's model has a range of values from 0 (or 0 percent) to 1 (or 100 percent), where 0 represents perfect equality and 1 represents perfect inequality. In a nation where every person has an identical income, the Gini coefficient of the nation would equal 0. In a country where one person alone earns the entire income of the nation, the Gini coefficient would equal 1.

For 179 countries worldwide, their average Gini coefficient (after taxes and transfers) in 2017 was 0.386.[7] Among the OECD countries listed in Table 7.1, the average was 0.311, a modestly more moderate outcome. Consider the ratio of the Gini coefficient of South Africa, the world's most unequal country (A), to the world's average Gini coefficient (B). The ratio of A:B is 0.634:0.386. A (the extreme) is 1.64 times quantity B (the average). That figure is close to *phi* (1.68), the golden ratio number, one of the most commonly occurring numbers in nature.[8] This suggests that there is a 'golden mean' between absolute

Table 7.1 Relative equality–inequality

Nation/territory	Market income Gini 2014–2016	Disposable income Gini 2014–2016	Market income Gini greater or lesser than disposable income Gini	Social spending as a percentage of GDP 2016*	Public employment as a percentage of total employment 2013*
South Korea	0.341	0.295	0.046	11	8
Switzerland	0.386	0.296	0.09	16	18
Iceland	0.386	0.255	0.131	15	N/A
Slovak Republic	0.4	0.241	0.159	18	27
Singapore	0.417	0.356	0.061	4	3
Norway	0.428	0.262	0.166	26	35
Turkey	0.429	0.404	0.025	13	13
Canada	0.431	0.307	0.124	17	20
Sweden	0.435	0.282	0.153	26	28
Israel	0.44	0.346	0.094	15	21
Netherlands	0.445	0.285	0.16	17	60
Czech Republic	0.448	0.253	0.195	19	34
Denmark	0.451	0.263	0.188	29	35
Slovenia	0.452	0.244	0.208	22	23
Hungary	0.455	0.288	0.167	21	27
Estonia	0.456	0.314	0.142	18	26
Poland	0.459	0.284	0.175	21	25
New Zealand	0.462	0.349	0.113	19	12
Australia	0.469	0.33	0.139	18	18
Latvia	0.475	0.346	0.129	16	31
Mexico	0.478	0.459	0.019	8	12
Luxembourg	0.482	0.304	0.178	22	26
Belgium	0.499	0.266	0.233	29	22
Austria	0.501	0.284	0.217	28	15
Japan	0.504	0.339	0.165	22	8
Germany	0.504	0.293	0.211	25	15

(Continued)

Table 7.1 (Continued)

Nation/territory	Market income Gini 2014–2016	Disposable income Gini 2014–2016	Market income Gini greater or lesser than disposable income Gini	Social spending as a percentage of GDP 2016*	Public employment as a percentage of total employment 2013*
United Kingdom	0.506	0.351	0.155	21	24
Finland	0.506	0.259	0.247	30	27
United States	0.507	0.391	0.116	19	14
Lithuania	0.515	0.378	0.137	16	71
Spain	0.516	0.341	0.175	24	17
France	0.516	0.291	0.225	32	20
Italy	0.517	0.328	0.189	28	17
Portugal	0.53	0.331	0.199	24	16
Greece	0.536	0.333	0.203	26	23
Hong Kong	0.539	0.473	0.066	5	7
Ireland	0.545	0.297	0.248	15	24

Source: OECD Statistics, Income Distribution and Poverty Data, 2014–2016; OCED Statistics, Social Spending, 2016 (Japan, 2015); OECD Statistics, Government at a glance 2015, Employment in the public sector, Table 3.1 Public sector employment as a percentage of total employment 2013 (Czech Republic and Germany, 2009); OECD Statistics, Israel, 2007; International Labor Organization, Employment by sex and institutional sector, Finland 2015, United States 2013, Netherlands 2016, Hong Kong 2013; Singapore Ministry of Finance, Before and after Taxes and Transfers, Singapore's Gini Coefficient, Chart 1: International comparison of Gini coefficients based on the square root scale, www.mof.gov.sg/Newsroom/Parliamentary-Replies/before-and-after-taxes-and-transfers – Singapore's Gini-coefficient; Singapore statistics, Employed Residents Aged 15 Years And Over By Industry And Age Group, Government Employees In The Civil Service By Sex, Government operating expenditure by sector (social and family development), 2013; Hong Kong Census and Statistics Department, 2016 Population By-census, Table E305: Gini Coefficient by household size, 2006, 2011 and 2016; Hong Kong Research Office, Legislative Council Secretariat, Information Note Fiscal sustainability of social welfare spending in selected places, Figure 3 – Public social spending in Hong Kong, 1997–2018. *Unless otherwise noted in sources

Note: The Gini coefficient ranges from 0 (or 0 percent) to 1 (or 100 percent). 0 represents perfect equality and 1 represents perfect inequality. In a nation where every person had an identical income, the income Gini coefficient would equal 0. In a nation where one person alone earned the entire income of the country, the income Gini coefficient would equal 1. Social expenditure comprises cash benefits, direct in-kind provision of goods and services, and tax breaks with social purposes. Benefits may be targeted at low-income households, the elderly, disabled, sick, unemployed, or young persons.

equality and absolute inequality, and that inequality/equality tends to gravitate around such a point. Countries like South Africa (0.634), Columbia (0.508), Panama (0.504), Chile (0.447), Malaysia (0.463), and Saudi Arabia (0.459) lie at a significant remove from the 'golden mean' point.

A modern social fantasy is that the state can create 'equality'. But equality is only possible by despotic means. Imagine that every person in a nation (bar one) has an identical income. That's only possible where one person, a despot, possesses the entire income of the society. A commonplace in functional societies are political movements that promise to make society 'equal'. Such promises are typically put forward by persons and groups hungry to accumulate moral status by offering conspicuous social pieties. Equality, ironically, is a vehicle to reassert a kind of hierarchy, dominated by those who are by their own self-measure morally superior.

There are those who claim that modern fiscal state methods of taxing and transferring income and wealth can make societies if not 'equal' then 'more equal' by means of redistribution. The assumption is that capital and labor markets distribute income in a manner that is 'too unequal' and state redistribution of income redresses that. What is achieved by taxing and transferring income is illustrated by OECD countries. The average before-tax market income Gini coefficient for those countries is 0.468. After taxes and transfers, it is 0.311, a substantial shift, though inevitably far from the mirage of 'equality'. What is particularly interesting about the OECD data, though, is that the distribution pattern of South Korea's, Switzerland's, and Iceland's *market* income (that is, income *before* taxes and transfers) achieves a Gini coefficient close to the OECD average for disposable income *after* taxes and transfers (Table 7.1). This raises an interesting issue: for it is conventionally assumed that a state's transferring of income reduces market-based inequalities. On the surface, this assumption seems obvious. Yet it supposes that social causation operates in one direction. But what if we assume that causation is bidirectional? Then a somewhat different picture emerges. What if the state creates market inequalities as well as obviating them?

The examples of South Korea, Switzerland, and Iceland beg the question: how is a moderate distribution of income achieved by the market alone? What do these nations have in common? Very little except one thing. Their governments are all cost effective or good-value governments (Table 4.3). They rank very high on those criteria. Iceland is a high-spending but efficient state; Switzerland and South Korea are relatively low spending and also efficient. Is it possible that paradoxically the tax-and-transfer solution to inequality creates – or perhaps more precisely part-creates – the problem that it is meant to fix. How might it achieve this perverse paradox? By instituting transfer schemes that reduce labor mobility, thus generating poverty traps, and by encouraging tax subsidies and fiscal allocations that lean toward low-productivity (and so low-income) economic activities or by financing state spending through debt, thereby redistributing income from a broader band of taxpayers to a narrower band of wealthier debt financiers.

But does that then mean that modernity is an age of inequality? Sometimes, simply put, that is true. Yet in the most successful modern societies inequality is substantially moderated. It is tempered. It cannot be eliminated but it can be mitigated up to a certain point. That represents neither a state of equality nor one of inequality but rather something else. That something else is proportionality. The concept of proportionality has its roots in ancient Greece. It lived on as a philosophical-political concept through Roman antiquity and the Christian Middle Ages. Its significance for the modern age takes off in the Renaissance.

Proportionality is a form of pattern thinking. The problem of equality or inequality is posed when a society has to combine factors that are large and small. How then to do that? Do we promise that everyone in the society can be big? Or do we make everyone small? The first is impossible. The second is despotic. What pattern thinking does is to combine the large and the small in pleasing ways. Patterns are created by combining opposites (antipodes) using the media of proportionality, symmetry, ratio, and so on. The effect of proportionality is not to eliminate inequalities (an impossibility) but rather to temper them in ways that if not everyone at least many people find satisfying.

Status (Redux)

Equality and inequality are not only a function of income and wealth. Just as important are relative degrees of status, that is, how a person is ranked in the eyes of society. The relatively anonymous nature of the operation of modern systems plays havoc with social arrangements that are fixated on status. This is because they are to a significant extent anonymous in the way they work. They are large-scale, impersonal in character, and quasi-automatic in their operation. This means that status is difficult to signal. In older pre-industrial societies, the opposite applies. Status hierarchies are common.

Modernity eliminates status hierarchies yet it also recreates them. Renovated hierarchies emerge. Often these are procedural and rule-based (legal-rational). But they also often reproduce characteristics that are neo-patrimonial, neo-feudal, or clannish in nature. Prosperity is a function of functional systems. But appetites for status ladders remain and tend to be quite insistent.

Sometimes, the working of status hierarchies is subtle. In the case of purely functional systems – those that are neither premodern nor legal-rational in structure – an ironic kind of hierarchy emerges. This is the insistence or the claim that one social sub-system is superior to another, that for example the engineering system is better than the price system or that the reading public is superior to markets. This both derives from and leads to the sense that economic and social systems are autarchic. But in fact in a modern autonomous or self-organizing society each social system paradoxically is the environment of another. Autarchy defies that principle. It creates the illusion that a system has no environment or at least that its environment is effete.

Do autonomous societies rank things? Yes, though their ranking principle is primarily functional not hierarchical. The principle is, *Does it work?* Or alternatively, *Does it work better?* Better is not quite the same as superior even if the words at points overlap in meaning. 'Better' implies variously the improvement, enhancement, recovery, or restoration of a condition or the kind of performance or state of operation that outdoes, surpasses, or exceeds another. Bigger, higher, grander, and loftier can apply to both superior and better but the former tends to have either an ascribed social status connotation or else a self-fixated, self-conscious connotation that the latter lacks.

The rise of Anon

The nineteenth century – and in a larger sense modernity – saw the gradual dissolving of traditional hierarchy as the cement of society. This happened unevenly, in different ways and to different degrees. Four typical responses to this phenomenon occurred, each offering a replacement for the traditional forms of hierarchy:

1. *The romantic society of equals.* In this society everyone is 'the same'. There is no division of labor and no state distinct from society. Karl Marx and Friedrich Engels described it this way:

   > as soon as the distribution of labor comes into being, each man has a particular, exclusive sphere of activity, which is forced upon him and from which he cannot escape. He is a hunter, a fisherman, a herdsman, or a critical critic, and must remain so if he does not want to lose his means of livelihood.

   In contrast, in the romantic communist society 'nobody has one exclusive sphere of activity'. Instead 'each can become accomplished in any branch he wishes'. It is

   > possible for me to do one thing today and another tomorrow, to hunt in the morning, fish in the afternoon, rear cattle in the evening, criticize after dinner, just as I have a mind, without ever becoming hunter, fisherman, herdsman or critic.[9]

2. *The horizontal society of spontaneous coordination.* Society has an intensified division of labor which is spontaneously coordinated through contracts and other kinds of horizontal bonds and ties.
3. *The vertical society of legal-rational hierarchies.* Old patrimonial and kin-based hierarchies are replaced by modern procedural hierarchies, the nub of the modern organization.
4. *The vertical society of renovated traditional hierarchies.* Patrimonial and kin-based hierarchies are preserved and transcended at the time. Neo-patrimonial systems develop in the form of authoritarian-presidential, single-party, extended-ruling-family, or despotic-militant loyalty hierarchies and resource-state patronage systems, oligarchies, and clientelism.

The French sociologist Émile Durkheim responded to the first three of these models in *The Division of Labor in Society* (1893). All but the most archaic societies, Durkheim argued, had a division of labor. Civilization developed – and modernity intensified – the division of labor. Society began in a condition where everyone was (more or less) 'the same'. That is, in hunter-gatherer societies the key social glue is resemblance. Each member of the society resembles each other member; each part of society is like each other part. Durkheim underestimated the age and sex hierarchies that were present in elemental societies but his basic point was not wrong. Across eons of history, societies differentiated themselves into parts that were as different as the merchant and the warrior are. If not resemblance then what is the glue that binds strongly differentiated societies together? Durkheim rejected the idea that such societies could rely on the horizontal coordination of their parts alone.

Herbert Spencer had argued that modern industrial societies were integrated through contracts. Durkheim thought contracts were insufficient. They were limited in time. They didn't last. So societies based on a division of labor required a durable directing intelligence – simply put, the state – to integrate their divided parts. Durkheim reasoned that segmental societies – those in which each part is much the same as any other part – were bound by a common punitive (i.e., repressive) law. Their integration was 'mechanical'. In contrast, societies with strongly differentiated parts (notably religious, political, legal, commercial, and artisan specialists) developed an 'organic' kind of integration. This involved a directing intelligence such as the state combined with forms of specialist law (commercial, public, administrative, procedural, and constitutional law).

In short, Durkheim argued societies were integrated through the media of resemblance and law. This is true – in part but only in part. The integration of social parts is more multifaceted than Durkheim allowed. At least nine kinds of media act to cement societies together. Resemblance and law each contributes something but so also do patterns, hierarchies, unions of opposites, functions, contracts, processes, authority, and commands. Broadly speaking, these different media fall into three major categories. These reflect different axes of society. Society is three dimensional. It is made up of vertical, horizontal, and orthogonal dimensions. The horizontal axis of a society is best represented by patterns, the vertical axis by hierarchies, and the orthogonal axis by rules. Each structures different kinds of behavior (Table 4.2).

All societies are mixes, hybrids, and amalgams of the three dimensions. Each society arranges the three dimensions in different ways. The vertical, horizontal, and orthogonal overlap and interact with each other in remarkably diverse ways. In each case, there is a tendency for one dimension to lead or over-determine the other dimensions. All societies have patterns, hierarchies, and rules. In the most successful modern societies, the pattern dimension leads the way. This does not mean it does or can eliminate rules and hierarchies. Not only do these persist but parties and factions arise that strongly gravitate to rules or hierarchies or both. Post-rational pattern-based action is not for all personalities. Some prefer the promise of rational mastery. Others prefer the emotional cocoon of rank, position, and status.

That said, pattern behavior is key to successful modernity. It creates an equilibrium of permanence and change, stability and dynamism, that is highly conducive to prosperity. Take one example – the question of identity. Individuals and societies have to have an identity. This is the sense that they are self-similar over time. Identity – 'who I am', 'who we are' – represents the continuity of self and society – the ability to see the resemblance of our own self or our own society across present, past, and future. Societies that lack an identity fall into incoherence and chaos. At the same time, a modern prosperous society has to be able to grow rapidly and expansively. Such growth requires various kinds of change – that is, dynamism. The ability to find an equilibrium point between continuity and change is important, even if it is not easy. It requires a taste for irony and conundrum. That's not the forte of the vertical or orthogonal axes of society. Hierarchies and rules are poor at striking effective balances between contrary forces and qualities. For the latter, something closer to mystery than rational mastery or status ascendancy is required. Adam Smith's invisible hand was a memorable way of describing such a mystery. It hinted at the enigmatic manner in which contrarieties – such as self-interest and social interest – are reconciled in modern paradoxical social systems.

The last major figure to foreground the role of equilibrium in political economy was Alfred Marshall, who wrote the *Principles of Economics* (1890–1920). By 1922, when Max Weber's treatise *Economy and Society* was published, the prevailing image of society had begun to trend toward a picture composed of mostly two-dimensional interaction between vertical and orthogonal social axes. Most notably, Weber contrasted legal-rational (procedural-rational) authority with traditional (patrimonial) authority. A legal-rational authority was an impersonal rather than a personal hierarchy. It was subject to rules and recruited persons on the basis of merit, that is, qualifications. This is what we mean by a contemporary 'organization'.

Business evolved across the nineteenth century from the owner-operated business through chartered companies, unincorporated associations, joint stock companies with their own legal personality, and companies that limited the liability of shareholders for losses. By the 1930s, the managerial corporation clearly separated ownership from control. In 1937, the economist Ronald Coase suggested that most economic activity in principle could be horizontal in nature, that is, mediated by contracts. The firm – which is a procedural hierarchy – exists, Coase argued, because it reduces the transactional costs of contracting.[10] Conversely, it should be noted that firms often also fail when the overhead costs of management and bureaucracy outweigh the savings on transactional costs.

Durkheim personified something that by the 1890s had become common among intellectuals. They had reacted against the idea of the self-organizing society. The reaction took many forms. Some embraced romanticism. They dreamt of a society of equals. Some were attracted to ideas that translated the perpetual warring, heroic sacrifice, and struggle of premodern pre-industrial militant societies into modern terms (Table 4.1). Others imagined a premodern community that was warm and intimate – organized around hierarchies that were beneficial, protective, secure, and embracing. Modern contractual society in contrast was cold, calculating, and callous. Better that society allocate goods hierarchically than expect persons to attain those goods through acts of symmetrical reciprocity requiring significant degrees of self-reliance and self-organization. Others thought that the medicine for the ills of modern 'bad society' was the state. Its directing intelligence could replace the automatic large-scale self-regulating rhythms of markets, industries, and cities. Planning, forecasting, designing, commanding, and regulating would erase the flaws of a bad society.

By the close of the nineteenth century the currents of romanticism and statism were often folded in together. They represented collectively an animus against self-organizing systems. Durkheim's view was more subtle than these. He anticipates the uneasy mix of system and state that solidifies in leading economies and societies in the second half of the twentieth century. As this happened, romantics, socialists, totalitarians, and statists tended to be pushed to the political margins, though each continued to attract support and influence public opinion – and each would enjoy periodic revivals. On the whole, though, by the 1950s, the typical outcome was an uneasy, often awkward compromise between big government and self-organizing systems. There are many versions of this compromise. Some lent towards a big government directing intelligence, others toward small-government self-organization.

While Durkheim argued that the scope and efficacy of spontaneous coordination was limited in nature, he also described beautifully many of the secondary characteristics of a self-organizing society. He noted the long-term historical move from clan-based to patrimonial-territorial-kingship societies and then after that to societies based on markets and cities. In the modern age, the latter step, he observed, entailed a shift away from relations of dependence to relations of interdependence, from low volumes of population to high volumes, from low material and moral density to high density, and from concrete and specific thought and action to belief and behavior that was general and abstract in nature.

Ratios

As traditional hierarchies gradually crumbled, organizational ties replaced personal relations, engineers replaced aristocrats, and political parties replaced kings and notables. Legal-rational procedures helped transform social classes into functional classes. The key to function is achievement in place of ascriptive status. The assumption of that is no matter 'who' you are – whatever your rank or status is – what matters is 'what you can achieve'. However, in practice, achievement is an elastic concept. Or more precisely the recipe for achievement is elastic. One common claim is that functional achievement is the result of knowledge (know-how and know-what). The knowledge of professional and skilled classes is touted as crucial. On the other side of the ledger, ethical behavior in the form of honesty, reliability, and trustworthiness is presented as the recipe for achievement, a key to good relations in societies where persons interact with large numbers of strangers. Notions of professional and vocational ethics attempt to merge the two functional precepts into one. Functional knowledge and personal reliability replace the loyalty, faith, and obedience of hierarchical orders.

The shift from a status to a functional society was one of a series of epochal transitions that created modern prosperous economies and societies. These transitions included shifts from metaphysical to positive knowledge (Comte), militant to industrial society (Comte and Spencer), consumer to producer society (Comte), producer to consumer society (Veblen), status to contract (Maine), community to society (Tönnies), feudalism to capitalism (Marx), uniformity to differentiation (Durkheim), ascription to achievement (Parsons), anarchic local power to pacified territorial power (Elias), and so on. Each of these shifts played a role in the creation of historically unprecedented prosperous societies.

Each of these transitions also posed a recurring question: amidst change, what integrates society? What ties it together? A more specific and more challenging version of this question then follows: is society possible without the binding agent of hierarchy? How do we explain the nature of spontaneous cooperation, adaptation, assimilation, evolution, and growth along with sympathies, pursuits, and actions that take place in economies and societies without the intervention of a directing intelligence?

A caricature of nineteenth-century social science supposes that spontaneous coordination is reducible to contracts (mutual promises). However, the shaping principle of self-organizing society is not the contract per se. Contracts and many other kinds of promises play a key but subordinate role in a self-organizing society. What is more important in large-scale self-organizing systems is the role of ratio. Ratio is a unifying and systemizing principle. It is an integrating force or glue of society. It influences some aspects of the city-states of classical antiquity. It reappears forcefully during the Italian Renaissance.[11] As self-organizing systems expand and multiply in the nineteenth century, driving prosperity and growth across a broad range of economic and social domains, action modulated by ratios finds numerous applications from markets to industries to cities to publics (Table 7.2).

Table 7.2 Ratios

Ratios	*Measures*	*Examples*
Business ratios		
Liquidity ratios	Measure of cash to pay creditors and vendors	*Working capital ratio* Current assets: current liabilities
Activity ratios	Measure of how long it takes a company to turn its assets into cash	*Days sales outstanding* Accounts receivable: Total annual sales ÷ 365 days
Debt ratios	Measure of the ability of a company to pay its long-term debts	*Debt ratio* Total liabilities: total assets
Profitability ratios	Measure of the efficiency of a company in using assets to generate profits	*Return on assets* Net income: total assets

(Continued)

Table 7.2 (Continued)

Ratios	Measures	Examples
Market ratios	Measure of the return on investment in a company	*Price/earnings ratio* Market price per share: Diluted earnings per share
Social ratios		
Housing ratios	Measure of the cost of housing as function of purchasers' ability to pay	*Housing multiple ratio* Median house price: median household income
Research power-law ratios	Measure of the ability of the total nominal researcher pool to generate research outcomes	*Researcher power-law ratio* Minor percent of university academics: major percent of research publication outputs
Good value government ratios	Measure of the return on government spending	*Good-value spending ratio* Public spending input: human development index outcome
Economic immigration ratios	Measure of the economic cost vs. benefit of immigration	*Economic migration ratio* Net additional growth due to migrant skills, capital: cost of public goods (welfare, infrastructure) to service migration
Higher education ratios	Measure of ability to undertake higher education studies	*Entrance score ratio* College-ready 19-year-old cohort: total 19-year-old cohort

In economic and social settings rarely do material quantities or social forces stand in a relationship of 1:1 or 50:50. Rather, it is much more common to find that they stand in ratios of 2:1, 3:2, 4:3, 5:4, and 6:5, that is, roughly 70:30, 60:40, or 55:45. These are all 'musical' ratios. They are comparable with the ratios of intervals of pitches that the human ear finds consonant and pleasing. The 80:20 ratio that the Italian–Swiss economist Vilfredo Pareto drew attention to is also a common way that economic quantities and social forces are structured. Such ratios emerge spontaneously in self-organizing systems. Persons find such patterns both intuitive and pleasing. This is because these patterns also echo patterns that are built into nature. In contrast, efforts to create 1:1 ratios of equality mostly fail. Often strenuous attempts are made to socially engineer such outcomes. They are almost universally unsuccessful.

Ratios shape economy and society not through the medium of actors and agents' intentions but rather as a by-product of an in-built sense of proportion that those actors and agents have. Contrary forces and qualities are united in proportionate relationships that are expressed, often tacitly or intuitively, in ratios. These are descriptive of what exists at a given point in time. They are also normative in the sense that there are 'ideal' ratios that economic agents and social actors feel comfortable with. These ratios are not codified. They are not inscribed in tablets of law. But they are nonetheless tacit measures of value that shape human behavior. For example, it would be a vain thing for a business to generate sales revenue only to find that its net profit after production costs and overheads was 1 percent. That's not a viable business. A stock portfolio that generated a long-term average return of 2 percent after inflation when the average long-term stock return was 7 percent is also not viable.

Persons have purposes, goals, hopes, expectations, and intentions. They mutually promise, commit to a vocation, choose a place to live, and marry. They inhabit a deeply subjective world. They expect their intentions to be realized. Sometimes those intentions are realized. Sometimes they are not. Whatever the case, be it positive or negative, their intentions are subject to factors that are objective. The scope of human purposes and goal-rationality is limited by the tacit self-organizing ratios that shape the long-run and large-scale dynamic of society.

A natural response to this is to look for a directing intelligence that will set these molding and sculpting forces aside when the outcomes they generate are unpalatable. If an enterprise earns 1 percent net annual profit, it will go out of business. Such a small return on investment is not sustainable. Government may offer the firm a subsidy to stay in business. But no grant will reverse or correct a poor business model. The company's products no longer generate strong sales. Overheads have been slashed. Yet the problem still remains. A government paying for part of the salary of the workforce can't obviate or change the lack of sales. Eventually the business will close. Its reprieve is only temporary. Moving costs from a business to the taxpayer will make no positive difference if the underlying ratio between sales revenue, production costs, and overhead costs is unsustainable and irrational.

The universal class

Even in the most successful societies, the pull of modernity's 'new feudalism' is strong. Across the twentieth century, we saw the spread of institutions that outwardly were modern, technological, procedural, and democratic yet inwardly were stratified, rank-ordered, and preoccupied with grants, allocations, and status creation. This was the phenomenon of the managerial society – first diagnosed by the American philosopher James Burnham in the 1940s.[12] It promised scientific government, expert knowledge, know-how, and efficiency. What it delivered were large organizational hierarchies preoccupied with rank, title, and status signaling. Managerial bureaucracies multiplied across the administrative state, the corporate firm, pressure groups, schools, universities, churches, charities, unions, sports, media, and arts bodies.

Premodern societies tend to be organized around ascriptive, that is, inherited, characteristics: sex, race, ethnicity, age, birth-class, ancestors, and kin. Behavior focuses on 'who you know' – on personal relationships with familiar figures, usually superiors, and subordinates. Distrust of strangers is prevalent. Nepotism is strong. Occupations are inherited.[13] Cliques and coalitions form around superstitions, taboos, fraternities, and group pride. Having one's personal status or one's status-group 'respected' is crucial. Conduct revolves around honor and shame. Prohibitions are effective if the eye of the community is watching. When not, transgressions are common. Accordingly, violence is pervasive. Warfare is chronic. Blood feuds and brutal abductions are widespread.

One of the great achievements of modern functional societies has been the massive drop in the level of human violence (Table 5.1). In part, this was because honor and shame culture was replaced by a conscience culture (doing good when no one is watching). This transformation occurred unevenly – more so among some people and some countries than others. Everywhere, the temptation to regress has persisted. Contemporary 'identity politics' is a case in point. As Durkheim observed, the most elementary human societies are segmental. Dividing them up is like chopping up a tape worm. Each part regenerates in a form that is essentially identical with any other part. The underlying impulse is that each social part is 'similar to' or 'identical to' each other part.

The drive to be part of a self-similar group made of 'people like me', to be 'identical' to them, may be an archaism yet it remains powerful. The search for segmental group identities and the motivation to reinvent aspects of feudalism in legal-rational form tend to go hand in hand. Legal-rational reinventions of grants, allocations, licenses, monopolies, privileges, and bounties are common. These often are blended with anti-industrial pastoralism and anti-machine handcraft utopias. Underpinning the procedural 'feudalisms' of the modern bureaucratic state is a personality type that is anchored in group identity. In the past the group was the village, guild, university, manor, monastery, clan, estate, or status rank. In the modern age, high-status groups began to be defined in non-traditional terms.

We see one of the early examples of this in the philosopher Hegel's nomination of the Prussian bureaucracy as a universal class. Marx followed Hegel by characterizing the proletariat as a universal class. By the beginning of the twenty-first century, Marx's proletariat had fallen out of fashion. Hegel's claim that the state bureaucracy is a universal class was remodeled into the claim that a larger knowledge class (the class with university qualifications) was the universal class. Expert, qualified, student, professional, and specialist status-groups all vied to assert their 'universal' nature.

The idea of a universal class was a paradox. It implied that there existed some social part (a class) that was identical with the social whole. The part that was the whole, it was implied, was the bearer of 'equality'. The promise of equality was undeliverable. So was the idea of a universal class in a differentiated society. Yet both were seductive concepts, for they promised something that appealed to the archaic human psyche – the idea of segmental sameness. This was the elemental image of being 'the same as' – which de facto meant 'equal to' – everyone else. This was a social mirage, but one that was repeatedly asserted in the most modern of societies.

Nietzschean inversion

The idea of the universal class was an answer to the question of how status-group hierarchy might be reborn in a modern functional society. Society might be differentiated but the idea of a universal class supposed that one part of society could symbolize 'sameness'. In doing so, it tapped into a wellspring of human need to believe that each slice, section, piece, or portion of society deep down resembles each other fragment. Another school of thought rejected the notion of universality. Its answer to hierarchy was to invert hierarchies, that is, stand them on their head.

If Hegel and Marx promised a universal class, Friedrich Nietzsche formulated the idea of the inverted hierarchy. Nietzsche called this the trans-valuation of values. This is the idea that the servant can dominate the master, the daughter can rule the mother, and the foe is better than the friend.[14] Nietzsche started by inverting the traditional hierarchy of Christian peace over aristocratic war. But in principle there is no hierarchy that cannot be inverted. Just war can be topped by perpetual peace, arms by disarmament, the hardy nation by the ethno-cultural nation, wealth by poverty, growth by de-growth, truth by error, two sexes by a fanciful infinity of sexes, biology by social construction, orthodox sexualities by heterodox sexualities, on and on it goes till the trans-valuation of values becomes permanent.[15]

A century or more after Nietzsche, the desire to invert value hierarchies has gradually filtered into the broader culture.[16] The Hegel-Marx idea of a universal class permitted the assertion of group status-claims in the name of equality (sameness). The Nietzsche idea of the trans-valuation of values encourages status-groups to reverse social hierarchies and invert differences. Today the latter notably applies in the case of groups defined by sex, gender, race, ethnicity, locality, provinciality, and sexuality. Claims based on group identities are routinely pursued in the name of 'equality'. Yet rarely do the claimants want to eliminate a real or presumed rank order. Rather, they wish to turn it on its head.

The aim is to climb up a perceived 'social hierarchy' not get rid of it. But in reality these 'social hierarchies' are more fallacious than anything, for this elaborate social drama is played out in largely functional societies whose motto is 'does it work?' not 'what's your status?' In reality, the social drama is a way of side-stepping the key (pragmatic) definition of truth in functional societies: 'does it work?' What conflicts based on the trans-valuation of values boil down to, and why they are seductive, is that they promise and often deliver access to a pool of social resources via tenures, benefits, grants and allocations. In archaic times the pool was the meat provided by the tribe's best hunters. Today it is the legal-rational or neo-patrimonial state's pot of tax revenue and the corporation's sales income.

Where status, rank, group affiliation, and title determine how much a person shares in these pools, the question 'what is your functional capacity?' is obviated. Claims of gender, race, or similar preference – however tacitly or awkwardly these might be stated and however many social pieties may attach themselves to the claims – are made to override the questions 'Are you good at this kind of work?', 'How well can you read?', 'Can you use a machine?', 'Can you interact with strangers?' – and perhaps above all 'How good are you at dealing with ambidexterity?'

The tension between status and function is not new. The archaic hunter's skill – and the protein it provided – was subject to overriding status claims of age and sex. At the same time, that skill was essential to the survival of the band. For most of human history, status edged out function. In modernity the reverse tends to occur, though status claims are persistent and resilient. In spite of the appeal of universal classes and inverted social hierarchies, the majority of persons in prosperous functional societies reject these neo-antediluvian temptations. They are at ease with contracts, technologies, and cities. They get on with strangers.[17] They use their own initiative. They move, settle, buy, sell, trade, travel, create, produce, adapt, and invent without the permission of a group, boss, patron, patriarch, godfather, guild, or government. They happily form voluntary associations and respond eagerly to the large-scale modern social systems that have created extraordinary economic wealth, broad-based prosperity, and general social uplift.

Equality and proportionality

Alexis de Tocqueville imagined the transformation of modern society as one from hierarchy to equality.[18] The outgrowth of this shift was democracy. Democracy – conceived as the offspring of equality – first emerged in the United States. The United States was a laboratory for inventing the future of the world. This happened because hierarchical ties were weak amongst the American colonists.[19] What developed from this crucible was a new type of society. It still had socially influential patricians, patrimonial political bosses, and chattel slavery. But, in many of its key aspects, its social constitution dispensed with traditional hierarchy. American social scientists gave various names to the kind of society that this produced. It was a society of people who were 'lonely' or 'marginal' and who constantly met other people they were unacquainted with and consequently developed dramaturgical skills to negotiate the expanding public world of strangers.[20] With these stage skills, they learnt to 'present' themselves in everyday public situations and manage other people's impressions of them. They also learnt to move adroitly between primary intimate relations, secondary work relationships, and tertiary long-distance anonymous relations.

Underpinning this was the growth of a large-scale pacified political territory in the United States. This was akin to what Norbert Elias observed of Europe but on a more extensive scale. The American polity was integrated by powerful communication networks and was achieved by multiple wars in North America in the eighteenth and nineteenth centuries. The influential French social theorist Auguste Comte (1798–1857) schematized the evolution of society from city-state to nation-state. He predicted a coming cosmopolitan order of mini-states. The American constitutional federation of states, arguably, realized a version of this before Comte even imagined it. The European transition from hierarchical order was rockier, more fraught, and slower than in the United States. The pressure on hierarchical order in Europe escalated as social cohorts emerged that did not easily fit into the framework of traditional hierarchies. Other cohorts proved difficult to assimilate to modern organizational hierarchies, including the categories of 'strangers' and 'entrepreneurs'.[21]

Among the dilemmas posed by this social reshaping was the question of what the role of equality was in all of this. Like achievement, equality is an elastic concept. So, also, it turned out is hierarchy. Race theorists invented new pseudo-hierarchies to replace traditional ones. Former European colonies embraced the rhetoric of proceduralism but practiced patronage. Some wondered whether the loss of hierarchy led to anomie and the 'twilight of authority'.[22] Others asked whether organizational hierarchies encouraged the formation of human beings who lacked character. Equality was meant to be levelling. It supposed that human beings were 'the same'. Yet relations between men and women firmly resisted such a notion. Influential movements pressed for the equality of the sexes while agitating that the sexes be treated differently. Equality could mean the equal right to run a business or vote in an election. But it could mean the romantic society of equals where being 'identical' implied a kind of equivalence, intimacy, and warmth that no society of strangers could ever achieve. Durkheim had argued that in the most elementary human societies persons resembled each other closely. Whether this 'sameness' ever applied to men and women is unlikely. Nonetheless the desire for 'equality' echoes the unease in some quarters of modern economies and societies that they have lost a paradisiac sameness, similarity, commonality, or community.

It is not surprising then that egalitarian movements are drawn to personalized hierarchies and collegial patrimonies. Equality in these cases is not a statistical equality but rather the 'sameness', 'identity', and 'fraternity' of a primitive, heroic, martial, or militant society. The nostalgia for this helps us to understand why it is that many currents in democratic societies proclaim equality but in practice are obsessed by status. Modern societies in part are the result of a shift from status to contract as their central load-bearing pillar. Yet the desire for status did not disappear when this happened. What disappeared was the notion that status was inherited and (mostly) couldn't be changed (a person was born with it and died with it). Status and rank consciousness didn't die. It just changed. It turned into the promotion and pecking order of managerial hierarchies. In the wider society, moral causes became key elements of status-seeking, the pursuit of being 'the good person in the bad society'. Along with this emerged the conspicuous consumption of dematerialized signs of the 'good (egalitarian) person' and the 'bad (unequal) society' that proliferate especially in media-saturated democracies.

Each newly discovered inequality in modern societies leads to the creation of an expert bureaucracy to manage it, which, in turn, creates new inequalities. The value horizon of modern equality is constantly in flux. The polarity between hierarchy and equality generates perpetual dissatisfaction. The forward march of equality always proves disappointing. The backward glance to old hierarchies is tinged with a painful sense of loss. The ghosts of the past whisper seductively about the certainty, intimacy, community, and immobility of the old order. The torn conscience worries that this is anti-modern and unprogressive yet it is enticing. A significant minority of modern personalities hanker after folkways and communal mores. Meanwhile, the various 'hidden hands' of modernity roll on, indifferent to this – industrializing, urbanizing, commercializing, and publicizing.

Modern economy and society is split in two powerful ways. One is the division between the self-organizing economy and the romantic consolations of hierarchy and equality, consolations that are often difficult to separate from each other. Second is the divide between self-organizing order and managerial organization. Order represents the tacit long-term patterning of society. Procedural organization is driven by explicit short-term goals or policies. The protagonists of self-organizing order are on the whole more contemplative than interventionist. They tend to observe trends rather than crafting policy rules. The pattern order of society is implicit. But it is also powerful. In modern societies the tacit order of society emerges from the numerous ceaseless daily actions of untold millions of individuals in cities, markets, households, publics, and industries. Economic and social actors respond variously to emergent patterns either by adapting to them or else by resisting them by attempting to control them.[23] Control tends to work in the short run but not in the long run.

Economic patterns are forceful in a quiet way. If policies and goal-rational actions are the surface noise of society, patterns run quietly but persistently under the surface. They are generally closer in kind to mathematical and aesthetic forms than they are to the purposive-rational rules, plans, strategies, and instructions of governments or firms. Patterns embody power laws and mimic natural configurations. Qualities such as symmetry, proportion, balance, scale, ratio, homology, and fractal self-similarity are exhibited in the deep background order of society where economic coherence and social meaning arises. Industrial technology along with cities, households, markets, and publics set in train long-term, anonymous cycles of behavior on a large scale. Millions of small interactions create large patterns of dynamic action. These interactions principally occur between strangers. Modern societies are societies of strangers. The personality types most at home in these societies are happy, confident, courageous, witty, and skeptical.[24]

Governments are not the panacea of modern economies. Their interventions on the whole tend to be modestly inconsequential when it comes to controlling the larger patterns of an economy. But governments are also a given. Modern social science tends to either want to eagerly defend the state or be rid of it. Sometimes this wrenched view is embodied in the same person. But the state is a given. Almost all societies – with the exception of Durkheim's segmental societies – produce states. The interesting question is not whether the state exists but whether the state is compatible with a larger enveloping self-organizing order. Markets, industries, publics, households, and cities are all, to one degree or other, limits on the state. At their peak, when they function well, the patterns that they create in their wake produce an abstract order of freedom and beauty. Dreams of hierarchy and equality compete with this image. Yet it is neither hierarchy nor equality – nor a mix of both – that is key. What matters is the compatibility of the state with self-assembling, morphogenetic, autocatalytic, economic and social processes. These animate prosperity and growth. States can neither produce nor direct the encompassing order that endows them with economic substance and durable prosperity. Legal-rational authority might set goals. But whether those goals are achieved depends on whether or not the actions of government facilitates or frustrates the enveloping patterns of economic and social self-organization.

Notes

1 The analysis that follows owes a part of its conception to Robert Nisbet's notion of unit-ideas in Nisbet, 1966.
2 Scruton, 2014, especially chapter three.
3 One of the building blocks of this is the history of mixed constitutions and city-states that runs from classical Athens and Rome to the Hansa cities onwards through Venice and Florence to Calvin's Geneva, the Dutch Republic, and England's mixed government. I discuss this route to successful modernity in Murphy, 2001. One can quibble about the degree to which prosperity is an immaculate conception or not. I am skeptical of claims of creation out of nothing. But, irrespective of this skepticism, what occurred was profound. A number of things mark off the era of generalized prosperity from prior history. One is technology. Ocean-going vessels changed the nature of trade and human settlement. Second, industrial technology magnified human productivity. Third, the focus of life shifted from the country to the city.
4 Goh (2013) emphasizes the role of cities in economic growth. The later work of William Röpke mirrored this. Röpke (1971 [1937]) was one of the earliest pioneers of the idea that from free markets arose a spontaneous social order – an order that is natural and spontaneous rather than organizing and commanding. See also Hayek (1944). *In A Humane Economy* (2014 [1960]), Röpke modulates this. He introduces the notion of beauty as a complement of markets, or as close observers of the early years of Lee Kuan Yew's premiership put it (Kwang, Fernandez, and Tan, 1998, 11): 'When jobs had to be created and communists fought in the streets, only the birds were interested in flowers and trees. But Lee was interested and he became personally involved in the project of transforming Singapore from just concrete and steel to concrete, steel, trees, shrubs, flowers and parks.' Lee began in 1963 with a tree-planting demonstration (Han, 2017, 8) and in 1967 he announced an official policy to turn Singapore into a 'garden city'. This was followed by successive programs of tree planting, park development, green corridors, and nature reserves. 'The country's prime minister from 1990–2004, Goh Chok Tong, once joked that Singapore's cabinet must be the only one in the world that read the meeting minutes of a Garden City Action Committee' (Sile, 2016). On Singapore as a garden city, see Warren, 2000; Waller, 2001.
5 Tocqueville, 2003 [1835/1840], Volume 2.
6 For the historical and philosophical background of proportionality or ratio as an organizing principle of society, see Murphy, 2001. The thinker who did most to re-emphasis ratio rather than equality as a precept of political economy and a fact of modern social structure and process was the Italian-Swiss economist and sociologist Vilfredo Pareto. See Pareto, 1963 [1917–1919, 1935], 2014 [1896–1897].

7 World Bank Gini Index, 2017.
8 Livio, 2003 [2002].
9 Marx and Engels, 1970 [1846/1932/1947], 53.
10 Coase, 1937.
11 Murphy, 2001, 163–191.
12 Burnham, 1941.
13 Until the government pursued reforms in Mexico in 2008, a teacher could pass on their occupation to a child, and if the child did not want to be a teacher, the office could be sold to someone else. 'Throughout history, the sons of carpenters have become carpenters.' Mexico's teachers unions controlled this *ancien regime* style of inheritable and saleable appointments. The going price for the sale of a post in 2008 was $6,000 in a country with an average annual income of $9,000 (Lloyd, 2008).
14 As the Irish-British playwright, Nietzschean, and Fabian-turned-fascist-admirer George Bernard Shaw conceived in his philosophic treatise-cum-drama, *Man and Superman* (1903). This kind of inversion echoes today in the style of British Labour Party politics under Jeremy Corbyn that seeks to replace armament with disarmament, philo-Semitism with anti-Semitism, markets with the state, and so forth.
15 Nietzsche's admirer, the German philosopher Martin Heidegger, observed how Nietzsche's 'revaluation of all values hitherto' became a system of 'perpetual reversal' (Heidegger, 1991, 29).
16 The desire to invert values takes many forms. Some of them are directly anchored in Nietzsche's own works. Take for example the preference among today's Nietzschean left for Islam over Christianity. This was originally advocated by Nietzsche in *The Anti-Christ* (1888), Section 60, where he claimed that 'Christianity destroyed for us the whole harvest of ancient civilization, and later it also destroyed for us the whole harvest of *Mohammedan* civilization. The wonderful culture of the Moors in Spain, which was fundamentally nearer to *us* and appealed more to our senses and tastes than that of Rome and Greece, was *trampled down*. . . . The crusaders later made war on something before which it would have been more fitting for them to have groveled in the dust – a civilization beside which even that of our nineteenth century seems very poor and very "senile".'
17 This is one of the many subtle inheritances from Christianity. As Calvin put it in the *Golden Booklet of the True Christian Life* (1550), 'Christ also teaches us we must live as strangers and pilgrims in this world, that we may not lose our heavenly inheritance.'
18 Tocqueville, 2003 [1835/1840], Volume 2.
19 Wood, 1993 [1992].
20 Park, 1967; Goffman, 1959.
21 Simmel, 1971; Schumpeter, 2017 [2011].
22 Nisbet, 2000 [1975].
23 Related to this is the tendency to anthropomorphize an economy, as if it behaved like a goal-rational person. On this psychological delusion, see Tuchtfeldt, 1982 [1973].
24 The social philosopher Agnes Heller called them Stoic-Epicurean types. Heller, 1978, 101–138.

Bibliography

Burnham, J. 1941. *The Managerial Revolution*. New York: John Day.
Coase, R. 1937. "The Nature of the Firm". *Economica* 4, no. 16: 386–405.
Goffman, I. 1959. *The Presentation of Self in Everyday Life*. New York: Doubleday.
Goh, K.S. 2013. *Wealth of East Asian Nations*. Singapore: Marshall Cavendish.
Han, H. 2017. "Singapore, a Garden City: Authoritarian Environmentalism in a Developmental State". *Journal of Environment and Development* 26, no. 1: 3–24.

Hayek, F.A. 1944. *The Road to Serfdom*. London: Routledge and Kegan Paul.

Heidegger, M. 1977. "The Question Concerning Technology". In *The Question Concerning Technology and Other Essays*, 3–35. New York: Harper.

Heidegger, M. 1991. *Nietzsche* Volumes 1 and 2. San Francisco, CA: HarperCollins.

Heller, A. 1978 [1967]. *Renaissance Man*. London: Routledge and Kegan Paul.

Kwang, H.F., W. Fernandez and S. Tan. 1998. *Lee Kuan Yew: The Man and his Ideas*. Singapore: Straits Times Press.

Livio, M. 2003 [2002]. *The Golden Ratio*. New York: Broadway Books.

Lloyd, M. 2008. "Striking Mexico Teachers See Jobs as Things to Inherit, Sell'". *Houston Chronicle*, October 13.

Marx, K. and F. Engels. 1970 [1846/1932/1947]. *The German Ideology*. New York: International Publishers.

Murphy, P. 2001. *Civic Justice: From Ancient Greece to the Modern World*. Amherst NY: Humanity Books.

Nisbet, R.A. 2000 [1975]. *Twilight of Authority*. Indianapolis, IN: Liberty Fund.

Nisbet, R.A. 1966. *The Sociological Tradition*. New York: Basic Books.

Pareto, V. 2014 [1896–1897]. *Manual of Political Economy*. Oxford: Oxford University Press.

Pareto, V. 1963 [1917–1919, 1935]. *The Mind and Society: A Treatise on General Sociology*. New York: Dover.

Park, R.E. 1967. *On Social Control and Collective Behavior: Selected Papers*. Chicago, IL: University of Chicago Press.

Röpke, W. 2014 [1960]. *The Humane Economy: The Social Framework of the Free Market*. Wilmington, DE: ISI.

Röpke, W. 1971 [1937]. *Economics of the Free Society*. Chicago, IL: Henry Regnery.

Schumpeter, J.A. 2017 [1911]. *Theory of Economic Development*. Abingdon: Routledge.

Scruton, R. 2014. *How to Be a Conservative*. London: Bloomsbury.

Sile, A.W. 2016. "Lee Kuan Yew Was Actually Singapore's Chief Gardener". *CNBC*, March 27.

Simmel, G. 1971. *On Individuality and Social Forms* (ed.) Donald Levine. Chicago, IL: University of Chicago Press.

Sombart, W. 2017 [2001]. *Economic Life in the Modern Age* (eds) N. Stehr and R. Grundmann. Abingdon: Routledge.

Tocqueville, A. 2003 [1835/1840]. *Democracy in America*. London: Penguin.

Tuchtfeldt, E. 1982 [1973]. "Social Market Economy and Demand Management". In *Standard Texts on the Social Market Economy: Two Centuries of Discussion*, 65–80. New York: Fischer.

Waller, E. 2001. *Landscape Planning in Singapore*. Singapore: Singapore University Press.

Warren, W. 2000. *Singapore: City of Gardens*. Hong Kong: Penplus.

Wood, G.S. 1993 [1992]. *The Radicalism of the American Revolution*. New York: Vintage.

8   Axial economies

The metaphysics of prosperity

Countries that display high levels of economic innovation and social ingenuity are the exception rather than the rule. So what explains the small pool of intensely creative nation-states and city-regions? These cities and nations are principally located on the world's maritime periphery in North-Western Europe, East Asia, Australasia, and North America. They share to varying degrees a set of common characteristics. One of these characteristics is a distinctive metaphysical temperament.

We tend to explain the metaphysics of creation in terms of models of either Enlightenment or Romanticism. But, arguably, the most important source of creative drive and energy derives from neither of these. Rather, its source is a 'third way'. That said, Enlightenment and Romanticism are unavoidable categories. They are components of a typology that is an almost inescapable shorthand guide to the modern life of the mind. But this typology is also misleading. For the Enlightenment subdivides into the rationalist Enlightenment and the skeptical Enlightenment, and Romanticism subdivides into meditations on the imagination and visions of society that are anti-rational, heroic, and militant.

If Enlightenment reason marks a departure from the idea of the militant society and is a precursor to industrial society, Romanticism marks the return of militant society, often different from yet continuous with the militant nature of pre-industrial societies. It may turn the artist into a hero but its hunger for a heroic society binds it to a past that Enlightenment reason separates itself from. The third way is not a model of Enlightenment or Romanticism but rather Renaissance – and on a deeper level, Axiality. It blends skepticism and imagination with order and pattern. It foregrounds neither rationality nor irrationality but rather emphasizes adaptability and shapeliness. Neither plan nor control, revolution nor belligerence, is to its taste. It is more comfortable with anonymity than heroics and with archetypes and gestalts than reasons and rationalizations, insolence and sullenness.

Modernity routinely splits between rationalist and militant forms. There are many permutations of each of these types. In competition with these is axiomodernity. It is anchored in forms of cognition that are ambidextrous, paradoxical, and often enigmatic. These are Janus-like ways of thinking, understanding, feeling, and behaving. They look one way and the opposite way simultaneously. Janusian behaviors are the strong sub-text of a set of efficacious if-not-always-easy-to-understand modern forms of economic and social behavior. These behaviors exist mostly in forms of tacit action, thought, comportment, and conduct subtly woven into the fabric of society. The Janus model is not an exclusive model of economic or social behavior. Rather, it exists in perpetual competition with other models – and in varying degrees of cross-over with them. Each of the competing models has moments of intensity and acceleration as well as moments of flaccidity and decline.

The two major competitors of the Janusian model are the Enlightenment social engineering model and the Romantic autocephalous model of economy and society. Enlightenment and Romanticism are conventional ways of writing modern intellectual history. If we assume that a significant part of modern life is axiological and Janusian in the way it operates, this plays havoc with the neat divide between Enlightenment and Romantic genres. For some aspects of Enlightenment thought and behavior are Janusian, some are not. Likewise, some threads of Romantic thought and its various off-shoots and successors have Janusian overtones, others do not.

Adam Smith and Immanuel Kant are as much Janusian in the style and character of their thought as they are personifications of the Enlightenment. The same is true of Samuel Coleridge and William Blake and their relationship to Romanticism. That is, from a Janusian or Axiological standpoint, Enlightenment and Romantic currents – and their Hydra-headed spinoffs – are not absolutes. Rather, they subdivide into Janusian affinities and antipathies. For Coleridge, the imagination balanced opposite and discordant qualities – sameness and difference, novelty and familiarity, steadiness and enthusiasm, the natural and the artificial. Conversely, a thread runs through the last two centuries that sees creation not as a union but rather as a hierarchy of contraries that can be inverted. In the latter case, creation is not an act of combination but rather one of radical inversion. Representative figures in the stream of creation-as-inversion include Johann Fichte, Friedrich Nietzsche, and Jacques Derrida.

In short models of creation can be sorted into three clusters. Each of these clusters has innumerable outgrowths and derivatives. *Cluster one* is composed of rationalist Enlightenment social engineering models of economic and social behavior. *Cluster two* is made up of Romantic or Romantic-inflected autocephalous models of economic and social behavior. Each of the two models – the Enlightenment knowledge economy model and the model of Romantic-modulated economic and social autocephaly – has been enduringly influential since the late eighteenth and early nineteenth centuries. Sometimes the two currents ally with each other. At other times they oppose each other. In addition both interact, coexist, compete, and argue with – as well as confront, subvert, and concede to – *cluster three*, the Janusian model.

The Janusian 'third way' coexists and overlaps with Enlightenment and Romantic models. Yet it is distinct from them and in many ways more important than them in explaining the deepest cradle of creation. The 'third way' draws on a broad spectrum of philosophical, anti-philosophical, religious, areligious, artistic, and sage traditions. These range from Pythagorean, Stoic, Skeptical, and Polybian views of the world to Zen Buddhist and Taoist quasi-philosophies or anti-philosophies to modern Neoclassical, Machiavellian, Pareto-Realist, Neo-Calvinist, New-Critical, quantum, and topological perspectives. The 'third way' resonates across an intellectual history that runs from Pyrrho and Polybius through Lao-Tzu, He Yan, Kuo Hsiang, and Hakuin Ekaku to Søren Kierkegaard, G.K. Chesterton, William James, Heinrich Wölfflin, Alfred North Whitehead, Kitarō Nishida, Carl Jung, Simone Weil, and beyond.

The most influential of the American Janusians, Ralph Waldo Emerson, thought that oppositions were pervasive and that the moments that make nature, society, and art interesting and powerful occur when contrasting forces – such as those of asceticism and business, fate and freedom, nearness and farness, shadow and light – are reconciled.[1] The Danish philosopher Søren Kierkegaard, Emerson's contemporary, argued that it was God's nature to join opposites and that the Christian apostles were called to paradox.[2] The English writer G.K. Chesterton agreed. For him also, creation was an act of paradox – two opposite things whose combination seemed impossible or absurd, and yet on reflection was valid or true. The Swiss art historian Heinrich Wölfflin defined classic art as composition by contrasts.[3] The French philosopher Simone Weil saw proportionality as the way in which the inherent contradictoriness of the world was resolved.[4]

The dominant school of literary criticism in the mid-twentieth century, the New Critics, stressed that literature operated through the media of irony and paradox.[5] The English literary critic I.A. Richards defined the act of imagination as an equilibrium.[6] The Hungarian-English writer Arthur Koestler defined it as the merger of two ostensibly incompatible frames of reference.[7] The American psychiatrist Albert Rothenberg dubbed it Janus-like in its style of thinking.[8] Antithetical images and concepts coalesce in the imagination. Rosalie Colie and Robert Grudin observed how the Renaissance imagination was permeated by paradoxes, the symbiosis of opposites.[9] The writer Joshua Wolf Shenk describes this symbiosis as the overlapping of connected opposites.[10]

Graham Priest argues that it is less language that contains contrasting truths simultaneously than reality itself.[11] Whether we can so clearly distinguish between the contradictions of speech and the oppositions of reality is debatable. Nonetheless human artifice – our made reality – is filled with mergers of opposing forces and qualities. Design, as one example, is built on the coexistence and intersection of dichotomies such as tactile material and immaterial structures. Successful design objects invariably have an uncanny aspect. In this aspect they are both X and not-X at the same time.[12] The synesthetic concept of being 'both at the same time' is, arguably, as good a definition of the creative imagination as any. The imagination is a cognitive coalescent. Through an exchange between poles, it conjoins subject and object, inside and outside.

There are various epistemologies of creation. One of the oldest is the Pre-Socratic and Platonic view of things.[13] More than two millennia ago, Plato stated in the *Phaedo* that all opposites are generated out of one another and that there is a passing or process from one to the other.[14] In the Platonic conception, opposites are united in forms and proportions. Of similar vintage is the insight of Aristotle, for whom creation is the work of analogies that generate resemblances between unlike things.[15] In both cases – form and metaphor – human cognition is able to perceive that not only are A and not-A alike in certain respects but also that A stands to B as B stands to C.

This epistemology of creation percolated down from classical antiquity via various threads of Stoicism, Platonism, and Aristotelianism to the Renaissance and beyond. Parallels exist in the East Asian traditions of Taoism and Zen Buddhism. All have a common source in the ancient Axial Age: a deep cognitive shift that occurred between 600 BCE and 200 CE. It happened not just because things were written down. The Babylonians, the Phoenicians, and others had already employed writing for functional purposes. Today statisticians point to the long-run rise in literacy rates across the world. This also is functional literacy. It is akin in significance to the clay tablets of Babylonian merchants 4,000 years ago. It is not cultural (bookish) literacy. Functional literacy is required to perform everyday tasks. Most of these are mundane. Cultural (bookish) literacy has a different, less obvious but more profound role. It facilitates abstract thought. It encourages conceptualization, invention, and imagination.

In the Axial Age, in addition to functional literacy, cultures of the book began to appear. This was a watershed in human history, so much so that the books and the ideas they gave birth to still flourish today, 2,000 years later. The Axial Age was characterized by a common way of thinking that emerged in parallel locations far apart. The intellectual geography of the Axial Era ranged across three specific zones, the Mediterranean and Black Sea littoral, the Ganges Basin, and the Yellow River Basin. These protean places were distantly linked by Indian Ocean and Silk Road trade routes. That is to say in a handful of distinct places, powerful, interesting, mobile, and heterodox forms of thought emerged. Their influence subsequently ranged across vast distances.

Gautama Buddha and Lao-Tzu, the Pre-Socratics, Plato, and Aristotle provided key Axial Age descriptions of the mean between antipodes. These were subsequently built on in the works of Cicero and Augustine, Nāgārjuna and Chuang Tzu.[16] In axiomodernity, the interest in the concept of 'the mean' and the related concept of a social or economic arrangement mediated by ratio rather than hierarchy or equality extends from the Renaissance Italians Luca Pacioli and Leon Battista Alberti to the twentieth-century Swiss Le Corbusier and Vilfredo Pareto.[17] At least philosophically speaking, axiomodernity is often found in dialogue with its Axial Era antecedents, for example when the mystic-syndicalist Jewish-Catholic French philosopher Simone Weil in the 1940s created a dramatically updated reading of the Pythagorean-Platonic tradition by blending it with Christian subtexts.[18]

It was the Frisian-Swiss psychiatrist and philosopher Karl Jaspers who brought the idea of the Axial Age to prominence.[19] He called its defining feature 'the coincidence of opposites'.[20] This type of thought marked the major intellectual systems of the Axial Age. It defined Taoism, the Pre-Socratics, the elegant puzzles of Mahāyāna Buddhist thinking, the 'union of opposites' of Plato's Republic, the yin-yang of the Warring States-era Zou Yan (whose works are lost), the Han-era's Dong Zhongshu Confucianism, Heraclitus' dynamic identity of opposites ('wet becomes dry'), and the Stoics blending of opposites. It included the Pythagorean idea of proportions that transform discord into concord, Aristotelian ratios that equate incommensurable qualities and quantities, the *coincidentia oppositorum* of Jewish mysticism, and the enigmatic nature of the biblical Jesus – the mortal son of a God whose two natures (human and divine) coalesce in a hypostatic union of one person.[21] The distinctive axial way of thinking created what we know as intellectual thought. The most imposing characteristic of Janusian or Axial thought is its sensitivity to the 'union of opposites'. Central to each of numerous strands are paradoxical monistic-dichotomies: singular-dualities or enantiodromia. These give the classic works of civilization their inexhaustible nature.

At times one finds echoes of these uncanny singular-dualities in Romantic and Enlightenment models of creation. Intellectual life after all is promiscuous. Nevertheless, the 'third way' is a distinctive worldview, one that is often underestimated by those who craft contemporary typologies of mentalities and systems of thought. Janusian behavior is built around a structure of ambidextrous or non-dualistic cognition. This structure is key both to the act of creation and to the analysis of it. Non-dualistic cognition bridges between artistic creation, social-scientific understanding, and practical economic enterprise. Whether it is the works of William Shakespeare and John Donne, the observations of Joseph Schumpeter and Arthur Koestler, or the methods of modern entrepreneurial and technological creation, contrarian pattern thinking is central to all of these.

Ambidextrous economies

Productive economies and creative societies are embedded in city-regions, nations, cultures, and traditions that have an easy familiarity with ways of 'thinking, feeling and acting' that are (often intuitively and at a deep level) rooted in intellectual 'unions of opposites' and their associated mental gymnastics. The most important models of creation tapped by these societies in the final analysis are not those of Enlightenment innovation or the Romantic imagination but rather the contrarian paradoxes, incongruous combinations, enigmatic matrimonies, and analogical unions of 'third way' acts of creation. It is true that today our standard models of creation tend habitually to hark back to Enlightenment or Romantic paradigms. These models dominate intellectual discussion. In contrast the 'third way' expresses itself less in the form of explicit intellectual templates and more via inexplicit background social dispositions. Humor, wit, irony, wryness, intellectual ambidexterity, and epigrammatic and epigrammatological behavior are key indicators of high levels of economic efficiency, technological creativity, and social ingenuity. This is because in prosperous economies there is no creation without destruction, no economic upswings without downswings, no growth without shrinkage, no competition without cooperation, and no cooperation without competition.

Successful modern economies are ambidextrous. Ambidexterity is expressed in different ways. One of the many ways it is expressed is via an equilibrium of opposing forces. Take the example of a manufacturer who creates an attractive product. Customers are seduced by it. So the manufacturer raises the price to increase the return on the sale. Customers continue to buy the product but each increment of price increase is met with an increasing resistance by consumers to paying the increase. At a certain point increased prices lead to decreasing sales.

This is a microcosm of the macrocosm of modern economies, which are cyclical. Share prices rise on the expectations of company performance. At each moment the rise is met by resistance from buyers who are more skeptical of the company's future, sometimes because of the general economy's future. Bears and bulls push against each other. Optimists and pessimists do battle. The resulting share price is a momentary equilibrium struck between the contending parties. As this equilibrium changes, it arcs into the cyclical upward and downward movements of the share market covering weeks, months, years, and decades.

The simultaneous up-and-down is not just characteristic of markets but of a number of key modern economic and social systems. Five of them are central: markets, industries, cities, publics, and households. Each of these systems is aided and abetted by lean government. To varying but significant degrees each of these systems is self-organizing. And to the extent that they are self-organizing they are also Janusian in character. They interpolate opposites. In so doing, they generate powerful economic and social dynamisms that are expressed in patterns of tension-and-release.

To give an example, the French economist J.B. Say proposed that supply creates demand. That's a paradox. Yet it is an operative paradox with important and widespread economic and social consequences, for when the manufacturer creates a product for which no demand exists but which goes on to create its own demand, the result is what we call 'innovation', one of the most important drivers of prosperous modern economies.

It is important to note that the peculiar dynamism-stability pattern of modern economies is not just the consequence of the operation of markets or alternatively of industries. Each of these has its partisans. Some people think everything good – or for that matter everything bad – is the consequence of the price system. Others focus on industries and technologies. But each of those viewpoints tends to myopia: for cities, publics, and households also contribute significantly to what in the end is a mosaic of behaviors that add to and subtract from the dynamic-stable pattern of successful economies. That pattern is a paradox. But it is only one of many – a box of paradoxes – that high-perform-ing economies and societies exhibit.

This picture is not new. A relatively small handful of societies over the past two centuries have shown themselves adept in a tacit everyday way at mastering paradoxes that energize large-scale participatory economic and social systems. The paradoxes lend those systems a dynamism that is born of a series of ten-sions. Those tensions resolve into unities and then back into tensions and then back into unities. The Swiss psychologist, C.G. Jung, observed that 'life consists of a great many pairs of opposites' and accordingly 'there is no energy without opposites'.[22] The energetic nature of a modern growing dynamic economy has its functional sources, many of them intensely prosaic. But deep underneath those pedestrian and functional forces, especially in the most successful socie-ties, is a metaphysics of the uncanny – signifying the capacity to blend opposites via paradoxes, pleasing conjunctions, powerful symmetries, inventive rhythms, beguiling rhymes, conjoined antitheses, delightful proportions, revealing ironies, caustic witticisms, and puzzling antimonies. We staple opposites together, more often than not unconsciously, with analogy, metaphor, anaphora, metonymy, aposiopesis, alliteration, and synecdoche.

Not all of these devices work when we use them. Sometimes they are oxy-moronic. Nevertheless, the better that we are at tacking together the polarities of innocence and experience, heaven and hell, mass and void, large and small, the more creative we manage to be and the greater the energy that we gener-ate. The remarkable thing in the past two centuries has been the application of this to economic behavior. After millennia of living off 3 dollars a day or less, modern political economy – in the broadest sense of that term – began to gen-erate economic energies out of the fusion of economic opposites. For millennia the up-down-up-down of cycles had been the province of politics. Applied to economic behavior the oscillating rhythm of the cycle gradually evolved into cycles of business and technology.[23]

Economic foxes and lions

The fusion of opposites is not just a linguistic phenomenon. It doesn't only occur in words. It is visual, auditory, material, spatial, and temporal as well. Nei-ther is it just an expression of the arts and sciences. It also applies on the general social level. It is true that it is easier to track evidence of the social incidence of paradox and all related phenomena through linguistic expressions than mate-rial embodiments – and through the ethereal arts rather than the anonymous workings of functional social systems. However, the evidence of the former is a proxy for the latter.

We also ought not to try and turn proxies into a mythical reality by try-ing to substitute creation in the arts for economic creation. The 1990s idea of 'the creative industries' engaged in this kind of contrived substitution. In reality such industries are minor ones. They reached the peak of their share of

GDP in major economies in 2000. Since then they've declined in economic significance. Arts and business, science and industry, run in parallel. The arts and sciences are tiny compared to business and industry. All four mostly operate in routine ways. But each has a component of paradox. In different times and places the component of paradox varies in weight and significance.

One of the pillars of great modern economies is technological and industrial innovation. This is the use of science to create machines that increase massively the productivity of labor. To do this science first looks for laws of nature. These the technologist 'obeys' in order to paradoxically 'dominate' nature. Obedience brings sufficient leverage over nature so that industries to a degree dominate it. This is not pure domination, nor is it pure obedience but rather a point of uncanny equilibrium between the two.

Something similar applies to the products of industrial innovation. The aim of the technologist in the first instance is to pioneer something new. But important technologies, the things that shape everyday life, are durable and lasting in nature. The Frenchman Nicolas-Joseph Cugnot built a steam-powered wagon in 1770; in 1816, the Czech Joseph Bozek engineered a steam-powered car. In 1806, the Swiss engineer François Isaac de Rivaz created an internal combustion engine. More than 250 years after Cugnot, there are today over one billion motor vehicles on the roads across the world. Two-hundred fifty years is no mean time span. Innovation generates duration. Freshness becomes maturity, surprise breeds familiarity. That's like the relationship between the foxes and lions in politics. The foxes are inventive. They pioneer new combinations of forces and interests. But a state cannot live by invention alone. It also needs the indomitable lions who endure and withstand the kinds of pressures that otherwise destroy nations.

Perhaps the most common delusion in modern economies is that human will trumps necessity. This delusion has many expressions and takes many forms. One is that the general will of the state can intervene in an economy to guarantee growth and prosperity or else halt and reverse an otherwise irreversible decline of industry sectors and social groups. However, the general will is but one among many wills – more concentrated certainly but not more powerful or efficacious than the millions and billions of wills, many of them mutually cancelling, which participate anonymously in functional self-organizing systems. The assertion of human will is accompanied by the expression of intention. Human beings describe what they intend to achieve when they decide courses of action. When states intervene in economies they describe the goals and outcomes – in short the intended consequences – of their actions. However, the actual consequence of an interventionist action often turns out to be the opposite of the intended consequence.

Not always but quite often, intention is paradoxical. An ego – including the collective ego of the state – intends to achieve an outcome. But in reality, often, the converse of that outcome is achieved. The consequences of the actions we decide on are both intended and unintended, predictable and unpredictable. It requires considerable levels of ambidextrous cognition to recognize and imagine both branching pathways simultaneously.

Successful decision-making requires a capacity for ambidextrous reflexivity – and a sense of humor attuned to the fallibility of the human will. The best economic and social actors have a sense of irony. This allows them to grasp that good can produce bad and goodness evil. It is useful to have a sense of tragedy, knowing that the best of intentions sometimes turn into the worst of outcomes. Successful societies embody or personify substantial degrees of humor, irony, and tragic understanding. This is not to say that they get bogged down in that. Reflexivity should not be confused with the paralysis of the will or the avoidance of making decisions or pursuing purposes. Reflexivity is not Hamlet-like doubt, the fear of the unknown consequences of any action.

A paralyzing fear of the unknown is the converse of an overconfident estimation of knowledge. Successful societies find ways, again to varying degrees, of avoiding both vices. Friedrich Hayek pointed to the paradox of knowledge.[24] In large-scale self-regulating systems (Hayek's interest was in markets) millions of persons with limited knowledge of the social whole participate. They know their own interests, needs, and ambitions well. But their system-wide or society-wide understanding is narrow and incomplete. The paradox of knowledge is that millions of persons with limited knowledge cooperating and competing together achieve much better economic and social outcomes than do a relative handful of persons (a knowledge class) with a nominally greater knowledge of the social whole.

The advocates of a policy-driven managerial society believe that the incomplete knowledge of interested human beings can be superseded by the complete and superior knowledge of 'disinterested' experts, planners, managers, executive agents, and others. Hayek correctly pointed out that this was a delusion, and wherever it was tried, it failed. Totalitarian economic planning (the command economy) was its most spectacular failure, but only because it pushed the notion that any human being could have a knowledge of the social whole the furthest. Rule-based, regulatory, legal-rational alternatives to totalitarian planning step back from claims of complete omniscience. Yet the history of corporate strategic plans, treasury projections, five-year budget cycle plans, and goal-rational action in general suggests that knowledge sufficient to direct even a partial domain of society is highly fallible and frequently wrong.

Vast anonymous functional systems take the limited and interested knowledge of each of their participants and sorts that scanty knowledge into prices that can be analytically described and adapted to but not knowingly or consciously willed. As with Hayekian prices in markets, measures of input-output efficiency in industries, cost-benefit ratios in cities, the relation of institutional learning to (speed-accuracy-expressive) fluency in reading publics, and the balancing of flexibility and stability in households play an analogous role. Each of these measures is ambidextrous. Each mediates between sets of antipodes. Each produces a mean (e.g., a 'golden mean') between the antipodes.

From axial exchange to axiomodern economy

The principle of antipodal balance is not unique or exclusive. It routinely faces stiff competition. The dominant organizing principle of most societies historically has been hierarchy not ambidexterity. Hierarchies do not disappear in the modern age. Rather, they are reinvented. Patrimonial bureaucracy is transformed into procedural bureaucracy. Master-and-servant is replaced by the firm's employer-and-employee. The status-defined relationship of 'service' is redefined as the 'contract of service'. The aristocratic class is pushed aside by the knowledge class. The Bonapartist bureaucratic class replaces the old courtier class. The Junkers are replaced by Bismarckians and the patricians by the social policy class. Birth hierarchy is replaced by merit hierarchy, the rule of the emperor by the rule of the one party filled with princelings.

Elites are inevitable and inescapable, as Vilfredo Pareto observed. We can circulate them and change them, but we cannot get rid of them. Pretending that we can simply seduces us into the thinking that the new boss is not just better than the old boss (which on occasions can be a plausible proposition) but that the new boss is an egalitarian intent on ushering in an age of equality. This is a delusion that persons in the modern age seem particularly susceptible to. A more interesting question to ask is whether a given elite is more or less compatible with self-organizing systems. Such systems don't generate equality, but they do generate proportionality and equilibrium between competing values, interests, needs, and classes.

In short, societies organize themselves in a hierarchical or antipodal manner – or some mix of the two. For most of human existence some kind of hierarchy dominated – be it in the shape of bands, tribes, monarchies or empires, and the rest. But antipodal ways of thinking were also latent in human cognition. From earliest times, it organized the universe into antipodal pairs even if these were then also commonly depicted in turn as hierarchical couplings. The uncoupling of hierarchy and antipode has been glacially slow over time, but nonetheless it has occurred in significant steps. The first decisive step occurred in the Axial Age from the eighth century BCE to the third century CE.

Aristotle hinted at the idea that there is a primary transaction or exchange that is constitutive of any given society.[25] The Greek-French social philosopher and economist Cornelius Castoriadis observed something interesting about this exchange. It cannot be thought of in terms of arithmetical equality. Rather, it takes place in terms of geometrical proportionality. Aristotle used the example of the farmer and the physician. Each is different. The primordial exchange of the two preserves what is different about each one while at the same time equating the two (making them the same). This is possible thanks to the paradoxical mechanism of geometric proportionality.[26] This mechanism allows the farmer to stand to the physician *as* the fisherman stands to the lawyer. Or alternatively, as Aristotle put it, it allows the builder (A) to stand to the shoemaker (B) *as* a house (C) stands to a shoe (D). In short A:B::C:D. The economic or social element (A) is not equated with (B). Rather (A) stands to (B) *as* (B) stands to (C). It is a ratio of ratios. This is an economic relationship whose point is not to equate things but rather arrange them in a series of proportional relationships that are satisfying or pleasant.

The economic relationship of builder and shoemaker operates not so that each can be equalized or 'made the same' but so that things may exist – at least in a dynamic sense.[27] The relationship of builder and shoemaker is economic but also ontological and generative in character. This supposes not that the parts of a society are 'the same' but rather that they are different yet commensurable. For there to be an exchange there must be comparability or commensurability (a way of treating things the same). But in the cases where exchanges are dynamic and grow, it rests on the paradoxical commensurability of what is incomparable, incommensurable, and unequal.[28] This is the paradox upon which prosperous economies rest. This ontological model of exchange evolves over time. The geometrically proportionate relationship of A:B::B:C may occur in accordance with skill, labor, wealth, technology but also in relation to status, nobility, merit, standing, and so on.

A parallel tradition with similar Axial Age roots is concerned with the 'balance of power' both *in* the state and *between* states. This idea has its ultimate source in the Pre-Socratic Greek concepts of *isonomia* and *isometria*. The notion of an equilibrium of political forces was given a potent practical expression in the relationship between the people and the Senate in the Roman Republic. It was encapsulated in the image of a 'mixed constitution' in *The Histories*, the work of the Greek-Roman historian Polybius, and in Cicero's *De re Publica*. The idea of a mixed constitution inserts itself influentially into modern British political history – as a balancing of the political antipodes of Crown and Parliament, Lords and Commons. It then assumes its most telling modern form in the guise of the 'balance of powers' that the American Founders inscribed in the US Constitution in 1788.

Aristotle in the fourth century BCE proposed a related concept – that of the political cycle. Aristotle's assumption was that all forms of rule, whatever their positives, have negatives. Because of this they tend to abruptly cycle from one form to another. Instead of *kýklos* or *anacyclosis* – maybe, thought Aristotle – if the better kinds of government were mixed together then their inherent weaknesses might offset each other – creating a longer-term stability. That was a political intuition. But the idea of society running through cycles – that is, oscillating or being caught up in a fluctuating, alternating, undulating pattern of activity and behavior – was to have its greatest practical effect not in modern politics but on modern economies. The latter exhibit a very strong cyclical pattern. This multi-layered oscillation of economies, notably across the past two centuries, contributes much to their atmosphere of dynamic stability – a sense that these economies both move forward and yet repeat themselves, like a wheel turning.[29]

There are different ways of understanding the 'revolutions' of this wheel turning. One way is via the concept of an equilibrium that is created by the interaction of opposing forces.[30] As it has been used in the modern world, the term 'equilibrium' takes off (gradually) after 1730. Its use rises more steeply between 1900 and 1960. After 1960 it declines somewhat.[31] It began its life as a term in physics – and for some time was principally used for that purpose. The eighteenth-century Swedish scientist-mystic-spiritualist Emanuel Swedenborg applied the concept in *Heaven and Hell* (1758) to explain spiritual phenomena.[32]

The French writer Pierre Boisguilbert in 1707 described the equilibrium of supply and demand as the 'unique preserver of prosperity'.[33] The French physician Francois Quesnay created a table of economic relationships (*Tableau Economique*, 1758) that outlined production and consumption in a balance that was liable to be upset by government taxes and spending, leading in turn to a decline in the national product. The Italian (Milanese) philosopher and economist Pietro Verri in *Reflections on Political Economy* (1771) discussed the balance between production and consumption, disequilibrium, and return to equilibrium in terms of the development of new industries, production innovation, and the emigration of labor. Verri recommended free market competition in the place of guilds, legally defined economic privileges, price and sales controls, and sumptuary laws.

A kind of economic moderation is built into the automatic balancing mechanisms of self-organizing economies. The nineteenth-century English economist William Stanley Jevons observed one of these kinds of tacit balancing mechanisms. Persons in a market seek to get the most utility or pleasure from what they purchase. Yet such maximizing behavior is subject to another countervailing reality: that of limited resources. Their purchases cannot be unlimited because their resources are limited.

The French-Swiss economist Léon Walras in the 1870s postulated a general equilibrium theory.[34] This set out to explain the interaction of supply and demand across multiple markets in an economy. It also sought to model it mathematically – though, subsequently, it has never been obvious that mathematical models of systems with untold billions of interactions really work. Given that the equilibrium in an economy is not something that is fixed or guaranteed but rather dynamic and contingent on the interaction of innumerable countervailing forces, Walras called the process in which prices rise and fall in relation to the scarcity of supply and the volume of demand one of trial-and-error or *tâtonnement*. Alfred Marshall's *Principles of Economics* (1890) substituted a partial equilibrium theory for Walras' general theory. In effect Marshall simplified the modeling of demand and supply interactions that are so numerous that they cannot be meaningfully mapped by a mathematical facsimile.

Notes

1 Murphy, 2008.
2 See especially 'Christian Discourses', 'Two Ethical-Religious Essays', and 'Concluding Unscientific Postscript to Philosophical Fragments' in Søren Kierkegaard, 2000.
3 Wölfflin, 1952 [1898], 258.
4 Weil's notebooks were written in Marseilles in 1941 and 1942 and posthumously published in an English-language edition as *The Notebooks of Simone Weil*.

5 William Wimsatt and Cleanth Brooks's *Literary Criticism: A Short History*, 1957, in many respects was a summation-to-date of a long tradition of aesthetic epistemologies of the imagination.
6 Richards, 1964 [1924].
7 Koestler, 1970.
8 Rothenberg, 1979.
9 Colie, 1966; Grudin, 1979.
10 Shenk, 2014.
11 He argues that 'contradiction (Widerspruch, the Latin contradictio) has to do with discourse (diction, sprechen, dicere). The world, with its non-mental and non-linguistic inhabitants – armchairs, trees, people – is not the right kind of thing that can be consistent or inconsistent, and ascribing such properties to (a part of) the world is ... a category mistake.' Priest, 2018 [1998]. See also Priest, 2002.
12 Folkmann, 2013.
13 Murphy, 2001, 45–78.
14 Plato, 1992.
15 'Metaphor consists in giving the thing a name that belongs to something else' (Aristotle, 1920, 1457 b6–9).
16 Cross-fertilization between axial streams has occasionally occurred. See for example the interest of the British philosopher Michael Oakeshott in the work of Chuang Tzu. See Cheung, 2012.
17 On the history of the social use of the concepts of 'the mean' and ratio, see Murphy, 2001.
18 Weil, 2004 [1956]. On Weil, see Winch, 1989 and McLellan, 1989. For a discussion of the model of society as a reciprocity of opposites – including *inter alia* Weil's image of the 'just union of contraries' – see Murphy, 1996.
19 Jaspers, 2010 [1949].
20 Jaspers, 2010 [1949], 3.
21 For a philosophical history of the 'union of opposites' from the Greek polis and Rome through the medieval West, the Renaissance, and America, see Murphy, 2001.
22 Jung, 2015. Letter to V. Subrahamanya, August 29, 1938, 247.
23 Röpke (1936) provides a classic account of the modern cyclical economy, as did Schumpeter (1939).
24 Hayek, 1960, 22–32.
25 Castoriadis, 1984, 299.
26 Castoriadis, 1984, 305–306.
27 Castoriadis, 1984, 306.
28 Castoriadis, 1984, 307.
29 For a classic account of the modern business and economic cycles, see Schumpeter, 1939.
30 The concept is extensively reviewed in Schumpeter, 2009 [1954].
31 Google N-Gram book analysis.
32 Swedenborg was an influence on Coleridge, Emerson, Blake, and Jung, among many others including Goethe, Schelling, Balzac, Baudelaire, Whitman, and Suzuki. See for example Ralph Waldo Emerson, 'Swedenborg; Or, the Mystic', *Representative Men* (1850). *Heaven and Hell* was translated into English as *Future Life*.
33 Faccarello, 1999, Introduction quoting Boisguilbert, *Dissertation de la nature des richesses* Volume 2, 1707.
34 Walras, 1954 [1874–1877].

Bibliography

Aristotle. 1920 [-335]. *The Poetics*, trans. Ingram Bywater. Oxford: The Clarendon Press.
Castoriadis, C. 1984. "Value, Equality, Justice, Politics: From Marx to Aristotle and from Aristotle to Ourselves" [1975]. In *Crossroads in the Labyrinth*, 260–340. Cambridge MA: MIT Press.

Cheung, C. 2012. "Skepticism, Poetic Imagination and the Art of Non-Instrumentality: Oakeshott and Zhuangzi". In C. Cheung and W.J. Coats (eds), *The Poetic Character of Human Activity: Collected Essays on the thought of Michael Oakeshott*, 19–40. Plymouth: Lexington.

Colie, R.L. 1966. *Paradoxia Epidemica: The Renaissance Tradition of Paradox*. Princeton, NJ: Princeton University Press.

Grudin, R. 1979. *Mighty Opposites: Shakespeare and Renaissance Contrariety*. Berkeley: University of California Press.

Faccarello, G. 1999. *The Foundation of Laissez-faire: The Economics of Pierre de Boisguilbert*. London: Routledge.

Folkmann, M.N. 2013. *The Aesthetics of Imagination in Design*. Cambridge, MA: MIT Press.

Hayek, F.A. 1960. *The Constitution of Liberty*. London: Routledge and Kegan Paul.

Jaspers, K. 2010 [1949]. *The Origin and Goal of History*. Abingdon: Routledge.

Jung, C.G. 2015 [1973]. *Letters of C. G. Jung: Volume I, 1906–1950*. London: Routledge.

Kierkegaard, S. 2000. *The Essential Kierkegaard*, ed. Howard V. Hong and Edna H. Hong. Princeton, NJ: Princeton University Press.

Koestler, A. 1970. *The Act of Creation*. London: Pan.

McLellan, D. 1989. *Utopian Pessimist: The Life and Thought of Simone Weil*. London: Palgrave Macmillan.

Murphy, P. 2008. "Nature's God: Emerson and the Greeks". *Thesis Eleven: Critical Theory and Historical Sociology* 93, no. 1: 64–71.

Murphy, P. 2001. *Civic Justice: From Greek Antiquity to the Modern World*. Amherst, NY: Humanity Books.

Murphy, P. 1996. "Classicism, Modernism, Pluralism". In P. Murphy and M. Crozier (eds), *The Left in Search of Center*, 118–139. Urbana: University of Illinois Press.

Plato. 1992. "Phaedo". In *The Trial and Death of Socrates: Four Dialogues*, trans. Benjamin Jowett. New York: Dover.

Priest, G. 2018 [1998]. "Dialetheism". In *Stanford Encyclopedia of Philosophy*. Stanford, CA: The Metaphysics Research Lab Center, Stanford University.

Priest, G. 2002. *Beyond the Limits of Thought*. Second edition. Oxford: Clarendon Press.

Richards, I.A. 1964 [1924]. *Principles of Literary Criticism*. London: Routledge and Kegan Paul.

Röpke, W. 1936. *Crises and Cycles*. London: William Hodge.

Rothenberg, A. 1979. *The Emerging Goddess: The Creative Process in Art, Science and Other Fields*. Chicago, IL: The University of Chicago Press.

Schumpeter, J.A. 2009 [1954]. *History of Economic Analysis*, ed. E.B. Schumpeter. Abingdon: Routledge.

Schumpeter, J.A. 1939. *Business Cycles: A Theoretical, Historical and Statistical Analysis of the Capitalist Process* Volumes 1 and 2. New York: McGraw-Hill.

Shenk, J.W. 2014. *Powers of Two: Finding the Essence of Innovation in Creative Pairs*. New York: Houghton Mifflin Harcourt.

Verri, P. 1993 [1771]. *Reflections on Political Economy*. Fairfield, NJ: Kelley.

Walras, L. 1954 [1874–1877]. *Elements of Pure Economics*. Routledge: Abingdon.

Weil, S. 2004 [1956]. *The Notebooks of Simone Weil*. London: Routledge.

Wimsatt, W.K. and C. Brooks. 1957. *Literary Criticism: A Short History*. New York: Vintage.

Winch, P. 1989. *The Just Balance*. Cambridge: Cambridge University Press, 1989.

Wölfflin, H. 1952 [1898]. *Classic Art: An Introduction to the Italian Renaissance*. London: Phaidon.

9　Creation

Tiny creation

Prosperity is a multifactor condition. It has no single cause. Rather, a range of factors coalesce into the pattern that we call prosperity. Creativity is one such factor. But what is creativity? The post-industrial model of economy and society equates economic creativity with 'knowledge'. It suggests that 'greater knowledge' means 'higher creativity'. This, though, is not the case. Economic creativity entails a combination of ingenious industrial technology and inventive economic and social forms – both organizational and self-organizing – possessing some kind of lasting value. Beyond a basic threshold, the contribution of qualifications, schools, and universities to this is of ever-diminishing marginal value.[1] Knowledge does not explain the act of creation. What does?

Modern self-organizing systems operate on a large scale. Millions of persons participate in these every day. Paralleling the self-organizing system is another self-organizing domain. It also is functional but rather than being mass in scale it is miniscule in size. This is the domain of intellectual creation. Intellectual creation runs parallel to social systems. It encompasses the arts and the sciences and extends beyond them. Individual modern societies can have relatively high levels of systemic functionality combined with relatively low levels of creative power in the arts and sciences. As with high-performing systems, intellectual creation is concentrated in a modest number of nations and city-regions. Creation clusters, as do systemic behaviors. In the case of creation, the power of transmission – that is mimetic behavior or copying – partly obviates this concentration.[2] Ideas are mobile. Modern society 'borrows' widely and freely from the limited number of cases of intellectual creation.

In the long run, maintaining high levels of prosperity requires ingenuity, invention, and creation. Yet most people do not participate directly in this. A degree of everyday problem-solving is common in economic and social systems. But only a tiny handful of persons ever engage in full-blooded acts of creation. While the publication of works is now vast, the number of ideas that are significant is small. The passage of time winnows our creations. Few works and even fewer names survive this winnowing process. That is to say, hardly any works outlive their creator and survive archival oblivion. Time is highly selective. One of the things that is most remarkable about human creation is how few works have a lasting impact. Most human creation is ephemeral. A tiny component of it is durable. Only a small number of countries produce such durable works in any kind of significant volume. We can measure this (Table 9.1). Reviewing creative objectivation per capita during the long modern age from the late Renaissance to the present day, what is evident is that few countries have managed to be continuously and intensively creative over the long run. This is true both of the arts and of the sciences.

The breakdown of creative significance by period and nation in Table 9.1 reworks raw data assembled by the American social scientist Charles Murray in his 2003 study on human accomplishment.[3] As part of the study he listed all creators prior to 1950 across most areas of the arts and sciences whom posterity has granted at least a modicum of mentions in selected standard reference works.[4] On the basis of entries in multiple standard reference works, he drew up comprehensive lists of named creators across time and space and from most intellectual disciplines in the past 3,000 years. In his inventory there are a total of 4,000 named figures, that is, on average about one per year for the entirety of human society since intellectual life made the transition from speech to writing.

Murray bent over backwards to include creators recognized by posterity. This is necessarily conditioned by the prior sorting and resorting processes of evaluation that societies constantly undertake and which are epitomized in reference works that themselves are subject to revision and winnowing over time. Before the cut-off point of 1950 everyone that you have ever heard of and many you haven't heard of and likely would never hear of are included in Murray's lists from a wide variety of times and places. His interest, like mine here, was not in making a critical judgment of who and what is 'in' or 'out' but rather to understand the pattern that has resulted from this long-evolving critical process. My interest, unlike Murray's, is how high-level creation manifests itself by nation and era.

The first thing to observe is numbers. Named creation is a tiny, tiny enterprise. This immediately puts it in contrast with economic phenomena. Modern economies are built around self-organizing systems: cities, households, publics, markets, and industries. These interact with each other. They also involve participation by millions, indeed billions, of people each day. Self-organizing systems are massive in scale. Human intellectual creation has been infinitesimally small by comparison. In the history of the human species it is estimated that 100 billion people have lived on our planet.[5] In the past 3,000 years, 4,000 persons have produced a sufficient glimmer of lasting creative significance to have managed to achieve at least a minor level of passing mention in standard reference works. Creation is not for the faint-hearted. The chances of anyone's name being remembered by posterity for intellectual creation is incredibly small.[6]

It is true that two modern systems (technological industry and reading publics) benefit substantially from – and in some major sense rely on – another kind of creativity, in this case institutionalized creativity that is measurable, namely the copyright industries that feed into reading publics and the patent industries

Table 9.1 Creative figures and significance, 1500–1949

Militant era	Named figures per ten million inhabitants. Weighted significance of figures per 10 million inhabitants								
Nation	1500–1549	1550–1599	1600–1649	1650–1699	1700–1749	1750–1799	1800–1849	1850–1899	1900–1949
Australia Arts Figures									
Australia Arts Significance									
Australia Sciences Figures									6.8
Australia Sciences Significance									106.8
Austria Arts Figures				4	11.5	31	4.8	8.9	31.8
Austria Arts Significance				4	34.6	593.1	44.1	75.6	187.9
Austria Sciences Figures		4				3.4	0.7	11.1	22.7
Austria Sciences Significance		4				69	11	204.4	277.3
Belgium Arts Figures		51.6	31.3	22.2		7.4		17	10.4
Belgium Arts Significance		271	43.8	22.2		37		73.6	51.9
Belgium Sciences Figures		12.9	12.5	5.6			6.7	9.4	9.1
Belgium Sciences Significance		251.6	168.8	33.3			30	113.2	67.5
Britain/United Kingdom Arts Figures	20.9	18.9	55.4	17.1	15	23.9	21.7	12.3	8.3
Britain/United Kingdom Arts Significance	69.8	149.1	424.6	130.3	154	163.2	233.3	84.3	44.1
Britain/United Kingdom Sciences Figures		9.4	13.8	21.1	18	35.9	45.7	26.1	13.1
Britain/United Kingdom Sciences Significance		154.7	172.3	835.5	275	654.7	906.5	398.9	151.3
Canada Arts Figures									
Canada Arts Significance									
Canada Sciences Figures								2.6	13
Canada Sciences Significance								5.1	159.8
China Arts Figures	0.8	0.3	0.4	1	0.3	0.1	0.03	0.1	0.44
China Arts Significance	15.7	11.2	6.2	19.9	3.1	2.2	0.34	0.3	N/A
China Sciences Figures									
China Sciences Significance									

Czech Arts Figures		5	5.6	9.5	3.2	14.6	10.7	7.8	12.5
Czech Arts Significance		60	5.6	19	6.5	**102.4**	29.8	46.8	90.4
Czech Sciences Figures							8.5	5.2	3.8
Czech Sciences Significance							89.4	123.4	26
Denmark Arts Figures				16.7	14.3	11.1	63.6	33.3	8.6
Denmark Arts Significance				**116.7**	**142.9**	22.2	**236.4**	**172.2**	22.9
Denmark Sciences Figures			15.9	50		22.2	5.3	16.7	22.9
Denmark Sciences Significance			**1,079.4**	**883.3**		**122.2**	**159.6**	**227.8**	**340**
Finland Arts Figures							18.2		6.1
Finland Arts Significance							54.5		39.4
Finland Sciences Figures							9.1		2.9
Finland Sciences Significance							**100**		**55.9**
France Arts Figures	6.5	11.1	9.5	14.5	9.5	9.2	12.7	19	19.5
France Arts Significance	40.6	52	92.1	**120**	75	55	**125.7**	**207.6**	**153.5**
France Sciences Figures	0.6	2.9	4.2	3.5	5.9	12.7	16.8	10.7	7
France Sciences Significance	9.7	**66.1**	**121.7**	55	75.9	**278.1**	**257.8**	**164.1**	74
Germany Arts Figures	10.8		4.1	14.4	10.4	18	17.8	7.4	9.4
Germany Arts Significance	97		4.8	47.4	**115.9**	**152.5**	**185.1**	63.8	51.6
Germany Sciences Figures	5.4		2.1	5.2	4.9	10.5	16.3	21.7	11.4
Germany Sciences Significance	66.9		14.5	**107.8**	28.7	**171**	**236.2**	**382.7**	**156.2**
Hungary Arts Figures							2		8.4
Hungary Arts Significance							9		90.4
Hungary Sciences Figures								1.5	13.3
Hungary Sciences Significance								30.3	**171.1**
India Arts Figures	0.2								0.3
India Arts Significance	1.5								N/A
India Sciences Figures		0.2							0.2
India Sciences Significance		2.8							0.9

(Continued)

Table 9.1 (Continued)

Nation	1500-1549	1550-1599	1600-1649	1650-1699	1700-1749	1750-1799	1800-1849	1850-1899	1900-1949
Ireland Arts Figures					10	2.8	4.2	5.8	1.3
Ireland Arts Significance					90	33.3	11.1	78.8	15.3
Ireland Sciences Figures						2.8	5.6	11.5	0.7
Ireland Sciences Significance						8.3	90.2	**142.3**	6.4
Italy Arts Figures	41.3	28.1	29.8	13.6	23.9	11.3	5.6	4	7.2
Italy Arts Significance	**430.3**	**148.8**	**196.9**	59.1	**110.6**	56.3	45.7	27	35.1
Italy Sciences Figures	5.5	8.3	7.6	3.8	2.1	2.5	3	2.5	2.6
Italy Sciences Significance	**101.8**	89.3	**229.8**	93.2	31	69.4	20.3	39.9	38.5
Japan Arts Figures	20	4	4	3.4	3.3	6.2	4.5	2.6	6.6
Japan Arts Significance	**450**	**156.1**	**106**	**171**	52	**134.5**	**116.8**	50.3	**162.6**
Japan Sciences Figures									0.5
Japan Sciences Significance									5.7
Netherlands Arts Figures	110	23.3	113.3	70.6	5.3	5		8.3	6.3
Netherlands Arts Significance	**360**	**271.3**	**1,115.3**	**449.1**	5.3	5		125	50.6
Netherlands Sciences Figures		7.8	26.7	41.2	10.5	10		27.8	16.5
Netherlands Sciences Significance		46.5	160	**976.5**	247.4	130		**486.1**	**174.7**
New Zealand Arts Figures									7.1
New Zealand Arts Significance									21.4
New Zealand Sciences Figures									14.3
New Zealand Sciences Significance									**692.9**
Norway Arts Figures							11.1	64.7	14.8
Norway Arts Significance							33.3	**464.7**	92.6
Norway Sciences Figures							11.1	17.6	7.4
Norway Sciences Significance							**266.7**	**176.5**	**174.1**
Poland Arts Figures		1.3					8.1	3.9	2.8
Poland Arts Significance		3.8					**140.5**	27.6	12.4
Poland Sciences Figures	1.3			1.1				1.3	2.8
Poland Sciences Significance	93.8			33.3				11.8	43.8

Portugal Arts Figures	30	30	8.3				3.3	2.3	0.3
Portugal Arts Significance	**140**	230	25				10	14	1
Portugal Sciences Figures									0.3
Portugal Sciences Significance									0.3
Russia Arts Figures						2	2.2	2.4	3.1
Russia Arts Significance						6.4	20.4	23.1	20.4
Russia Sciences Figures						0.4	0.6	1	1.2
Russia Sciences Significance						5.2	6.9	9.2	10.4
Spain Arts Figures	12.9	15.6	13.8	3.5		2		3.7	7.4
Spain Arts Significance	31.4	**111.7**	**180**	9.4		42		15.4	76.1
Spain Sciences Figures		1.3				1.4	0.8	0.6	0.9
Spain Sciences Significance		33.8				5.7	5.7	2.5	6.5
Sweden Arts Figures			12.5		14.3	10.5	20	9.8	5
Sweden Arts Significance			25		71.4	36.8	84	90.2	20
Sweden Sciences Figures				10	21.4	21.1	24	17.1	11.7
Sweden Sciences Significance				100	**700**	**557.9**	**552**	**224.4**	63.6
Switzerland Arts Figures	14.3				16.7	40	16.7	15.4	27.5
Switzerland Arts Significance	57.1				41.7	**586.7**	72.2	96.2	**130**
Switzerland Sciences Figures	14.3	23.2	20	9.1	58.3	26.7	33.3	19.2	27.5
Switzerland Sciences Significance	**971.4**	**523.3**	**110**	**327.7**	**1,625**	**500**	**394.4**	**207.7**	**212.5**
United States Arts Figures						6.9	8.1	5.7	6.1
United States Arts Significance						31	70.1	39.3	24.7
United States Sciences Figures						8.6	16.2	11.4	10
United States Sciences Significance						**225.9**	**255.6**	**164.7**	**135**

Source: C. Murray, Human Accomplishment, New York, HarperCollins, 2003

Note: From 1700 Ireland's population, figures and works are counted separately from Britain/United Kingdom. Dating: Each named figure and their corpus of work is dated to their fortieth year. The fortieth year is a standardized point of creative maturity. Nationality: The nationality of each named figure is their nation of origin (their birth place).

Incidence of intellectual figures listed by Murray (2003) and their weighted significance. Named figures per ten million inhabitants. Weighted significance of figures per 10 million inhabitants:

Significance measured by the quantity of scholarly text and event mentions related to the figure in reference works. Bold figures indicate a high incidence of science or arts productivity. Dotted cells indicate militant eras.

Table 9.2 Institutional creativity

Rank	Number of Books Published Per Capita 2016–2017, 2013–2015	Forward citations of patents 2004	Patent generality 2004	% share of total breakthrough patents [top 1 percent of forward-cited patents] 2004	Patent radicalness 2009	Average duration of patents 2015, for patents filed in 1998
1	United Kingdom	Korea	Finland	Japan	Israel	Japan
2	Iceland	Belgium	Belgium	United States	United States	Norway
3	Denmark	Italy	Denmark	Germany	Netherlands	Ireland
4	Hong Kong	Switzerland	India	Korea	Canada	Denmark
5	Slovenia	Spain	United States	Switzerland	Denmark	Belgium
6	France	Germany	Netherlands	Netherlands	Ireland	Sweden
7	Spain	France	Ireland	France	China	United States
8	Czech Republic	China	Japan	Italy	Japan	France
9	Switzerland	Taiwan	United Kingdom	Finland	Belgium	Switzerland
10	Netherlands	Canada	Canada	Canada	France	Netherlands
11	Norway	Finland	Germany	Austria	Austria	Austria
12	Taiwan	Singapore	Switzerland	Sweden	Finland	Germany
13	Australia	Austria	Spain	Taiwan	Germany	Australia
14	Germany	Luxembourg	Sweden	Spain	Switzerland	Finland
15	Italy	Sweden	Luxembourg	United Kingdom	United Kingdom	Canada
16	United States	United States	Australia	Australia	Brazil	United Kingdom
17	Georgia	Denmark	France	Denmark	Luxembourg	Italy
18	Hungary	India	Israel	Belgium	Sweden	Israel
19	Korea	United Kingdom	Korea	-	Korea	Luxembourg
20	Bosnia	Ireland	Italy	-	Austria	Spain
21	Sweden	Israel	Austria	-	India	South Africa
22	Argentina	Norway	Singapore	-	Spain	Hungary
23	Finland	South Africa	China	-	Norway	Taiwan
24	Singapore	New Zealand	Taiwan	-	Turkey	-
25	Japan	Australia	Norway	-	Italy	-

Rank	H-index physics and astronomy papers 1996-2017 by country	H-index mathematics papers 1996-2017 by country	H-index computer science papers 1996-2017 by country	H-index engineering papers 1996-2017 by country	H-index social science papers 1996-2017 by country	H-index arts and humanities papers 1996-2017 by country
1	United States	United States	United States	China	United States	United States
2	Germany	United Kingdom	United Kingdom	United States	United Kingdom	United Kingdom
3	United Kingdom	Germany	Germany	Japan	Canada	Germany
4	Japan	France	Canada	Germany	Netherlands	Canada
5	France	China	France	United Kingdom	Germany	France
6	Italy	Canada	China	France	Australia	Japan
7	China	Italy	Switzerland	India	France	Netherlands
8	Switzerland	Netherlands	Italy	Korea	Sweden	Switzerland
9	Canada	Switzerland	Australia	Canada	Italy	Australia
10	Netherlands	Australia	Netherlands	Italy	Switzerland	Italy
11	Spain	Spain	Israel	Taiwan	Israel	Sweden
12	Australia	Japan	Spain	Spain	Spain	China
13	Korea	Israel	Hong Kong	Australia	Denmark	Israel
14	Sweden	Hong Kong	Japan	Iran	Hong Kong	Spain
15	India	Belgium	Singapore	Netherlands	Belgium	Denmark
16	Israel	Sweden	Korea	Poland	China	Austria
17	Poland	Korea	Belgium	Brazil	Norway	Belgium
18	Austria	Denmark	Taiwan	Sweden	New Zealand	Finland
19	Denmark	Taiwan	Sweden	Singapore	Finland	Norway
20	Belgium	Singapore	India	Switzerland	Taiwan	Korea
21	Taiwan	India	Austria	Turkey	Japan	New Zealand
22	Brazil	Austria	Finland	Malaysia	Singapore	Brazil
23	Singapore	Finland	Denmark	Hong Kong	Austria	South Africa
24	Hong Kong	Brazil	Greece	Belgium	South Africa	Taiwan
25	Finland	Poland	Turkey	Portugal	Korea	Hong Kong

(Continued)

Table 9.2 (Continued)

Source: OECD, 'Measuring the technological and economic value of patents', 2015, chapter 2, Figure 2.9 Forward citations, average index by economy 2004; OECD, 'Measuring the technological and economic value of patents', 2015, chapter 2, Figure 2.12 Generality, average index by economy 2004; OECD, 'Measuring the technological and economic value of patents, 2015', chapter 2, Figure 2.11 Share of economy in breakthroughs, percentages 2004; OECD, 'Measuring the technological and economic value of patents, 2015', chapter 2, Figure 2.14 Radicalness, average index by economy 2009; OECD, 'Measuring the technological and economic value of patents, 2015', chapter 2, Figure 2.15 Patent renewal, average duration of patents filed in 1998 in number of years; International Publishers Association Report 2017 and 2014; Book Registration Office, HK Leisure and Cultural Services Department Annual Report 2016–2017; Singapore data based on annual average of books deposited with Singapore legal depository library https://catalogue.nlb.gov.sg; SCImago Journal and Country Rank, 1996–2017, H-Index, calculated from information in the Elsevier Scopus database.

Note: This table excludes resource-dependent states: Saudi Arabia ranks 20 in number of books published per capita. Russia ranks 20 in forward citations of patents, 12 in H index physics and astronomy, 24 in H index mathematics, 12 in H index engineering, and 23 in H index arts and humanities.

Definitions: the H index is a country's number of published articles (H) that have received at least H citations, 2017; patent forward citations is the count of citations garnered by a subject patent five to seven years after its original publication, an indicator of the technological value and innovative power of a patent; patent generality is a form of forward citation scoring where a patent scores higher if it is cited by later patents belonging to a broad range of fields rather than just its own specific technology field. The average strength of a country's patent generality is calculated using a modification of the Herfindahl–Hirschman Index, HHI, calculation method; breakthrough patents are the top 1 percent of patents measured by citations five to seven years after their publication; the radicalness of a patent is a measure of the average degree (ranging from 0 to 1) to which a country's patents cite patents in technological classes other than their own; average duration of patents is the number of years on average a nation's granted patents are kept alive.

that feed into industry technology innovation (Table 9.2). That said, institutionalized creativity adapts and teases out creation proper. The former relies on the latter. The latter involves hardly more than a handful of persons across time.

Religion

The most notable point of comparison of named creation is with religion. Religion is a mass phenomenon. However, within the macro world of religion there is the micro phenomenon of small heterodox intellectualized religious currents that have an outsized influence on societies without necessarily attracting a large following. Whether it is the intellectual or moral demands of these religions that tacitly restrict their size is an open question. However, Calvinism, Judaism, Jansenism, Pietism, Mormonism, Zen Buddhism, and a number of others have had an influence on modernity far exceeding their number of adherents, whether actual or nominal.

Take one small but instructive example: the Arab world. Its contribution to significant works in the arts is principally in the years 500s to 1200s. The contribution was small relative to population. After the 1200s it was negligible, with a tiny upswing relative to population in the first half of the twentieth century. In that latter case, of the 13 key figures listed in Murray's 2003 inventory, Jurji Zaydan was born into an Orthodox Christian Lebanese family, Mikhail Naimy came from an Orthodox Christian Lebanese background, and Khalil Gibran came from a Lebanese Maronite Catholic family. The point is not about religion per se but rather the role that heterodox minorities including religious minorities – and also heterodox nations – play in high-level named creation. In this case Lebanon both harbored Christian minorities and was a classic case of a 'torn' country. It was serially partitioned after the fall of the Ottoman Empire by clans, religious groups, inter-communal violence, and struggles for control with France and Syria. A significant number of intellectually productive societies likewise are 'torn'. No one would wish such a condition on any society. Yet the correlation between the two seems too common not to note (Table 3.2).

Often it is from small groups that big things come.[7] Today in the United States, Mormons and Jews are the most successful of any social groups in business and education.[8] Yet they are also among the smallest of America's socio-religious cohorts. This underscores a larger point about modern business and industry. In many respects it was not the generic 'Protestant ethic' that helped modern capitalism along but rather minority currents within the broader ranks of Protestantism. The role of Calvinism is well-known. It had several discrete centers of influence: Calvin's Switzerland, the Puritans in East Anglia, the Puritan emigres from England to New England (and their descendants in the Utah West), and the migration of the Ulster-Scots Calvinists to the America's Upland South.[9] Another influential minority were the Quakers who migrated from the East Midlands to Pennsylvania and the Mid-Atlantic states and then dispersed to the Mid-West and Lower Mid-West.

If Protestantism represents the large scale, then Lutheranism represents the middle scale of the Protestant religion. On the small scale within Lutheranism was

Pietism. As Calvinism was to Protestantism so Pietism was to Lutheranism. They were both paradox-inflected heterodoxies of Protestant orthodoxies. It is notable that Emanuel Swedenborg's father, Immanuel Kant's parents, Johann Georg Hamann, Kierkegaard's father, and Max Weber's mother were Pietists. Pietism emphasized practical piety and opposed theological disputation. It valued private meeting rather than the institutional church. Pietism's a-dogmatic worldview underwrote the practical spirit of modern functional societies. It emphasized self-scrutiny according to objective criteria. Pietistic self-inspection – 'Have I lived up to the moral law?' – prefigures the self-examination of the person who asks 'Have I been productive?' or 'Have I been efficient?' or 'Have I wasted my time or your time?'

The past two centuries have produced few great religious writers. Among them were Kierkegaard and Chesterton. One was a Protestant, the other Catholic. But both agreed that Christianity was a religion of paradox – maybe even that paradox was another word for God.

The truth of a modern self-organizing functional society is not the truth of a hierarchical church or an institution – what Hegel called 'positive Christianity'.[10] The Pietist conventicles (private meetings) were in fact an incipient form of modern self-organization. Echoes of this repeat in surprising places, as in contemporary Mainland China, which has experienced a remarkable (and unlikely) surge of Calvinism but one that stresses informal 'house' meetings rather than formal church assembly.[11] This in a society where the ruling and officially atheist Communist Party, mirroring its own trenchant hierarchy, is only comfortable with compliant institutional churches that it regulates. What is at stake in this is much less religious truth than self-organizing truths.

Among the Chinese, beliefs tend to be syncretic and on the whole more demotic or philosophical than religious, liturgical, or salvationist in nature. Confucianism defines truth in terms of an ethical hierarchy; Buddhism distinguishes between conventional truth and ultimate truth. For Legalism truth is the state. For Taoism truth is paradoxical. Accordingly, for the latter, in the greatest action, nothing is named; in the greatest disputation, nothing is said. Those Taoist paradoxes remind us that creation is not simply named creation. For most purposes, not least of all, the very large economies that have emerged in the past two centuries, creation is anonymous. That is, named creation is part of the tiny tip of the very large polyhedron of anonymous creation. Modern societies are autonomous societies. When and where these societies are most effective, they work away 'automatically', that is, for the most part without specific direction. Everyday millions – billions even – of persons participate in the classic quintet of markets, industries, cities, publics, and nuclear households. Most of this behavior is routine and repetitive. We do not remake the world every time we get out of bed. On the other hand, modern autonomous societies expand and grow. They are generative. What explains this?

Consider what it means to be part of an autonomous system where both rules and directions are reasonably modest in scope. If you buy a car, no one tells you what make or model you must buy, how much you can spend, or what color is best. Millions of people daily engage in such transactions and yet a remarkably lucid order emerges from this spontaneously. In Immanuel Kant's terms this order appears to be a result simultaneously of causality and of spontaneity. This is possible because the interactions in autonomous systems are to a significant degree based on neither rules nor directions but rather on patterns. Patterns are unions of opposites. That is, they bridge antinomies: mass-and-void, large-and-small, curved-and-straight, and so on. Rules and directions are not good at producing growth. Patterns on the other hand are very extensible. They do not multiply in unlimited ways. Pattern growth itself is a pattern. It combines expansion and recession, increase and decline. The cyclical nature of modern economies is a clear example. Businesses, investment, technology, markets all cycle.

The greater the degree of pattern thinking across a society, the more likely its economy and society is to be generative. The arts and sciences are not the anvil forging pattern thinking. Rather they are part of a larger syndrome. They are the conscious (and invariably self-conscious) tip of the iceberg of anonymous creation. Named (self-)conscious creation and collective anonymous creation interact with each other. They are co-causal. They expand and retract in tandem. Each nourishes the other and starves the other. Golden periods of named creation suddenly appear, in spontaneous upsurges. Those extemporaneous moments in intellectual history appear like fireworks. They burn brightly in the night sky for a time. They are genuinely spontaneous. They can't be planned for. Their bright lights can't be preserved in the mausoleums of museums and universities. Nonetheless they are conditioned. Their spontaneity has a causal ground, for these surging moments are embedded in the larger anonymity of autonomous societies and systems that themselves experience tremors of creation and waves of imagination embedded in a deep background of demotic pattern-thinking and social irony.

Epigrammatology

Murray's data recast here provides a descriptive picture of what happened to named creation over five centuries. The overall pattern is pretty clear (Table 9.1). First, very few countries contribute to the inventory of significant human creation. Over five centuries of evidence this is clear. Second, a still smaller number of countries manage to be more or less continuously creative at a high level per capita. Even more difficult is to be continuously creative in both the arts and the sciences. Italy achieved high levels in the arts and sciences for two centuries from 1500 to 1700. Britain managed the same Herculean outcome for three centuries between 1550 and 1850. Then its arts performance collapsed. France achieved a similar two-track outcome across the nineteenth century. Then the intensity of its sciences collapsed in the first half of the twentieth century. With some half-century gaps, Denmark performed intensely in the arts and sciences from 1650 to 1900. Then its arts intensity subsided. Between 1600 and 1700 the Netherlands managed high per capita levels of significant works in both the arts and the sciences. Then the significance of its arts mostly retreats in favor of the sciences. Conversely, from 1500 to 1950 Japan had a strong track record of producing bodies of significant work in the arts. Yet it produced little in the sciences.

Across five-and-a-half centuries it is evident that consistency of high-level performance in the sciences has been easier to achieve than in the arts. Britain, Denmark, Germany, the Netherlands, and more recently Norway have managed this. The most consistent science nation over the long historical stretch of five-and-a-half centuries has been Switzerland. In the relatively more recent era, from 1750 to 1950, the United States was a fairly weak performer per capita in the arts and strong in the sciences, though typically on a per capita basis not as strong as the European science nations.

Three inferences can be drawn from this.

First, it is wrong to think of intense creation as a 'European' or 'Western' phenomenon. Just as in the case of the geography of prosperity, the spatial distribution of creation is much more specific than that. In fact it is very specific. As Table 9.1 makes clear, most European countries are not intensely or continuously creative in the arts and sciences, nor for that matter is most of the world. Significant levels of intellectual creation is the exception not the rule.

Second, it is easier to sustain creation in the sciences than in the arts. A number of science nations exist (Table 9.2). These nations also tend to do well on technology measures while doing less well on measures of market performance (Table 4.3).

Third, the most difficult thing to sustain is creation in the arts. Why so? There is a sharp decline in the high-level arts in Britain after 1850 and in Denmark, Norway, and the Netherlands after 1900 (Table 9.1). France avoids this decline because of an intellectual life that is fueled by political militancy – a militancy that also has had a long-term deleterious effect on the country's economy. The United States has never delivered a high level of arts intensity.[12] Austria had a burst of creativity in the first half of the twentieth century. The story of Austrian modernism is well known. In the second half of the century, that shrank to virtually nothing.

France and Japan perform well in the first half of the twentieth century. But like almost every nation the incidence (per capita) of major figures creating bodies of significant work declines in the second half of the twentieth century. The per capita decline in significant works in the arts is evident (measurably) since the 1950s.[13] The decline is also evident in the sciences (Table 9.3).

How can it be that the more nations spend (in real terms per capita), the less works of significance and lasting value they create? How is it that the world produces an ever-greater quantity of intellectual works through institutionalized mechanisms (Table 9.2) yet the quality of works in the upper range of creation deteriorates?

A fallacy of the second half of the twentieth century was to suppose that creation was institutional – and capable of being produced in a legal-rational

Table 9.3 Prominent scientists by decade

Cohort	Number in cohort	Population Europe	Population North America	Number of higher education students
Cohort A, born 1910s, active 1950s, typical recognition apex 1970s	24	1900: 291 million	1900: 106 million	United States 1930: 1.1 million
Cohort B, born 1920s, active 1960s, typical recognition apex 1980s	37			United States 1940: 1.4 million
Cohort C, born 1930s, active 1970s, typical recognition apex 1990s	25			United States 1950: 2.2 million
Cohort D, born 1940s, active 1980s, typical recognition apex 2000s	15	1950: 366 million	1950: 217 million	United States 1960: 3.6 million

Source: Great Minds: Reflections of 111 Top Scientists, New York, Oxford University Press, 2014, edited by Balazs Hargittai, Magdolna Hargittai and Istvan Hargittai. Population figures: R. Cameron, *Concise Economic History of the World*, New York, Oxford University Press, 1993; student enrolment figures: National Centre for Educational Statistics, 120 Years of American Education, A Statistical Portrait, Table 24.

Note: Analysis of three groups of scientists (physicists, chemists, and medical biochemists) included in Hargittai et al. The 111 figures chosen for inclusion in *Great minds* were selected from a larger of body of hundreds of scientists who were interviewed for the six volumes of Candid Science published by Imperial College, London (2000–2006). Nine of the interviews in *Great minds* were recorded as late as 2005, and most were recorded between 1994 and 2005. Between population growth in Europe and North America, and the ageing of Cohorts A and B, it might be expected that Group C and Group D would be considerably larger in relative terms than they are. The 1930s and 1940s-born cohorts underperform despite their 60-plus years of life and work.

manner by the analytical methods and procedural norms of arts, educational, and research institutions. At its core, creation is neither analytical nor procedural but rather synthetic and analogical. In its most pronounced form, it is a union of opposites. This is a view that begins explicitly in the Axial Age with the ancient Greek thinker Heraclitus and more generally with the Pre-Socratics and the intellectual traditions of Taoism and its reconfiguration of Buddhism in the form of the maritime East Asian tradition of Mahāyāna Buddhism and most notably its Zen strand. These currents from the Axial Age reproduce themselves over two millennia and enter the blood stream of modernity.[14] This then raises the question: if there is an intellectual axiomodernity, how can we measure it empirically?

To do the latter I have taken the case of the epigram (Table 3.3). Arguably the epigram – and the witty and paradoxical cast of mind that underpins it – is the most succinct, compressed form of human creation there is. It lays bare the way in which the human mind compresses contradictory observations into penetrating insights. It easily and strikingly communicates – and it is exhibited widely through time and space. It also reminds us that it is not rationalist logic that makes the most interesting creations but rather the cognitive ability to fuse opposites into variously pleasing, startling, and revealing patterns of thought, where void and mass coexist in the same thought simultaneously in opposition and union.

To purse this empirical epigrammatology, I have drawn on raw data provided by M.J. Cohen's *Dictionary of Epigrams*.[15] This includes an inventory of 1,000 creative figures, whose birth-dates range from 604 BCE to 1965 and who each produced notable epigrams. I break down this inventory by time and space (Table 3.3). Like the arts and sciences in general, epigrammatical behavior clusters in time and space. There are marked flowerings of epigrammatical thought and marked declines. France's and Britain's lengthy courses of intensive creation in the arts is echoed in this matrix, likewise is Ireland's early twentieth-century efflorescence and just as quick fading. So is America's persistent record of creation since 1750 but also the degree to which the American scale of creation is conventionally overestimated. Overall two epigrammatical periods predominate: the second half of the eighteenth century and the first half of the twentieth century. The latter is weaker than the former. Almost everywhere the level of epigrammatical power declines in the second half of the twentieth century.

Why does this matter to the question of prosperity? Because paradoxes have powerful practical productive effects. For example, modern economies create employment by replacing labor with machines.[16] That's a paradox, and a potent one, not least for public policy, which has to understand and explain the enigma that only by getting rid of labor can we expect a society's labor force to grow. Automation of old industries allows new industries to rise.

Conversely, how do we explain the (belated) rise of a once poor country like the Republic of Ireland into the ranks of very prosperous nations (Table 1.1)? There is the matter of location: being on the maritime rim of North-Western Europe. On the other hand its history of militancy held it back. Militancy – against the English and in favor of a grim clerical hierarchy and later against that clerical hierarchy – exhibited a pugnacity typical of the brutal fighting ethos of pre-industrial societies. Counter to this, though, was a hidden vein in the culture or at least one submerged since the time of Edmund Burke. In any event a series of prominent exilic Irish-born cultural figures – Oscar Wilde, George Bernard Shaw, James Joyce, and Samuel Beckett among them – tapped into this vein. In Beckett's case his interest in the antinomies of logic and the paradoxes of reality echoed an early interest in Jansenism that in turn echoed in his exile in Paris.[17]

In order for late-twentieth-century Irish prosperity to accelerate, a route (at least partially) out of the constraints of a militant society had to be found (France comes to mind here as well). The cultural exiles did not engineer this or even necessarily directly influence it. What they did rather was to lay bare a latency in Irish culture that had been dormant since the age of Oliver Goldsmith, Laurence Sterne, and Edmund Burke. By the 1990s the antinomies of a strong economy rose to the surface. This was the practical demotic expression of a culture latent with the kind of double-coding that one also finds in literary devices such as double-entendre, dual narration, recursive structures, circularity, self-generation, and literature about literature. But in the case of Ireland, as in the case of France, a shadow of militancy continued to haunt the practical antinomies of a late-arriving prosperous economy. Militant societies prefer status to function, loyalty to persistence, hierarchy to task, retaliation to remedy, activism to adaptation, regimentation to freedom, war to peace, swarms to individuals, offense to defense, and aggression to cooperation.

Prosperous societies trade militancy for paradox. Thus we find that paradoxy is the substrate of a diverse range of features of modern growth economies; the following are examples:

Sampling is consuming. This is the paradox of information goods.[18] Before an information good (e.g., software) can be purchased it has to be trialed but in trialing it the consumer may derive all the useful value they require from the good and have no need to actually purchase it.

Zero pricing increases prices. A business gives away part of its product for free. What remains is scarcer, and its price goes up, more than compensating the business for its giveaways.[19]

More is less. The paradox of freeway expansion indicates that a society may expand its freeways to reduce congestion but if non-freeway users as a result are induced to become freeway users or non-peak-hour drivers are induced to join the peak-hour traffic or public transport users are induced to become freeway drivers, what results is worse congestion.[20]

Lower prices lead to less consumption. Usually, persons consume more of a product when the price of a product decreases. But in the case of status goods, where high price is a signifier of high status, a lower price leads to a fall in consumption.[21]

Price subsidies increase prices not lower them. State subsidies for goods such as housing or education are intended to reduce their prices, thereby making them more affordable for those on lower incomes. In practice though the greater the subsidy the higher the price, as producers (both public and private) raise their prices or fees as subsidies increase.[22]

Success means failure. Companies develop a method for successful business. It works for a long time. Then the method hardens into an inert formula. It is routinized and bureaucratized, entrenched and unresponsive, making it incapable of meeting new challenges. The company goes out of business.[23]

Goal-rationality means pattern irrationality.[24] For example, a retail business opens extra hours. This adds labor costs but increases the competitiveness of the business. Its competitors respond by opening extra hours. This cancels out any competitive advantage while raising costs across the board.

Thrift begets indulgence. Economic generations alternate. A cohort marked by work, thrift, prudence, personal responsibility, gratitude, and sacrifice will alternate with one marked by leisure, complaint, entitlement, indulgence, and status-seeking.[25]

Some of these paradoxes are negative, while some are positive. No matter, the point is that quite a lot of ordinary human behavior can be uncanny in nature. Prosperous societies find ways of harnessing this, not least by understanding it. Whether it is Adam Smith's 'paradox of value' or Joseph Schumpeter's 'creative destruction' or alternatively Niels Bohr's 'principle of complementarity', Democritus-Beckett-Malone's 'Nothing is more real than nothing' or Beckett-Nell's 'Nothing is funnier than unhappiness' – all these display a common structure of thought.

The era 1500–1800 saw the creation of many of the institutions of modern capitalism, among them the insurance industry and the stock exchange. In both of these cases the human appetite for economic risk was increased by decreasing risks. Insurance decreased risk by pooling it among many individuals. Joint-stock companies spread risk among multiple shareholders and multiple stock holdings. The limited liability company later on reduced risk by reducing liability for failures. In each case, less risk increased a person's readiness to assume risks and engage in uncertain but potentially rewarding and productive ventures.

The incidence and influence of the structure of thought that underwrites this kind of behavior varies over time, both in intellectual culture and in everyday life. In the latter part of the twentieth century we see a measurable decline in this structure of thought (Tables 3.3 and 9.3). This was the era of the 'knowledge society'. It was a time when general education and the universities rapidly expanded. Therein lay the problem, for the institutions of knowledge are institutions. Their impulse is to push aside imagination and intuition. Paradox, antinomies and the *coincidentia oppositorum* sit uncomfortably with institutional rationalism. So began a process to try and rationalize these irritating phenomena out of sight and mind. Where possible they were replaced with 'best methods' and routinized, codified, and standardized practices. Annoying head-bending antinomies were pushed aside where they could be, by a stolid unidirectional 'correctness'. Wherever institutions could manage it, the ironies and paradoxes of wit and imagination were replaced by a stifling language of norms, appropriateness, and acceptability. In short in the arts and sciences and elsewhere, skeptical reason was supplanted by legal-rationalism.

Notes

1 Murphy, 2015.
2 The social science of mimesis was developed by the French sociologist Gabriel Tarde in *The Laws of Imitation* (1890).
3 Murray, 2003.
4 Murray (2003, 476–478) describes a three-step process of selection. For each field in the arts and sciences he began with an encyclopedic source and a non-encyclopedic source to define a parent population of intellectual figures. Then he identified 'qualified sources' (reference works) that included at least 18–20 percent of the parent population. He used anywhere between 9 and 16 reference works for each field and a median of 13. A total of 19,794 figures were mentioned in these reference works across the entirety

of human history. Of those, 'significant figures' were mentioned in at least 50 percent of the relevant 'qualified sources'. A 'major figure' was one who was in 90 percent of the sources.

5 Kaneda and Haub, 2018.
6 Google (Taycher, 2010) estimates that 130 million books (printed bound volumes) have been published in the entirety of human history. Assuming 4,000 significant figures with an average of 2.5 printed books (including collections of papers) of importance (that have been read by successive generations), peak literate print creation represents 10,000 volumes out of 130 million, or 0.0077 percent.
7 Clark, 2014.
8 Rubenfeld and Chua, 2014.
9 Salvesen, 2018.
10 Hegel, 1971 [1948].
11 Zylstra, 2017; Chow, 2014; Fällman, 2013.
12 Alexis de Tocqueville had already observed this in the 1830s.
13 Murphy, 2015, Table 1.1, 1.2, 1.3.
14 Both echo earlier oral societies' myths of creation, that is, the structure of thought of these societies summed up in Claude Levi-Strauss' view that myths are composed of elements that oppose or contradict each other and further elements that resolve those oppositions. This represents in the most elementary form the deep structure of the human imagination (Levi-Strauss, 1963 [1958]).
15 Cohen, 2001.
16 Murphy, 2017.
17 Foehn, 2009; Breuer, 1993.
18 Arrow, 1962.
19 Aumann and Peleg, 1974.
20 Schneider (2018) observes that 'Rather than thinking of traffic as a liquid, which requires a certain volume of space to pass through at a given rate, induced demand demonstrates that traffic is more like a gas, expanding to fill up all the space it is allowed. Transportation researchers have been observing induced demand since at least the 1960s, when the economist Anthony Downs coined his Law of Peak Hour Traffic Congestion, which states that "on urban commuter expressways, peak-hour traffic congestion rises to meet maximum capacity".' See also Downs, 1962 and Vadim and Avineri, 2015.
21 Leibenstein, 1950.
22 As this applies to public goods and specifically universities, see Murphy, 2015.
23 Miller, 1990.
24 Stützel, 1979
25 Salamone and Morris, 2012.

Bibliography

Aumann, R.J. and B. Peleg 1974. "A Note on Gale's Example". *Journal of Mathematical Economics* 1, no. 2: 209–211.

Arrow, K.J. 1962. "Economic Welfare and the Allocation of Resources for Invention". In Universities-National Bureau Committee for Economic Research, Committee on Economic Growth of the Social Science Research Council (ed.), *The Rate and Direction of Inventive Activity: Economic and Social Factors*, 609–626. Princeton, NJ: Princeton University Press.

Breuer, R. 1993. "Paradox in Beckett". *The Modern Language Review* 88, no. 3: 559–580.

Chow, A. 2014. "Calvinist Public Theology in Urban China Today". *International Journal of Public Theology* 8, no. 2: 158–175.

Clark, G. 2014. *The Son Also Rises: Surnames and the History of Social Mobility*. Princeton, NJ: Princeton University Press, 2014.

Cohen, M.J. 2001. *The Penguin Dictionary of Epigrams*. London: Penguin.

Downs, A. 1962. "The Law of Peak-Hour Expressway Congestion". *Traffic Quarterly* 16, no. 3: 393–409.

Fällman, F. 2013. "Calvin, Culture and Christ? Developments of Faith among Chinese Intellectuals". In F.K.G. Lim (ed.), *Christianity in Contemporary China: Socio-cultural Perspectives*, 153–168. London: Routledge.

Foehn, M. 2009. "'Is That the Word?' Samuel Beckett and the Port-Royal Philosophy of Language". *Études irlandaises* 34, no. 2: 43–54.

Hegel, G.W.F. 1971 [1948]. *Early Theological Writings*. Philadelphia: Pennsylvania University Press.

Kaneda, T. and C. Haub. 2018. *How Many People Have Ever Lived on Earth?*, Population Research Bureau, March 9.

Leibenstein, H. 1950. "Bandwagon, Snob, and Veblen Effects in the Theory of Consumers' Demand". *Quarterly Journal of Economics* 64: 183–207.

Levi-Strauss, C. 1963 [1958]. *Structural Anthropology*. New York: Basic Books.

Miller, D. 1990. *The Icarus Paradox: How Exceptional Companies Bring about Their Own Downfall*. New York: Harper Business.

Murphy, P. 2017. *Auto-Industrialism: DIY Capitalism and the Rise of the Auto-Industrial Society*. London: Sage.

Murphy, P. 2015. *Universities and Innovation Economies: The Creative Wasteland of Post-Industrial Societies*. Farnham: Ashgate.

Murray, C. 2003. *Human Accomplishment: The Pursuit of Excellence in the Arts and Sciences, 800 B.C. to 1950*. New York: HarperCollins.

Rubenfeld, J. and A. Chua. 2014. *The Triple Package: How Three Unlikely Traits Explain the Rise and Fall of Cultural Groups in America*. London: Bloomsbury.

Salamone, C. and G. Morris. 2012. *Rescue America: Our Best America Is Only One Generation Away*. Austin, TX: Greenleaf.

Salvesen, A. 2018. "What 770,000 Tubes of Saliva Reveal About America". *Ancestry.com*, February 8. https://blogs.ancestry.com/cm/what-770000-tubes-of-saliva-reveal-about-america/

Schneider, B. 2018. "CityLab University: Induced Demand". CityLab, September 6. https://www.citylab.com/transportation/2018/09/citylab-university-induced-demand/569455/

Stützel, W. 1979. *Paradoxes of Money Economy and Competitive Market Economy (Paradoxa der Geld- und Konkurrenzwirtschaft)*. Aalen: Scientia.

Tarde, G. 2013 [1903/1890]. *The Laws of Imitation*. Patterson Press Kindle Edition.

Taycher, L. 2010. "Books of the World, Stand Up and Be Counted! All 129,864,880 of You". *Google Books Search* blog.

Tocqueville, A. 2003 [1835/1840]. *Democracy in America*. London: Penguin.

Vadim, Z. and E. Avineri. 2015. "Braess' Paradox in a Generalised Traffic Network". *Journal of Advanced Transportation* 49(1): 114–138.

Zylstra, S.E. 2017. "Young, Restless, and Reformed in China". *TGC The Gospel Coalition*, March 27.

10 Ambidexterity

Maritime East Asia

Axial Age societies were concentrated in two places: the Mediterranean and Maritime East Asia. In the third Axial zone, the Ganges Basin, Buddhism began. The latter though quickly exported itself to maritime South-East Asia and maritime East Asia. Today it clusters around these two regions. Theravada Buddhism is focused on Thailand, Cambodia, Burma and Laos, and (adjacent to these) South-Western China. Theravada's more paradoxical cousin, Mahāyāna Buddhism, is mustered in Japan, Singapore, Taiwan, and China's coastal Fujian and Zhejiang provinces near Taiwan. Taoism's heartland is the southern Chinese provinces of Guangdong, Guangxi, and Guizhou bound by the Pearl (Zhujiang) River system together with Hunan province, an appendage of the Yangtze River system. Confucianism is most densely represented in the northern Chinese provinces that surround Bohai Bay and on the nearby Korean peninsula.

Just as China was influenced socially and politically by the administrative legalism (*Fajia*) of Shen Buhai, Shang Yang, Shen Dao, and Han Fei, so in Europe and America during the twentieth century we saw the rise of Max Weber's legal-rational 'iron cage'. Administered states, firms, universities, churches, and scientific and charitable organizations proliferated. For four decades mid-century China detoured through the economic fantasies of Communist (Maoist) totalitarianism. Where the bureaucratic iron cage was procedurally rational, totalitarianism was irrational. Its command economics, magical science, and hostility to capitalism proved to be economically disastrous. Deng Xiaoping's unleashing of China's commercial potential (by creating special economic zones) closely followed in geographical scope the footprint of the despised nineteenth-century treaty ports. What is striking is that both Deng's 'special economic zones' and the earlier treaty ports closely adhere to a metaphysical geography of coastal and riverine regions where Taoism, Mahāyāna Buddhism, and Confucianism are concentrated.

Maritime East Asia has long been receptive to axial intellectual culture. That applies much less to territorial China. The post-Maoist Beijing model proved to be a potent mix of bureaucratic legalism and latent patrimonialism. Rules and connections, impersonal methods and personal influence, control and corruption, performance and cronyism, administrative standards and neo-patrimonial princelings (relatives and descents of powerful party officials) coexisted cheek by jowl in an ambitious developmental state. Much is made of the national humiliation of China in the nineteenth century when it was forced to open up to foreign trade. But arguably what happened in the British colony of Hong Kong was a connection between the two axial seedbeds through economic behaviors. The same was true of the British equatorial colony of Singapore and might even be true of the multinational 'concessions' in Shanghai. In any event, the most materially successful societies in the modern age have been North-Western Europe, the settler societies of North America and Australasia, and maritime East Asia. The most recent of these, the economies of maritime East Asia, are underpinned by tacit background mixtures of Axial-era Taoism, Confucianism, and Mahāyāna Buddhism along with more recent imports including Presbyterianism in South Korea and a still-more generic non-institutional Calvinism in China. We have even seen the official take-up in China of Alfred North Whitehead's enantiodromia-flavored process theology.

In step with this is high literacy. While the cities, provinces, and states of contemporary maritime East Asia are well known for their industry, they are also great readers. According to the OCED's Program for International Student Assessment (PISA), 15-year-olds in Japan, 'Beijing, Shanghai, Jiangsu and Guangdong', Singapore, and Taiwan are among the world's best readers.[1] Japan and Singapore have very high rates of daily newspaper readership, among the highest in the world.[2] Taiwan is the number 2 per capita book publisher in the world after the United Kingdom; Korea is number 14. Japan at number 20 is evidently less interested in books than in newspapers. Intellectual literacy expresses itself in different ways.

The tropics today are the most hard up of the world's major geographic regions. Climate – that is, heat and humidity – once played a decisive role in tropical economies. Since the spread of air-conditioning, working in the tropics and the subtropics has become significantly more pleasant. So climate now is only a lesser factor in economic performance. Geography on the other hand remains a central element in economic and social success. Overall today, the world is a lot less poor than it was even three decades ago. In 1981, 52 percent of the population in developing countries lived in extreme poverty; by 2010 that figure had fallen to 21 percent. In the tropics, the number of extreme poor over the same period dropped from 51 percent of the total population to 28 percent. In the rest of the world, extreme poverty fell from 53 percent to 14 percent of the population. The whole globe has improved markedly, although the tropic zone least so.

The most improved parts of the tropics have been Southeast Asia and Central America, while extreme poverty in Central and Southern Africa has gotten worse. A key reason for the latter's worsening condition is the geography of Africa – or rather its coast.[3] Simply put, coastal Africa has few natural harbors or ports and hence a poor history of portal trade.[4] In contrast, three out of fifteen of the top-ranked by GDP per capita nations in 2016 (Table 4.3) are in the tropics: Hong Kong, Singapore, and Taiwan. In 50 years, these countries went from poverty to impressive wealth (Table 1.1). They achieved this because they emerged as nodes in a major maritime economy zone.[5] Singapore in 2018 was the number 2 container port in the world; Hong Kong was number 5. Taiwan's Kaohsiung was number 15 (Table 2.1).[6]

The idea of 'the port' does not only signify a functional economic node. It is also a metaphor for ceaseless 'in-and-out' transactions. A transactional society is only possible where process and paperwork, the life-blood of bureaucracy, are kept to a minimum. Hong Kong, Singapore, and Taiwan are at times called 'Confucian' societies. Yet in the case of Hong Kong, Singapore, and Taiwan, a more decisive if less visible developmental influence has been the diffuse, heterodox, minority demotic philosophy-religion of Taoism. In Taiwan, a third of the population identifies as Taoist; 10 percent of Singaporeans do as well, as do 14 percent of Hong Kong citizens. Taoism is part popular religion and part popular philosophy. Most significant of all, it is a belief system filled with paradoxes.

Philosophical Taoism encourages those interested in it to think in syncretized opposites: solid-and-void, black-and-white, presence-and-absence, abundance-and-scarcity, above-and-below, agreement-and-disagreement, entrance-and-exit, internal-and-external, frequent-and-rare, hard-and-soft, and so on. This mental approach has myriad implications. Thinking-in-opposites – fusing them, combining them – is linked to human creation. Merging antitheses is what the imagination does. Forms, patterns, and shapes are created by the coalescence of opposites. The act of creation – in art, business, science, technology, and in life generally – occurs when we look at something going up and can see it in our mind's eye going down simultaneously, like an E. M. Escher lithograph. The person who says 'let us meld Amazon's retail model and the sale of enterprise software' or 'let us put themes into amusement parks' or 'let us blend academic citations and web searches' takes two things not normally connected and associates them in an act of creation.[7] Modern commerce and industry regularly combines antitheses – such as the warehouse and the shopping outlet or the new manufactured pair of jeans designed with frayed knees. Images of wholesale and retail, new and old, are fused in antithetical combinations whose attractiveness, salience, and efficacy lie in that fact. The more radical the association, the more it has the feel of being uncanny, the more it resembles the quantum paradox that a wave is a particle and a particle a wave.

We see this uncanny *both-and* mentality echoed in the ambidextrous attitudes of the Taiwanese today, who are both armed against mainland China and yet do vast business in that country. The case of Hong Kong is similar. It is a part of China and yet it is a Special Administrative Region (SAR) with its own ways of doing things. Mainland China is a bureaucratic state. In contrast the background Taoist ambience of Hong Kong shies away from the deliberate action of the state. The Taoist attitude is '*Let it be*': leave it alone; adapt to the cycles of the world rather than try and rule or direct them.[8] Background Taoism looks to the tacit 'pattern of things' rather than to methodical state, institutional, or bureaucratic intervention and organization. Hong Kong, Singapore, and Taiwan are not libertarian societies by any means. They have plenty of laws and regulations. Yet, by orthodox Confucian standards, let alone by legalist standards, they are relatively free. They have a greater tolerance for the spontaneous order of markets, industries, cities, nuclear households, and publics than their neighbors do. They are more ready to pay attention to patterns rather than persons and replace patrimonial connections with impersonal abstractions.[9]

The paradox factories

Peak modern societies are 'automated societies', that is, autonomous societies. In varying degrees, they are dominated by five self-organizing systems: industries, markets, cities, nuclear households, and publics. In autonomous or highly automated societies, patrimonial connection is edged aside by impersonal order. This impersonal order begins with 'the rule of law'. Laws replace personal direction and connection. But eventually laws in their turn are displaced by impersonal patterns. Cycles and ratios emerge as more important than procedures, policies, and rules. It is not that the latter disappear – any more than personal interaction disappears in an automated or self-organizing society. It is not a matter of *either-or*. Rather, it is a matter of relative weighting. In the most advanced societies, that is, in the peak automated societies, patterns, abstractions, and quasi-aesthetic qualities like ratios and proportions acquire increasing and outsized significance in the overall way that a society functions.

In miniature, we see this operate in the case of industry automation – the technological correlate of the automated society. Today we can observe office work and sales work being gradually replaced by machines (computers and robots).[10] The age of the twentieth-century white collar 'knowledge economy' is winding down. This also means that today work of a non-routine, problem-solving, pattern-based kind is becoming increasingly important as a means of replacing the work that is being replaced by machines. The post-industrial path from agricultural and manufacturing work to routine service and office work is being incrementally computerized out of existence, gradually replaced by an auto-industrial path. Where this happens the paradox-and-pattern path to prosperity becomes ever more important.

But this then raises the question, Are some societies more able to navigate this than others? The answer is 'yes' to the extent that some societies rest more easily on 'paradox-and-pattern' matrices and axionomic behaviors than do others. But why is that so? Is there some kind of social 'paradox factory'?

If there is such a thing, then one of its sources is religion or rather the subset of heterodox religions. I have already pointed to the role of Taoism as an agent of paradox in maritime East Asia. For a comparative example take the case of the Mormons.[11] They make up 2 percent of the American population. Small perhaps – but size is not the only measure of influence. Jewish Americans, who make up 2 percent of the US population, constitute 7 percent of US corporate board members. The presence of Mormons in American business is similarly outsized.[12] By the measure of mainstream Christianity, the doctrinal views of Mormons are clearly heterodox. However, what is important for the present discussion is neither doctrine nor creed but rather the way in which certain belief systems generate paradoxes.

The American literary and religious scholar Terry Givens calls the Mormons a 'people of paradox'.[13] He argues that the Mormon mind is structured by a series of paradoxes: those of 'authority and radical freedom,' 'searching and certainty,' 'the sacral and the banal' and 'election and exile'. The thing about paradoxes is that they are not dualisms but rather dualities that are compressed successfully into singularities – single doubles, if you like. Thus, in the Mormon case, the divine is found in everyday life, moral freedom is achieved through thoughtful obedience, certainty makes searching possible, and religious election leads to exile in the larger culture. While this matrix might reflect the specificities of the Mormon mind, it also has some generalizable implications.

The Mormon divinization of the material, a classic paradox, parallels the Protestant spiritualization of work. Both are types of paradox that energize a material civilization. They invest inert matter with a dynamic sense of spirit. They animate the inanimate. The compression of duality into singularity is the way that creation in general works. So perhaps it is then not so surprising that among the most successful Americans today are persons from Mormon backgrounds. The Mormons have been especially successful in corporate America because they fruitfully interpolate the paradox of freedom and authority – a paradox tailored to innovation in plodding institutional environments. Notably, many high-achieving Mormons come from modest backgrounds. This fact is both a metaphor for countries climbing the economic and social ladder and a pointer to the kinds of social groups that engineer such upward mobility.

In addition to the Mormons, Jed Rubenfeld and Amy Chua also point to the success in America of immigrants from Iran, Lebanon, India, China, and the Caribbean along with those with Jewish backgrounds. They cite a 'triple package' among such groups: a sense of being exceptional or special ('chosen'), feeling (as a group) insecure, and having a high degree of impulse control in an otherwise self-indulgent culture.[14] Broad-brush geographies such as 'India' or 'China', though, disguise more powerful distinctions. Indian immigrants to the United States come predominately from the Gujarati, Punjabi, and Tamil regions – the first a portal zone, the second India's 'five rivers' zone, the third abutting the Palk Straits zone – echoes of the Indo-Gangetic Axial Age.

The Chinese diaspora is similar. It comes predominately from the Chinese coastal provinces of Fujian and Zhejiang. One might add ditto for the Caribbean and Mediterranean-hugging Lebanon. Many of the 'Iranians' in the United States are actually Jewish, Armenian (Armenian Christian), and Assyrian (Syriac Christian) minorities from Iran. The Armenian religious doctrine of miaphysitism (Christ as a union of divine and human nature) and the Western Syriac Church view of dyophisitism (Christ as a loose union of divine and human nature) and the Eastern Syriac Church view of monophysitism (Christ as one divine and human nature) all deal in the common metaphysical question of the union of contrasting things, a question that is not just religious but has pertinent application to the modern professions such as engineering, law, science, and economics – as well as business and management.

Small heterodox religious groups or milieu with such obscure interests or backgrounds paradoxically do especially well in modern societies. Why among the nations of ex-Soviet-controlled Eastern Europe has Slovenia (Table 4.4) done so well? It is historically a Catholic Counter-Reformation country. Yet its culture effectively began with a Lutheran religious leader and late Renaissance era humanist Primož Trubar (1508–1586). In any event, economic mobility, individual or national, does not arise solely from conventional economic formulae. That is not to say that conventional fiscal, market, education, and health prescriptions and functions are not important. They are. But behind such formulae lie more subtle considerations. In 1945, the Republic of Korea was in a state of absolute poverty. Excluding resource-dependent states (in this case Qatar, United Arab Emirates, Kuwait and Oman), South Korea in 2016 ranked 22nd in per capita GDP (US$ 2011) at US$36,103 per head.[15] This compared with Australia, which was ranked seventh at US$48,854 per head. Syngman Rhee, the strong-man first president of the Korean Republic, was a Protestant convert, and many members of his inaugural cabinet were Christians: this at the time when in the country only 3.75 percent of the population was Christian (by 2015, 28 percent of South Koreans were Christians).[16] South Korea adopted a flag whose centerpiece was the Taoist *yin-yang* symbol. At one point in his life Rhee had also been a Taoist convert.

In Singapore, Taiwan, and Hong Kong, Christian minorities contribute something key to the latent background of social creation. Singapore has 11 percent Protestants, 7 percent Catholics (and 10 percent Taoists); Taiwan 4 percent Christians (and 33 percent Taoists); Hong Kong 7 percent Protestants, 5 percent Catholics (and 14 percent Taoists).[17] The argument is not that a percentage of people say they are 'Christians' or 'Taoists' and then 'creative activity' or 'productive activity' magically follows from that. That is an implausible proposition not least when religious identification in a modern society is often nominal. Rather, the proposition is that religion becomes relevant to prosperity to the degree that it conveys a paradoxical metaphysics. This is not necessarily common. Yet it does happen. At times small heterodox religious groups play an outsized role in the generation of economic and social prosperity.

Notes

1 OECD PISA reports, 2000–2015.
2 United Nations Educational, Scientific, and Cultural Organisation (UNESCO) Institute for Statistics, 2002–2004.
3 Landes, 1999; Sowell, 2015.
4 Cf. the 'very limited number of good natural harbors along both coasts of Africa' (Duignan and Gann, 1975, 296).
5 'Maritime transport is essential to the world's economy as over 90% of the world's trade is carried by sea and it is, by far, the most cost-effective way to move en masse goods and

raw materials around the world.' International Maritime Organization https://business. un.org/en/entities/13

6 These rankings are measured by the total number of twenty-foot equivalent units (TEUs) handled by the ports.

7 The allusions are to Salesforce (the customer relationship management company), Disney Corporation, and Google (Dyer, Gregersen, and Christensen, 2011, 17–40).

8 The ethos of 'let it be' directly parallels the view of one of the principal architects of Hong Kong's powerful economy, Sir John James Cowperthwaite (1915–2006), who was the then-colony's financial secretary between 1961 and 1971, and who advocated 'positive non-intervention'. In 1962 Cowperthwaite insisted that '[over] a wide field of our economy it is still the better course to rely on the nineteenth century's "hidden hand" than to thrust clumsy bureaucratic fingers into its sensitive mechanism' (Reed, 2014). Positive non-intervention meant that '[personal] taxes were kept at a maximum of 15 per cent; government borrowing was wholly unacceptable; there were no tariffs or subsidies. Red tape was so reduced that a new company could be registered with a one-page form. Cowperthwaite believed that government should concern itself with only minimal intervention on behalf of the most needy, and should not interfere in business. Reflecting on what became the world's most successful economy, Cowperthwaite remarked, "I did very little. All I did was to try to prevent some of the things that might undo it".' (Obituary, 2006).

9 On Taiwan, Hong Kong, and Singapore as low-trust familial societies, see Fukuyama, 1996, 10, 29, 30, 50, 56, 57, 84–95.

10 Murphy, 2017.

11 The Mormons belong to the Church of Jesus Christ of Latter-day Saints.

12 Lears, 2012.

13 Givens, 2007.

14 Rubenfeld and Chua, 2014.

15 Groningen Growth and Development Centre, Maddison Historical Statistics, 2018, Real GDP per capita in 2011US$.

16 Grayson, 2006, 14–15; Statistics Korea, 2015.

17 CIA *World Factbook*, 2019 based on 2015 Singapore data, 2005 Taiwan data and 2016 Hong Kong data; United Nations Statistics Division, Demographic Statistics Database, Population by religion, sex and urban/rural residence, Singapore 2010 data; Hong Kong Government Yearbook, 2010, chapter 18, 377–379.

Bibliography

Duignan, P. and L.H. Gann. 1975. *Colonialism in Africa 1870–1960*, Volume 4. Cambridge: Cambridge University Press.

Dyer, J., H. Gregersen and C. M. Christensen. 2011. *The Innovator's DNA: Mastering the Five Skills of Disruptive Innovators*. Boston, MA: Harvard Business Review Press.

Fukuyama, F. 1996. *Trust: The Social Virtues and the Creation of Prosperity*. New York: Free Press.

Givens, T.L. 2007. *People of Paradox: A History of Mormon Culture*. Oxford: Oxford University Press.

Grayson, J.H. 2006. "A Quarter-Millennium of Christianity in Korea". In R.E. Buswell and T.S. Lee, *Christianity in Korea*, 7–25. Honolulu: University of Hawaii Press.

Landes, D.S. 1999. *The Wealth and Poverty of Nations*. London: Abacus.

Lears, J. 2012. "The Mormon Ethic and the Spirit of Capitalism". *The New Republic*, October 19. https://newrepublic.com/article/108787/the-mormon-ethic-and-the-spirit-capitalism

Murphy, P. 2017. *Auto-Industrialism: DIY Capitalism and the Rise of the Auto-Industrial Society*. London: Sage.

Obituary. 2006. "Sir John Cowperthwaite". *Telegraph*, January 25.

Reed, L.W. 2014. "The Man behind the Hong Kong Miracle". *The Freeman*, February 10. https://fee.org/articles/the-man-behind-the-hong-kong-miracle/

Rubenfeld, J. and A. Chua. 2014. *The Triple Package: How Three Unlikely Traits Explain the Rise and Fall of Cultural Groups in America*. London: Bloomsbury.

Sowell, T. 2015. *Wealth, Poverty and Politics: An International Perspective*. New York: Basic Books.

11 Antinomy and economy

Imagination

Intellectual generation occurs through the imagination. The imagination is a cognitive faculty. It parses the world around it into contrary qualities and forces – large and small, hot and cold, bright and dull, animated and tranquil, up and down, near and far, and so on.[1] The imagination is the intellectual medium that enables these antonyms to become synonyms. It synthesizes antitheses. It turns difference into likeness and disparity into similarity. It unifies oppositions and does so in pleasing and striking ways.

How does the imagination manage this? First, through the organizing power of form. Proportion, ratio, harmony, balance, oscillation, rhythm, rhyme, homology, and symmetry are some of the principal means that enable the human mind to structure relationships between antipodal qualities so that they appear to us as being somehow 'just right'. The imagination also deploys the structural power of analogy. Similes, metaphors, allegories, and symbols create resemblances out of things that are normally experienced as dissimilar. Form and analogy operate through multiple mediums – linguistic, visual, auditory, tactile, and so on. The imagination creates equivalences out of things that are not equivalent and comparisons out of what seems incommensurable. It produces unity out of opposition and forges meaning by translating the terms of one thing into those of another.

By the sixteenth century, many Europeans had begun to use the word 'imagination' to portray a mental faculty much like that just outlined. It denoted a cognitive processing capacity that performed various kinds of gymnastic analogical and patterning operations. It is these that underpin the uncanny equivalences that distinguish the act of creation. The epistemology of the imagination evolved from Francis Bacon's power of perceiving resemblances and Shakespeare's faculty that 'bodies forth the forms of things unknown' through the 'wit' of John Dryden, Thomas Hobbes, and John Locke to Joseph Addison's pleasures of the imagination and Alexander Pope's dangerous art.[2] William Hazlitt thought that the imagination was the faculty for finding 'something similar in things generally alike', while wit was what allowed us to find something the same where we least expected it 'in things totally opposite'.[3] Denis

Diderot pointed to the paradox of great actors who do not feel the emotions that they act out.

The idea of wit suggests both laughter and imagination, humor and creation. These are all closely related. The eighteenth-century Scottish poet and philosopher James Beattie proposed that laughter arose from a 'view of things incongruous united in the same assemblage'. We laugh where 'two or more inconsistent, unsuitable, or incongruous parts or circumstances' are 'united in one complex object or assemblage'.[4] This kind of incongruous 'mutual relation' defines both the nature of humor and the character of creation.

It is observable as well that the early modern period saw the coining of an alternative theory of humor: laughter as the expression of superiority. As modern societies make the transition, uncertainly, from heteronomy to autonomy, they equivocate on whether or not to abandon the social-structuring principle of hierarchy. After all, from band to tribe to patrimony to feudalism to courtly empire, different versions of hierarchy provided the primary social bond. Giving that up was difficult. So in many cases the bond was reinvented. Procedural hierarchies, absolutist hierarchies, totalitarian hierarchies, managerial hierarchies, and moral hierarchies were among the many kinds that found a footing in the modern era. Post-modern attempts to re-found hierarchies by inverting them proved influential from the late nineteenth century onwards. In all these cases, irrespective of type or period, renovated hierarchy was accompanied by assertions of superiority.

Just as wit creates things, so humor can disparage, sneer, and belittle them. This distinction is replicated in multiple forms of economic and social organization. Just as once the lord was superior to the peasant, the patriarch to the matriarch, patron to client, monarch to courtier, courtier to servant, and so on, the modern era produces new impersonal hierarchies. Some of these are organizational in nature, others systemic in nature. All are nominally functional in character. Yet status often over-writes function. Social actors become subsumed with intense desires to demonstrate that they or 'their' system or organization is superior to others, just as organization-loyalists strive to show that they are superior to 'exiteers'. All manner of condescension, haughtiness, aloofness, pomposity, and self-importance follow. Since the beginning of the nineteenth century, such haughtiness has often taken the form of ideologies and 'isms'.

Laughter as an expression of superiority is an assertion of status. Thomas Hobbes in *Leviathan* (1652) gave a powerful description of the 'sudden glory' that accompanies this kind of laughter. The glory comes from humorous jibes in which we compare ourselves with others' lack of ability or deformity. When we compare ourselves with the defects and imperfections of others, we applaud ourselves. The effect is to elevate our own status. We are superior. In humor we do this suddenly. The nature of a joke is that its punch line is unexpected. In the imaginative use of wit, the amusing person sets up an expectation in the listener that is confounded by its unexpected opposite. As James Beattie put it, incongruous things (set-up and punch line) are 'united in the same assemblage'. The same is true of all different kinds of creation. They share a paradoxical character.

We can assert both superiority and paradoxy by means of laughter. The former kind of humor communicates our scorn and derision of others, the latter our capacity for invention or creation.

The economy of laughter

During the eighteenth century, the theory of paradox found an application in the understanding of the nature of modern economy and society. Bernard Mandeville's paradox of private vice and public benefits, set out in his satire *The Fable of the Bees* (1714), suggested that private self-seeking led to the public good and that self-love was the foundation of social virtue. In *The Wealth of Nations* (1776), Adam Smith raised this paradox into the most important economic doctrine of the modern age. Human beings, he observed, have an almost constant occasion for the help of their brethren. It is in vain for them to expect that help from benevolence alone. They are more likely to prevail if they can interest the self-love of others in their favor. In short, Smith argued, I have to show others how providing help for me is an advantage to them.[5]

The Wealth of Nations is filled with economic ironies. Among these, Smith recounts how, in the case of thriving countries, we find a great number of people who not only do no labor but many of whom consume the product of ten times, frequently a hundred times, the labor of those who do work. Yet the produce of that same society is so great that everyone can be abundantly supplied. As long as they are frugal and industrious, the humblest and poorest worker can enjoy a greater share of the necessaries and conveniences of life than they could in any nominally more egalitarian premodern society.[6] Great prosperity for all rests not on equality but paradoxically on inequality. Conversely, Smith observed that no society can be flourishing and happy if the greater part of the members are poor and miserable. It is a matter of equity that those who feed, clothe, and lodge the whole body of the people should have such a share of the produce of their own labor as to be themselves tolerably well fed, clothed, and lodged.[7] A sense of proportionality informs a happy society.

Such happiness is underpinned by another paradox. As Smith observed, from the experience of all ages and nations, the work done by freemen comes cheaper in the end than that performed by slaves.[8] Why freedom? Smith argued that the natural effort of every individual to better his own condition, when compelled to exert itself with freedom and security, is such a powerful principle that it alone, without any assistance, can carry a society to wealth and prosperity.[9] Such efforts paradoxically conjoin two antithetical things: nature and freedom, necessity and spontaneity. The biggest problem that the effort of individuals faces is government. Its laws contribute to the security of property and person. Yet its laws also create 'a hundred impertinent obstructions' that encumber the effort of the individual and encroach on its freedom and diminish its security. The public good often turns into the public bad.

That said, there are wheels within wheels. For individual effort, even unencumbered, is itself not free from the demands of paradox. Smith is a fluent master of pattern thinking. This rests on the cognitive ability to reverse opposites – as in the highest forms of wit. For every mass there is a void and vice versa. The successful modern personality finds cognitive reversal – the switching back and forward – congenial. This has crucial practical consequences. Take the case of production. Modern production, Smith observes, exists for its opposite: consumption.[10] Consumption is 'the sole end and purpose of all production'. Thus the interest of the producer properly is to promote that of the consumer. The philosophy of mercantilism, which periodically asserts itself in the modern age, supposes the purpose of production is production. Thus, the manufacturer's interest is the manufacturer not the consumer. This is the modern equivalent of the medieval guild. What happens in a mercantilist atmosphere is that the state tries to draw to a particular type of industry 'a greater share of the capital of the society than what would naturally go to it'.[11] Politically out-of-favor industries experience the converse. Employing regulations and directions, the state tries to re-route from a particular un-favored species of industry some share of the capital that would otherwise be employed in it. What follows is the misallocation of resources to inefficient industries and away from efficient industries.

Persons who are left alone to exercise their natural liberty are able, subject to the laws of justice, to employ their own industry and capital in their own way, competing and cooperating with others to do this in the most effective manner. This is a key to prosperous society.[12] But assuming that natural liberty flourishes, the need for thinking that switches rapidly from one pole to another and grasps the subtle interaction of polarities and the ironies that they produce does not disappear. One among many examples is the irony of money. A great stock with small profits, Smith notes, generally increases faster than a small stock with great profits. Likewise, when you have a little money, it is often easier to get more. But the great difficulty is to get that little amount in the first instance.[13] If persons and societies cannot easily negotiate such practical ambidexterity, then they will fail or at least not do so well.

Antinomies

The ambidexterity syndrome appears at all levels of modern societies. All societies have to deal with it. Successful societies are more proficient by degrees in mastering the challenges of ambidexterity. Adam Smith preferred persons to be left alone by the state to exercise their natural liberty. That observation is generally reduced to platitudes about freedom. But Smith's words imply more than that, for the idea of natural liberty is a paradox. It points both to the causality of nature and the freedom of will simultaneously. How is such a thing possible? The answer to this is partly stated by Smith's contemporary, the philosopher Immanuel Kant.

Kant's philosophy is peppered with paradoxical locutions: lawful external freedom, unsocial sociability, purposiveness with no purpose. In his *Critique of Pure Reason* (1781), Kant proposed a theory of antinomies.[14] Antinomies are statements that are contradictory yet equally true, such as 'the world begins in time' and 'the world has no beginning in time' or 'everything occurs in a law-like and causal manner' and 'everything is spontaneous'. How are these resolved? How can we think in antinomies – indeed, *can* we think in antinomies? For Kant there is a world independent of us. We know that world through experience. The world that we experience Kant called the phenomenal world. Yet there is also the world 'in itself' which is *noumenal*. The noumenal world is outside what we ordinarily understand as experience. It is the world of antinomies where both causality and spontaneity are equally true. Causality assumes a chain of causes and effects. But where does that chain begin? A beginning cannot have a preceding cause. If it doesn't have a preceding cause then it is spontaneous – that is, it is free not caused. To try and avoid that paradox, we can dispense with the idea of a beginning and have instead an infinitely receding chain of cause and effect. If we do that, though, the explanatory power of cause and effect dissipates and disappears. If the nominal cause of something infinitely recedes to ever-more distant causes, the idea of causation becomes meaningless. The first term of any series of conditions has to be unconditioned.

In the noumenal world, human beings tussle with antinomies. These lie at the deepest and most interesting level of cognition. Yet Kant only provides a sketch, and no more, of what the noumenal world looks like. The fact that Kant goes on to propose that the noumenal world is an unknowable 'thing in itself' as opposed to the rationally knowable phenomenal world implies that, at a certain point, Kant gives up his struggle with the problem of antinomies. A similar struggle is evident in the theory of humor that Kant proposed in his *Critique of Judgment* (1790). Kant's theory circles the insight that creation and the imagination unify opposites yet also pulls back from it.

Kant says of humor: in everything that excites a 'lively convulsive laugh' there must be something absurd.[15] Reason or 'the Understanding' – logic, argument, and the like – finds 'no satisfaction' in it. Laughter, Kant goes on, is 'an affection arising from the sudden transformation of a strained expectation into nothing'. Reason does not find laughter enjoyable – and yet it does, because, suggests Kant, absurdity pleases our body, though not our mind (the noumenal world is unknowable). How, after all, could a delusive expectation be gratifying? Well, in truth, the delusive expectation of the humorous set-up – the set-up that is suddenly transformed into its opposite in the punch line – *is* cognitively satisfying, often exquisitely so. But to explain that, Kant would have needed to explain how antinomies are reconciled, which is to explain the generative power of the union of opposites, the power of paradoxy. Kant, almost knowingly, does not go down this path. Instead he says that humor brings about an equilibrium of vital forces in the body rather than the mind.

To show this, Kant proceeds to tell a series of jokes. One of them is about an Indian at the table of an Englishman in Surat, the Gujarat seaport. The Indian watches a bottle of ale being opened. The beer turns into froth and overflows. The Indian exclaims his great astonishment at this. The Englishman is puzzled. Why is his guest so excited about a bottle of beer frothing over? The Indian explains: 'I am not at all astonished that it should flow out, but I do wonder how you ever got it in.' A second Kantian joke goes like this: The heir of a rich relative wished to arrange for an imposing funeral for his departed relation. But he laments that he could not properly succeed. The reason for that? 'The more money I give my mourners to look sad', he says, 'the more cheerful they look.'

Both of these Kantian jokes lay bare the structure of creation. They conjoin polar opposites. The outward flow raises the puzzling image of the inward flow of froth. The mourners' melancholy is actually joy. No, Kant says, we don't laugh because of this. Reason does not get pleasure from the absurd. We get pleasure from it because the set-up *strains* our expectation and the punch line *relieves* our expectation. Laughter is like an economy; it gives us gratification. Our satisfaction comes because the corporeal *tension* that was induced by the expectation that the joke maker raised in us is *released*. Laughter is a release of body tension. That's not a wrong theory, but it is not a complete theory either.

A joke, Kant explains, works like this: it begins with something that deceives us for a moment. Then the deception is dispelled. Once that happens, in a flash, the mind very quickly considers, backwards and forwards, the deception and the revelation in the punch line. As the mind moves from one to the other, it experiences a 'rapidly alternating tension and relaxation', that is, it is 'put into a state of oscillation'. This happens very suddenly. The 'understanding' (intelligibility or reason) may be unimpressed by this but not so the body. Mind and body, Kant argues, are coordinated. The 'sudden transposition of the mind, now to one now to another standpoint' corresponds to the 'alternating tension and relaxation' of our intestines and our diaphragm. We laugh, even despite ourselves, convulsively.

Kant's explanation of laughter is corporeal not mental. It's our body not our reason that laughs. It is true that reason (logic, argument) is not easily amused. But equally arguable is that the whole of us laughs, mind and body. As the mind moves rapidly from deception to revelation, the mind in the form not of reason but imagination sees in two things one thing. The imagination apprehends not the duck or the rabbit but the duck-rabbit. It perceives both at once. It sees inflow and out-flow, sadness and joy, as one thing in one instant.

Notes

1 For a more detailed exploration of what follows, see Murphy, 2017, 117–132.
2 'bodies forth', Shakespeare, 1979 [1595/1596], 163.
3 Hazlitt, 2004 [1818], 436.
4 Beattie, 1809 [1779].
5 Smith, *Wealth of Nations*, book one, chapter 2.
6 Smith, *Wealth of Nations*, Introduction.
7 Smith, *Wealth of Nations*, book one, chapter 8.
8 Smith, *Wealth of Nations*, book one, chapter 8.
9 Smith, *Wealth of Nations*, book four, chapter 5.
10 Smith, *Wealth of Nations*, book four, chapter 8.
11 Smith, *Wealth of Nations*, book four, chapter 9.
12 Smith, *Wealth of Nations*, book four, chapter 9.
13 Smith, *Wealth of Nations*, book one, chapter 9.

14 Kant, 1998 [1787/1781], Division 2, Book II, chapter one and chapter two.
15 Kant, 1951 [1790], Section 54.

Bibliography

Beattie, J. 1809 [1779]. "On Laughter, and Ludicrous Composition". In *Essays*, Volume 3. Philadelphia, PA: Hopkins and Earle.

Hazlitt, W. 2004 [1818]. "On Wit and Humor". In Geoffrey Keynes (ed.), *Selected Essays of William Hazlett 1778 to 1830*. Whitefish: Kessinger Publishing.

Kant, I. 1998 [1787/1781]. *Critique of Pure Reason*. Cambridge: Cambridge University Press.

Kant, I. 1951 [1790]. *Critique of Judgment*. New York: Free Press.

Murphy, P. 2017. "Design Research: Aesthetic Epistemology and Explanatory Knowledge". *She Ji: The Journal of Design, Economics and Innovation* 3, no. 2: 117–132.

Shakespeare, W. 1979 [1595/1596]. *A Midsummer Night's Dream*, ed. Harold F. Brooks. London: Methuen.

Smith, A. 1993 [1776]. *Wealth of Nations*. Oxford: Oxford University Press.

12 Romantic economies

Hierarchy and autarchy

Johann Georg Hamann and Immanuel Kant were contemporaries, friends, and philosophical jousters. They both lived in Königsberg, today the Russian enclave city of Kaliningrad that looks out across the Baltic Sea towards Sweden. Hamann was a witty critic of rationalism. He thought that the most important ways that we grasp the world work more like humor than reason. They are closer to enigmatic faith than to phenomenal knowledge. That is, they function more like holistic association than analytic separation. Hamann was a tormenter of unreconciled dualisms and dichotomies. Realism and idealism, faith and reason, ignorance and knowledge, the natural and the supernatural belong as much together as apart. Hamann was a defender of the *coincidentia oppositorum*, the reconciliation of contraries. This was the view that all opposites coincide in God, where the infinitely great and the infinitesimal coincide. What Kant hinted at in his treatment of the antinomies in *The Critique of Reason* Hamann made explicit in his *Metacritique on the Purism of Reason* (1784),[1] namely that the world, at least so far as it is an artefact of creation, is a function of the union of opposites.

That said, Hamann also stood at a philosophical crossroads. He tapped into the long history of the epistemology of the *coincidentia oppositorum*.[2] Yet his work also pointed in another, very different direction: towards romanticism, historicism, and linguistic-nationalism. This begins with Hamann's proposition that language precedes reason. This is not the notion that the imagination complements reason. Rather, it is the idea that language is superior to reason, that it precedes it in importance. That's the core of his criticism of rationalism. Contrary to claims of the universality of reason and logic, Hamann suggested that words have meaning only in the context of a specific time and place. In *Aesthetica in nuce* he proposes that 'poetry is the mother-tongue of the human race, as the garden is older than the ploughed field; painting, than writing; song, than declamation; parables, than logical deduction; barter, than commerce.'[3] This is Continental romanticism *in nuce*. It is a search for an aesthetic origin that is superior to logic and reason. It also anticipates Nietzsche's post-modern trans-valuation of all modern values, Martin Heidegger's transposition of death over life, nature over technology, nearness over distance, finiteness over infinity, and Jacques Derrida's inversion of writing over speech, margins over the center, and so forth.

Metaphor and simile are models of the act of creation. Shakespeare's dogs of war and the winter of our discontent illustrate the fusion of contraries in language. The greater the distance between the terms, the more powerful the metaphor. As soon as rationalism's hierarchy of logic over poetry is inverted for the hierarchy of poetry over logic, simile over conclusion – a procedure that is starkly different from that of the *coincidentia oppositorum* – almost without realizing it we enter an alternate intellectual universe.

Hamann's student, Johann Gottfried Herder, exemplifies this. He emphasized the allegorical, metaphorical, and symbolic – that is, the poetic – structure of archaic myth and legend. But what ends up being important is less the poetics or the moment of archaic origin or even the counter-position of poetry *to* logic but rather the inverted hierarchy of poetry *over* logic. Late in life, Hamann criticized his friend Kant's essay 'What Is Enlightenment?'. Kant spoke of enlightenment as 'the departure of human beings from their self-incurred incapacity', which later became an influential definition. Hamann responded by replacing the word 'incapacity' with 'domination'. What being unenlightened means is not a failure to 'think for yourself' (much as the Calvinists had said, 'read it for yourself') but rather the domination of a knowledge class – namely, the party of logic – that considers itself more rational than others and in possession of a truth that others lack.

The more skeptical view is that the party of poetry is no less supercilious than the party of logic. Both have their own presumptive intellectual hierarchies. Each is the mirror image of the other. This is in effect far removed from the ironies and paradoxes of Mandeville and Smith – and just as far removed as barter is from trade. As these currents diverged, what emerges is a conspicuously different kind of irony: not the kind born of Mandeville's satire but rather romantic irony. The kind of irony that suffuses Smith and Mandeville's works operates to create a distance from the self. It casts a skeptical eye on what we unthinkingly think the self is, such that under certain conditions our vices may turn out to be virtues and our virtues vices. This is the kind of self that (to an extent) is enigmatic, a mystery of sorts, a riddle, a puzzle, a conundrum.[4] Romantic irony in contrast is the product not of a skeptical distance from the self but rather of intensified self-consciousness.

For the German philosopher Johann Fichte, the source of the self was the self's self-consciousness – not just the self's awareness of itself or even its self-conscious awareness of itself but rather a hyper self-consciousness. This is the crucible of romantic irony – the self that is fixated on the self, interrogating 'who am I, who are we?' The larger significance of this is that the Romantic image of the ardently 'self-conscious self' became a model for all kinds of human behavior and institutions. It encouraged the idea of the state as an intensely self-conscious formation – obsessed, even militantly obsessed, with its own origins, history, language, and culture. This produced a specific kind of political economy. It was mercantilist, statist, willful, protectionist, closed, closely supervised, and minutely regulated. It eventually mutated into a command economy that is embedded in a totalitarian society – the almost complete antithesis of Smith and Mandeville's economy of paradox.

The difference between the two types of political economy in part lies in competing theories of creation. Hamann was right. Logic is not enough. We can do many interesting things with reason. Take one simple example. We can make inferences from the number of housing approvals: if these decline sharply, we can infer that the housing market is declining. That is a very useful thing to know but the logic we use to do that does not drive, let alone create, the market or the housing industry or the cycles of buying and selling or cycles of technology, and so on. Animation and creation are poetical not logical. There are two notably influential modern theories of creation: one is the *paradoxical union of contraries*. The other is the *hierarchical inversion of contraries*. The former is happy to wryly blend poetics *and* logics. The latter wants in various ways to have poetics rule *over* logic.

At a deeper level the difference in political economies is bound up in the divergent nature of the word-forming element *auto-*, meaning 'self, one's own, by oneself' from the Greek *auto-*, meaning self, same, directed from within, and spontaneous. The Greek root appears in many contemporary English-language words: automatic, autocratic, autochthonous, and autodidactic, to name a few. Two distinct kinds of modern society both have *auto-* as their prefix. Yet the two have little in common. One is the autonomous society; the other is the autarchic society. One is self-organizing; the other is self-ruling. What's the difference? The first assumes self-organizing systems: nuclear households, markets, industries, cities, and publics. Autarchic societies are different from autonomous societies. If we think of the phrase 'directed from within', the autonomous society works on its own, anonymously, forming and reforming intelligible patterns. In the case of the former, the autarchic society, 'directed from within' means conscious direction using commands or rules to reach targets.

Unhappy in paradise

Modern prosperity is puzzling. Why do so many people who benefit from it oppose it? Why have they done that not just today but over the past two centuries? The world has never had it so good. So why does a third of humanity routinely detest modernity's prodigious prosperity? The disaffected despise world trade, market efficiency, and industrial productivity. In varying degrees, they hate these: not least intellectuals – 95 percent of them loath the remarkable achievement of the past two centuries. As prosperity has grown, so have the 'isms' opposed to its beneficial mix of merchants, metropolises, and machines.

The opposition begins with romanticism. It is soon followed by laborism, socialism, populism, nationalism, vitalism, fascism, and totalitarianism. Modern autonomous societies have produced massive gains in per capita GDP, wealth, and income. The counter-movements have devoted untold energies to undoing this. Millions of people who benefit everyday from prosperity wish to end it. This is a very puzzling thing.

While human happiness has expanded dramatically in the past two centuries, in ways that were inconceivable to previous millennia, happiness has been matched by a wellspring of brooding discontent. For many, prosperity has proved to be unbearable. For those persons, all is not right in paradise. Rising standards of living often have been met not with jubilation but with dissatisfaction and disaffection.

Why do so many people end up being so masochistically dissatisfied with an economic and social system that produces so much human happiness? Consider how human beings across the eons of unprosperous times organized their societies. Bands, tribes, monarchies, aristocracies, feudal relationships, and patrimonial states were the norm. These were organized around personal ties, hierarchies, extended kinship systems, communal family structures, statuses, and rank orders. Even today, a large minority of people, often unconsciously, feel that this kind of structure is 'natural'. It communicates an image of personalized warmth and care along with the apparent security of being a step in a hierarchy. The image of hierarchy is anchored in nature. Hierarchy is a common organizing principle of nature. But so also is symmetry, ratio, proportionality, rhythm, fractal scaling, and so on.

One of the difficulties that a lot of persons have, even after two centuries of remarkable human development, is that many individuals just want to interact with 150 people, the largest number of personal connections that typically a human being can have.[5] Axiomodernity in part is a world of strangers. There are many zones of intimacy but also numerous spheres where persons interact with those they do not know, have never previously met, nor will ever meet. What interacting with 150 people promises is warmth, empathy, and personal contact even if the reality of such a limited scale of interactions may be toxic, claustrophobic, and demeaning.

It's not so surprising then that, in spite of the epic spread of modern markets, cities and industries along with the dramatic increase in living standards across the world, a majority of countries still have neo-patrimonial, client-patron, kin-based, clan-anchored, and tribe-like social structures with influential status power systems based on personal connections. Most still focus on pooling rather than production. Where this prevails, the rule of law is weak and everyday life is marked by high levels of violence.

Where functional societies have become most deeply rooted, it is notable that in these societies numerous 'isms' have emerged to cater to society's latent hostilities to modern industrial and urban civilization. These 'isms' promise individuals a 'warm' community in place of a 'cold' society. Militancy is idolized in preference to industry. Status is eulogized in place of contract. Rural life is venerated in contrast to urban life. Most 'isms' do not prescribe a literal return to the archaic past. Even so, in the past two centuries a surprising number of them have exhibited some pretty extreme back-to-the-earth and *völkisch* tendencies.

Romantic nature worship – a mix of pantheism and Gnosticism – is never far from the surface of modern societies. Its attractions evolve with time. A century ago in Europe it was the promise of living close to the cleansing spring waters of the burbling brook among the happy smiling peasant farmers in harmony with nature away from the dirty overcrowded city teeming with 'alienated' factory workers and middle-class 'philistines'. Today semi-rural or provincial rust-belt industries are sanctified in opposition to urbanized high-tech industries. How little things change. The Agriculturalists (the School of Agrarianism) was one of the contending schools of thought that preceded the rise of China's Legalist Qin dynasty (221 BCE). Society, it believed, was based on the propensity to farm. It argued, as do all modern egalitarian movements, against the division of labor and for the kind of economic self-sufficiency that is found in segmental-type societies.

The same kind of argument was made by the philosopher Jean-Jacques Rousseau. His first objection was to artifice. For Rousseau modernity's material civilization enslaved rather than liberated. Its refinements were corruptions. They degraded human goodness. Goodness, Rousseau argued, is the preserve of 'simple men'. Among the happiest people in the world were 'bands of peasants regulating the affairs of state under an oak tree'.[6] The simple guileless peasants in unison created a 'general will' that was wise. In contrast modern 'refined nations' were both 'illustrious and wretched'. Rousseau was influential. What he began branched in several different directions. No matter how it cleft, its underlying complaint was always the same. Modern prosperity – and its core mix of capitalism, industrialization, urbanization, and materialism – is the cause of spiritual ills. These strip life of 'meaning'. Prosperous modernity is disenchanting. It destroys 'meaning' because it is inauthentic. It has no purity. It lacks originality. It is tainted by admixtures. Because it is not first, unpolluted, unique, indigenous, or simple, it lacks validity.

Fichte extended Rousseau's vision of romanticism. He did so in part in response to Napoleon's effort to create a Continental French imperial superstate. In his later years, Fichte's concern was to see the creation of a German nation. Echoing Hamann and Herder, Fichte thought that a people was formed by language. A nation was a poetic creation. Accordingly, the German nation-state was co-extensive with German speakers. And because German was a literary language, the German-speaking people was special. Still more special was their history. That history symbolized, Fichte thought, the self-determination of a national super-ego.

Fichte built a philosophical system around the concept of the absolute ego.[7] His notion of the state echoed this idea.[8] He imagined the nation as a self-contained super-subject – a super-ego. God was expunged from this concept of the state. There was no place in it for natural law or even the divine right of kings. God was replaced by the nation conceived as a divine super-subject. Self-determination meant a nation free from external forces. For Fichte the primordial resistance of German tribes to the Roman Empire was the original model of national self-determination.[9] From the self-determination of the national super-subject emerged a divine people. The symbol of permanence and eternal life previously had been God. Now the divine people took the place of God. Ordinary selves were emanations of the national super-ego. They gladly sacrificed themselves for it.

The economic correlate of Fichte's national super-ego was a 'closed commercial state'. This entailed a state-managed economy insulated from external trade, diplomacy, and travel. Science and communication were partly exempted from this national solipsism but still regulated through state-funded institutions. The key to political-economic romanticism is the idea of a super-subject that is 'free'. Freedom means separating the nation from external forces – treaties, agreements, wars, markets, and industries – that it cannot control. Conversely, freedom means control. Complete freedom is complete control. In practice this is impossible to achieve.[10] So when unavoidable external pressures impinge on the national super-ego, feelings of persecution, suspicion, and paranoia spread. Fear, scapegoating, and conspiracy theories proliferate.

Fichte was a nationalist. Yet, like Rousseau, he was also a trans-nationalist. Rousseau proposed a federated European super-state that could legislate a 'common law' for all its members in order to secure 'a lasting peace between all the peoples of Europe'.[11] In effect this was the first model of what became in the twentieth century the European Union. Fichte argued that perpetual peace was only feasible if the component states of Rousseau's super-state were no longer economically competitive but rather had economies that were planned and self-sufficient. Perpetual peace could be attained if nations severely reduced relations with each other – restricting commercial, political, and intellectual interaction or regulating these through government agencies.[12]

Johann Herder, Fichte's older contemporary, thought that the world was made up of equally valid cultures. This is where the post-modern ideology of 'diversity' comes from. Each culture is the collective mind of a group that has a common language, literature, tradition, experience, history, and memory. Each culture is separate and distinct. There is no 'chemistry' that can bond them together. In the pan-national version of this, a single hermetic culture is the basis of a super-state that incorporates multiple states. The classic example was the German-speaking principalities that were amalgamated in the nineteenth-century German Wilhelmine Empire.[13] This state fused Herder's idea of an immaculate culture and history with a Fichte-style tariff-protected, regulated economy symbolized by the technique of amalgamating German-speaking states around a custom's union (*zollverein*) – a technique used again in the creation of the trans-national European Union.

Super-state nationalism was reconfigured as a kind of super-state trans-nationalism by the philosopher Friedrich Nietzsche.[14] The model for this was Friedrich II, the thirteen-century Holy Roman emperor. Nietzsche was an anti-romantic romantic.[15] He regarded nationalism – cultural, racial, or pan-German – as a neurotic sickness.[16] He proposed instead a European Union.[17] But there was a catch. The original Central European multinational super-state was the Holy Roman Empire. It was in need of updating, for Napoleon had abolished the old empire and created by conquest his own European Empire (1804–1814), roughly the scale of the Holy Roman Empire at its height. Nietzsche eulogized Friedrich II and declared that God was dead.[18] Out this strange crucible emerged the idea of a trans-national super-state deferential not to God but to a class of Supermen – inspired, Nietzsche said, by 'aristocratic commonwealths' like Venice.[19] This echoed Fichte's root concept, the super-subject or super-ego, which similarly had replaced God. The Nazi Reich (1933–1945) pushed this in a totalitarian direction. Just six years later, the search for a continental super-state began yet again, this time with the creation of the European Steel and Coal Community in 1951, the first institutional step toward a European Union.

Romantic economy

As the romantic idea of the nation came into wide circulation, so did the modern anti-romantic conception of the nation. Its outlook is stoical. Its people are 'hardy'.[20] The latter don't deny external determination. Rather, they adroitly adjust to it. They face external forces with thrift, industry, discipline, work, enterprise, grit, and persistence. The hardy nation, like the romantic nation, is a collective subject. But unlike the romantic nation, the hardy nation is an unself-conscious subject.

Let us for the moment accept Fichte's equating of the state and the self. Human selves are purposeful beings. They have conscious aims that they strive for. They are also self-conscious about those aims. But peak human performance is unlike this. It does not obviate conscious purposeful striving but rather adds another dimension to it. Peak human achievement tends to be un-self-conscious. The model for this is the person who is absorbed in a task. Persons over time develop skills. This permits them rational mastery of the world. They can rationally organize means to achieve ends. But high performance adds a dimension, that of the complete absorption in a task. Absorption is post-rational.[21] It is a kind of letting-go of the self.[22] Such persons unify disparate often opposing forces, skills, and materials in an act of concentrated effort. Absorption is quietist. It shies away from noisy ideologies.

The letting-go of the self is reflected in a readiness to adapt to the pattern behavior of large-scale social systems, which are a little like machines in that, to a degree but only ever to a degree, they run automatically. In contrast a considerable number of modern political economies conceive of action as modelled on rational mastery – that is the purposeful achievement of ends. This is the idea that the state, as the nation's super-ego, can instruct, plan, and direct economic outcomes. Rational mastery on that scale is impossible and self-defeating. More simply, it doesn't work. Economic romanticism does something different. It aims not for rational mastery but rather irrational mastery. It equates freedom with control, that is, the mastery of social or economic outcomes. But the super-ego of the romantic state acts irrationally in the sense that the super-ego state behaves in ways that are narcissistic, vindictive, paranoid, aggressive, arrogant, conceited, demanding, and overconfident.

The national super-ego is a type of glorified self.[23] As a collective entity, it is intensely self-conscious. It constantly appraises itself in grandiose ways. Its metaphoric head is swollen with self-attributed virtues. Its admiration for itself is inflated and ostentatious yet also anxious and insecure for it can never match in reality its own claims of mastery and control. At the best of times control is an elusive human capacity. The mix of inflated ego and insecurity leads to a condition where rivals cannot be tolerated. They have to be eliminated. The super-ego must triumph over competitors. Rivalry is *either/or* not *both/and*. In parallel with this, the economic focus on efficiency turns to a focus on self-sufficiency. The underlying implication of this is that in some way the economic division of labor is dispensable even if only at a global level in the intercourse between nations. The super-ego both seeks to triumph over rivals and retreat into isolation from rivals. The super-ego state readily and loudly criticizes other nations but is super-sensitive to any criticism made of it.

If we think of nations as lying on a spectrum, the hardy adaptive nation sits at one end of the spectrum, the romantic self-determining nation at the other end. There are many points in between. One of the things that distinguishes a hardy nation is that a hardy nation is not self-fixated. It has needs and interests, purposes and aims, but it pursues these functionally rather than psychologically. The motto of a functional society is '*does it work?*' Its truth is pragmatic. Its deeper truth – that which underpins exceptional societies that achieve high levels of prosperity – is its capacity to act on and assimilate forms and patterns, absorbing these on a large scale and finding interesting 'purposeless purposeful' ways of working, acting, and organizing human effort.

The Faustian economy

Fichte's idea of a closed economy generated several future political economies. The severest of these was the mid-twentieth century model of the totalitarian economy. Totalitarian societies had command economies that were owned, managed, directed, and 'planned' by the state. These were to a high degree autarchic and insulated from the global economy. Totalitarianism though is not the only form of political-economic romanticism. A second notable kind is the Faustian economic model. Among the most influential arguments for a Faustian economy was Oswald Spengler's *Decline of the West* (1918–1922). In Spengler's case, the 'West' meant a gothic 'German-Roman' Middle European culture.

Spengler thought this gothic culture had originally emerged in the 1100s along with the Holy Roman Empire – the original model of so much Continental territorial European politics.[24] This was the hook around which he developed a cultural hierarchy. In the 'West' the country 'gentleman' was superior to the 'parasitic' city dweller. Likewise, the provinces were superior to world-cities and culture was superior to civilization. To that point Spengler's argument recapitulates a fairly conventional style of agrarian romanticism. There have been to date in modernity numerous versions of this kind of romanticism, ranging from dreams of 'arts-and-craft' handicraft economies to anti-urban Catholic 'back to the land' movements to anti-industrial and de-industrializing 'green' economies replete with animistic forms of wind and solar power. But as well as these kinds of earthy tellurian semi-agrarian romanticisms there are also forms of industrial romanticism, a kind of romantic Prometheanism.

Spengler paid obeisance to telluric romanticisms but also reflected the reality that earth-and-land romanticism was an ever-receding prospect in modernity. So Spengler, the thinker who ranked the country higher than the city and culture higher than civilization, also proposed that Faustian becoming was superior to being, and measurelessness was superior to form and boundaries. Provincialism and boundlessness in a tense ungainly merger typify a 'reactionary modernist' economy.[25] This is an economy that is industrially or perhaps more precisely military-industrially propulsive with a large authoritarian state founded on a society that is urbanizing and an economy composed of large firms, cartels, and monopolies. This molten mix coexisted in early twentieth-century Germany along with persistent agrarian romanticisms and fears of the diseases of 'civilization', literal and figurative.[26]

Germany's urban population grew from 10 percent in 1850 to 28 percent in 1890. In many respects it was the pre-eminent science nation of the second half of the nineteenth-century. It made significant industrial applications of that science. Yet it pursued industrialization and urbanization with reservation. The German sociologist and economist Werner Sombart epitomized the conflict in the German soul between the industrial behemoth and the pre-industrial *volksgemeinschaft*.[27] He observed the industrial proletarian, as if in mourning. '[Like] all city people [the proletarian] distinguishes himself from the earth-bound, rooted, child of the land through the predominance of the understanding over the feeling and instinctual faculties' (*Das Proletariat*, 1906). Yet Sombart didn't straightforwardly reject industrial-scientific abstraction in favor of fantasy or its utility in favor of a rooted nature. Rather he distinguished between the good 'entrepreneur' and the bad 'trader'. The former had the faculty of 'quick perception' and 'sharp judgment' while the latter 'calculates everything in terms of money' (*Das Bourgeois*, 1913). Objection to such calculation characterized opposition to finance capitalism, the financialization of modern economies, and the abstractions of interest rates ('usury').[28] This view was encapsulated in widespread social antipathy to 'Jewish capitalism'.[29]

Pattern behavior, which is to say the abstract nature of an axiomodern economy, came under intense pressure. This feeling expressed itself in many ways, not just in racial antipathy, but also in preferences for the business 'house' rather than the business 'firm', for the conduct of face-to-face business rather than the abstractions of markets filled with strangers, and for movements of aristocratic militancy and aesthetic decadence in preference to rational mastery.[30] 'America' was a symbol of individualism and unalloyed competition. The 'Slavonic East' represented an economy and society of serf-like morbid dependency. 'Germany' symbolized an economy in which the revolutionary energy of industrialism might be (somehow) squared with extended-family domesticity and the warmth of community. Personal relations might be fastened together with impersonal systems. The old warehouse economy might continue amidst the new factory economy. Nineteenth and early-twentieth century German political-economic aspirations walked uneasily between these polarities without ever reconciling them, which the country's eventual mid-twentieth century slide into totalitarianism confirmed.

In the middle of all of this was the kind of rational mastery promised by Enlightenment liberalism. It offered the prospect that the German-Lutheran work ethic would prevail over the romantic economy of the socialists and the reactionaries, and its diligence, perfectionism, and pervading sense of duty at work would prove more compelling than the Stoic-Epicurean detachment and distance of those drawn to the wry-cosmopolitan or abstract-national ambience of large-scale markets, publics, cities, and industries and their impersonal forces and enveloping oscillations.[31] It was expected that the 'social political' policy of a large Bismarckian welfare state would obviate the waves of laborism, socialism, populism, nationalism, vitalism, fascism, and totalitarianism that kept welling up from the roots of romanticism. None of these prospects came true.

While German political economy in the first half of the twentieth century was not agrarian or segmental in a Rousseauist or Maoist sense, it was earth-fixated and anti-thalassic in Carl Schmitt's sense.[32] The liberal-Enlightenment promise of diligent rational mastery was not sufficient to avert the attraction of a transnational-linguistic culture with racial overtones and expressive of a collective preference for authenticity over artificiality. Unlike agrarian romanticisms, Germany's Faustian economy did not react against the division of labor but rather against civilization and in favor of culture. Accordingly, Germany fought World War I in the name of 'German culture' against 'French civilization'.

The Faustian imperatives of becoming and boundlessness fed an impulse to recreate an empire that was as expansive as the old 'German-Roman' West. The result was the disaster of World War I and the even greater disaster of World War II. Eventually, at enormous cost, romantic culture lost its battle against material civilization. Yet the appetite for a political economy of control was not sated. Twice, 'war economies' had been mobilized in pursuit of the goals of Faustian industrialism, Continental empire, and some kind of authentic earth-bound culture. The failure of this stimulated a drive toward another political economy, less Faustian yet still motivated by the search for economic and social control as an alternative to axiomodernity and its political economy of patterns, paradoxes, cycles, and ratios. Out of the ashes of economic romanticism and totalitarianism, post-war Germany pivoted back to the idea of an economy based on the Enlightenment conception of knowledge and its derivations, including the ideas of expertise, management, direction, and specialization. Even so by 1980 yet another romantic social current emerged: green parliamentary and lobby politics with a strong undercurrent of pantheism, Gnosticism, and millenarianism attractive to about 10 percent of the voting population.

Protectionism

Over the course of time, there have been many variants of the romantic 'closed commercial state'. The most strident ones were the totalitarian states: Nazi Germany, the Soviet Union, and Maoist China prominent among them. These mixed high degrees of economic autarchy with a centralized politicized command economy and various kinds of economic 'planning'. Milder versions of romantic economics resorted to techniques such as high tariff walls, the cessation of immigration intakes, the nationalization of industry, and de-industrialization.

A classic example of diluted romanticism is the influential theory of 'national economics' developed by the German economist and sometime American resident Friedrich List. In *The National System of Political Economy* (1841), List combined a neo-romantic policy of high tariffs with the promise of Faustian industrialism. That mix echoed two related views. One was that of Alexander Hamilton, America's first secretary of treasury, who argued in his *Report on Manufactures* (1791) for high tariffs in order to encourage the development of infant industries. The second was Henry Clay's *American System* speeches (1832), a public policy system that interwove tariffs to promote industries, a national bank to support commerce, and federal government subsidies for transport infrastructure ('internal improvements' – roads and canals) designed to take agricultural products to distant markets.

Hamilton's, Clay's, and List's economic protectionism promised a blend of national greatness, economic prosperity, and industrial innovation. In the case of the United States, the average tariff rate on *all* imports rose to over 50 percent in the 1820s (the Tariff of Abominations, 1828), falling to 15 percent in the 1850s, rising to 50 percent during the Civil War of the 1860s, falling to 7 percent in the 1920s, rising to 20 percent in the early 1930s, falling to 6 percent in the 1950s and 2 percent in the 2000s. A regime of low tariffs worldwide, sanctioned by the 1948 General Agreement on Tariffs and Trade (GATT), accompanied the rapid, unprecedented and generalized growth in global prosperity after 1950. In 1950, the average per capita wealth of all countries with reliable records was US\$3,767 in constant 2011 dollars. In 2016, it was US\$18,958. As prosperity increased the trend was for tariffs to decrease. Average global tariff levels declined from an estimated 22 percent in 1947 to 4 percent in 1999.[33] To an extent, other protectionist measures replaced tariffs – including regulatory barriers to trade and the subsidization of domestic producers by the state. But the long-term trend did not favor protectionism and was hostile to neo-romanticism.

Yet, economic romanticism has remained a persistent thread in modern life. Underlying it is a distinct discomfort with axiomodernity. There are three sources of this. One is the dream of a beatific-agrarian or earth-rooted society living close to nature. The second is the feeling that 'society is bad'. Rousseau invoked the latter feeling when he said that man was born free but everywhere is in chains. The third is the idea that economic Prometheanism can be reconciled with economic Sentimentalism.

A huge tension is repeatedly played out even within romantic currents in modernity between the power of industrialism and sentimental objections to it. A classic example of this schizoid view is Karl Marx and Friedrich Engels's 1848 *Communist Manifesto*. In a romantic-Promethean manner they hymn capitalism's development of productive forces, condemn capitalism, hymn proletarian trans-nationalism, and offer a Fichte-like program for state control of capital. 'The bourgeoisie, during its rule of scarce one hundred years, has created more massive and more colossal productive forces than have all preceding generations together,' relished Marx and Engels.

> Subjection of Nature's forces to man, machinery, application of chemistry to industry and agriculture, steam-navigation, railways, electric telegraphs, clearing of whole continents for cultivation, canalization of rivers, whole populations conjured out of the ground – what earlier century had even a presentiment that such productive forces slumbered in the lap of social labor?

Indeed so. Yet for all its world-transforming power this Faustian industrialism came with periodic crises (namely, the business cycle) that Marx and Engels decried. They believed that as capital accumulated the lot of labor necessarily grew worse. In reality, it didn't: quite the contrary. But for a significant and influential minority of persons the myth of immiseration was more compelling than the reality of generalized prosperity.

Notes

1 This was a criticism of Kant's *Critique*. It was unpublished though it circulated in Hamann's life-time.
2 On that history, see Murphy, 2001.
3 Hamann, 2007, 63.
4 Murphy, 2009, 225–236.
5 Dunbar, 1998, 77.
6 As long as 'several men assembled together consider themselves as a single body' then they have only 'one will' directed towards their 'common preservation and general well-being'. That being the case then all the animating forces of the state will be 'vigorous and simple' and its principles 'clear and luminous'. There will be no incompatible or conflicting interests. The common good will be manifest. Rousseau, *The Social Contract*, book IV, chapter 1, paragraphs 1 and 2.
7 Fichte, 1982.
8 Fichte, 2012, 2013.
9 In Rousseau and Fichte – and far beyond – culture is the antidote to civilization. The French aristocrat Arthur de Gobineau and the British-German Wagnerite Houston Stewart Chamberlain were among many for whom the numerous social anxieties triggered by modern dynamic economies were placated by culture. For them, culture was the work of superior races. In Oswald Spengler, in contrast, culture is something provincial. It is rooted. Where civilization is moored to the non-provincial world city, culture is anchored in peasant-like wisdom. It 'grows' while civilization only 'expands'. Civilization is bourgeois rather than aristocratic, nomadic rather than dynastic, outwardly focused rather than inwardly facing. Culture produces meaning and enchantment. Civilization produces alienation and disenchantment.

10 In his more philosophical mode in *The Science of Knowledge*, Fichte understood that while the source of all reality is the absolute self, the absolute ego also creates the 'not-self' – a reality that in some sense must check or limit the absolute self's self-determination. Such a reality-check might apply by analogy to the closed commercial state, except that the 'non-self' lies outside the national super-ego – in the form of other states. The philosophical delusion that the self-determining subject is both limitless and limited by virtue of its own activity neatly encapsulates the ruin of all post-colonial failed states that got drunk on the wine of national self-determination after Word War II.

11 Rousseau imagined 'a form of federal Government as shall unite nations by bonds similar to those which already unite their individual members, and place the one no less than the other under the authority of the Law. . . . [This form of Government would combine] the advantages of the small and the large State, because it is powerful enough to hold its neighbors in awe, because it upholds the supremacy of the Law, because it is the only force capable of holding the subject, the ruler, the foreigner equally in check.' He further argued that 'the Federation must embrace all the important Powers in its membership; it must have a Legislative Body, with powers to pass laws and ordinances binding upon all its members; it must have a coercive force capable of compelling every State to obey its common resolves whether in the way of command or of prohibition; finally, it must be strong and firm enough to make it impossible for any member to withdraw at his own pleasure the moment he conceives his private interest to clash with that of the whole body.' Jean-Jacques Rousseau (1756).

12 Fichte, 2012.

13 The national unification of German speakers left four problems. First, what to do with those who didn't speak German as a first language? That is, the significant number of Poles, Sorbs, and Danes in German principalities. Then, what to do with German speakers who also had a parallel experience, tradition, history, and memory – namely, German Jews? Third, what to do with German-speaking provinces that identified with France and French Catholic culture, for example, Bavaria. Fourth, what to do with the German speakers who headed a multinational Empire, the Austro-Hungarian Empire, and were uninterested in German unification? Nazism provided answers to all the these questions. It slotted the Poles and Sorbs into a racial hierarchy that treated Slavs as an inferior race. It conquered Denmark. It exterminated the Jews. It occupied Austria and Hungary.

14 Middle European pan-nationalism is represented by the Wilhelmine German Empire (1871–1918) and later the Nazi Third Reich.

15 About the Romantic composer Richard Wagner, whom he had known well, Nietzsche observed, 'He is one of the late French romanticists, that high-soaring and heaven-aspiring band of artists, like Delacroix and Berlioz, who in their inmost nacres are sick and incurable.' *Ecce Homo: How One Becomes What One Is* (1888). Yet even while Nietzsche castigated romanticism, he created his own steely version of it.

16 'Nationalism, this national neurosis from which Europe is sick.' *Ecce Homo* (1888).

17 'That great free spirit, that genius among German emperors, Frederick II.' *The Anti-Christ* (1895).

18 'God is dead; but given the way of men, there may still be caves for thousands of years in which his shadow will be shown. – And we – we still have to vanquish his shadow, too'; 'God is dead! God remains dead! And we have killed him. How shall we comfort ourselves, the murderers of all murderers?' *The Gay Science* (1882).

19 'Man is something that shall be overcome. Man is a rope, tied between beast and super-man – a rope over an abyss. What is great in man is that he is a bridge and not an end.' *Thus Spoke Zarathustra* (1883). 'Those large hothouses [*Treibhäuser*] for the strong, for the strongest kind of human being that has ever been, the aristocratic commonwealths of the type of Rome or Venice, understood freedom exactly in the sense in which I understand the word freedom: as something one has and does not have, something one wants, something one conquers.' *Twilight of the Idols* (1888).

20 This is the term used by the Singaporean statesman Lee Kuan Yew. See, for example, Lee, 1965a and 1965b.

21 Heller, 1985, 203–250.

22 John Carroll (2008, 37–42) characterizes this as the point where the human soul over-determines the mentality and actions of the ego. He introduces a Zen model of the human personality to explain this. There is the ego with its normal range of ambitions, goals, and interests. The ego acts by controlling and dominating things. The soul behaves differently. Its modus operandi are persistence (sticking at things), focus, dedication, and the capacity to step out of oneself and lose oneself in the objective law of the activity (the vocation) that one is pursuing. The strong soul insists to the ego that good work is the result not of ego's free will and self-determination but rather of the necessity of things. Persistence, focus, dedication, and letting-go of the self's egoism culminates in grace. Grace is the balanced fusion of mind, body, and external environment. The grace-ful person acts with poise, skating and weaving through all kinds of opposing forces and creating a balance between them. Success is not the result of a proud dominating ego but rather the soul's 'expansive embrace of the greater all'.

23 The national super-ego has parallels in individual psychology. A good description of the grandiose self in pursuit of expansive mastery is provided by Karen Horney, 1950, 187–213.

24 Spengler, 1991 [1926, 1918].

25 Herf, 1984.

26 The German philosopher and neo-pagan Ludwig Klages in his *Man and Earth* speech (1913) declared: 'Progress is devastating forests, exterminating animal species, extinguish-ing native cultures, masking and distorting the pristine landscape with the varnish of industrialism, and debasing the organic life that still survives.'

27 Sombart, 2017 [2001].

28 The Austrian-born Marxist and German finance minister Rudolph Hilferding in *Das Finanzkapital* (1910) distinguished between classic-liberal merchant entrepreneurial cap-italism and bank-financed large corporate, cartel, and monopolistic forms of industrial capitalism, a.k.a. 'finance capitalism'. Progressive-era American intellectuals displayed a similar animus to finance though with markedly less practical effect. See, for example, Thorstein Veblen in *Theory of Business Enterprise* (2017 [1978/1904]).

29 The German economist Gottfried Feder inspired Hitler in 1919 with a call for the 'breaking of interest slavery'.

30 On this and what follows immediately, see Doidge, 2019, 13–73.

31 On the roots of the Stoic-Epicurean synthesis, see Heller, 1978 [1967].

32 Murphy, 2017, 130–145.

33 Bown and Irwin, 2015.

Bibliography

Bown, C. and Irwin, D. 2015. "The Urban Legend: Pre-GATT Tariffs of 40%". *Vox CEPR Policy Portal*, December 19.

Carroll, J. 2008. *Ego and Soul: The Modern West in Search of Meaning*. Melbourne: Scribe.

Doidge, S. 2019. *The Anxiety of Ascent: Middle-Class Narratives in Germany and America*. Abing-don: Routledge.

Dunbar, R. 1998. *Grooming, Gossip, and the Evolution of Language*. Cambridge, MA: Harvard University Press.

Fichte, J.G. 2013 [1808]. *Addresses to the German Nation*. Indianapolis, IN: Hackett Publishing.

Fichte, J.G. 2012 [1800]. *The Closed Commercial State*. New York: SUNY Press.

Fichte, J.G. 1982 [1802, 1794–1795]. *The Science of Knowledge*. Cambridge: Cambridge University Press.

Hamann, G. 2007. *Writings on Philosophy and Language* (ed.) K. Haynes. Cambridge: Cambridge University Press.

Heller, A. 1985. *The Power of Shame: A Rational Perspective*. London: Routledge and Kegan Paul.

Heller, A. 1978 [1967]. *Renaissance Man*. London: Routledge and Kegan Paul.

Herf, J. 1984. *Reactionary Modernism: Technology, Culture, and Politics in Weimar and the Third Reich*. Cambridge: Cambridge University Press.

Horney, K. 1950. *Neurosis and Human Growth*. New York: Norton.

Lee, K. Y. 1965a. *Speech to Students of Canterbury University*. Christchurch, New Zealand, March 15.

Lee, K. Y. 1965b. *Proceedings*. Political Study Centre, Goodwill Hill, Singapore, April 15.

Murphy, P. 2017. "Land Versus Sea". *Thesis Eleven: Critical Theory and Historical Sociology* 142: 130–145.

Murphy, P. 2009. "I Am Not What I Am: Paradox and Indirect Communication, or the Case of the Comic God and the Dramaturgical Self". *Empedocles: European Journal for the Philosophy of Communication* 1, no. 2: 225–236.

Murphy, P. 2001. *Civic Justice: From Ancient Greece to the Modern World*. Amherst, NY: Humanity Books.

Nietzsche, F. 1964 [1872–1888]. *The Complete Works of Friedrich Nietzsche*. New York: Russell and Russell.

Rousseau, J.J. 1968 [1762]. *The Social Contract*. Harmondsworth: Penguin.

Rousseau, J.J. 1917 [1756]. *A Lasting Peace through the Federation of Europe and the State of War*, trans. C. E. Vaughan. London: Constable.

Sombart, W. 2017 [2001]. *Economic Life in the Modern Age*, ed. N. Stehr and R. Grundmann. Abingdon: Routledge.

Spengler, O. 1991 [1926, 1918]. *The Decline of the West*. New York: Oxford University Press.

Veblen, T. 2017 [1978, 1904]. *The Theory of Business Enterprise*. Abingdon: Routledge.

13 Enlightenment economies

Scientific socialism

Axiomodernity has generated societies that are freer and more prosperous than any in the entirety of human history. Yet many of its denizens, perhaps as many as a third of them, feel that society is bad and has placed human beings in shackles. The disenchanted 'third' routinely turn to the state to break these restraints and free them – ironically by means of the manacles of organization, administrative regulation, and the age-old techniques of the state allocation of resources. The sentimental hope is to replace contract with community and function with status. The means to this end is organization. The mix of community and status is pursued by having procedural bureaucracies extend their control over economic and social processes. The state, the firm, and the organization stand in for community. They offer status hierarchies in place of lateral functions.

In successful societies, we see degrees of this ranging from the minimal and incidental to the quite extensive. But beyond a certain modest level, though, the administered economy and the managerial society is counterproductive. Status and function are like oil and water. In pure romanticism, de-industrialization or alternatively a dysfunctional nationalized industrialization dominates. The alternative aspiration following World War II was for a 'mixed economy'. It was promised that this would tap the deep vein of modern productivity yet offset it with administrative regulation, state allocation, and enterprise organization. The economies of Core Europe and the Nordic region today are examples of this mix. They combine high and at times claustrophobic levels of market regulation and the extensive state allocation of resources with elevated levels of industry (technology) innovation (Table 4.4).

These nations echo the preferences of an ageing Karl Marx working on *Capital* (1867). Marx's mature political economy was premised on the idea of a scientific socialism. This was not what the philosopher Karl Popper assumed it was: namely a science of immutable laws of history. Rather, it was a socialism that grew out of the fruits of science – and the application of science to economic production. Modern industry, Marx observed, made science 'a force of production distinct from labor'.[1] Machinery necessitated the substitution of 'natural forces for human force' and the 'conscious application of science instead of rule of thumb'. Including natural sciences in the process of production, 'modern industry raises the productiveness of labor to an extraordinary degree'. Marx didn't like the fact that machinery had turned the instruments of labor into an 'automaton' or that the skills of any operative could be acquired now in six months, nor did he like that the 'automatic factory' required the replacement of desultory work habits with work discipline. The 'mysteries' of trade guilds disappeared, as did handicrafts, the execution of production 'by the hand of man'. That said, Marx saw that the conscious and systematic application of natural-science-based production gave rise to useful effects. Technology discovered that the productive action of the human body, seemingly so complex, in fact could be reduced to a few simple motions.

The technical basis of modern industry, Marx observed, is 'revolutionary' compared with earlier modes of production that were 'conservative'. The result is that masses of capital and labor are 'incessantly' launched from one branch of production to another. Modern industry necessitates 'variation of labor, fluency of function [and the] universal mobility of labor'. Science and technology 'give capital' a 'power of expansion' independent of the 'magnitude' of the capital invested.[2] Indeed, some of that invested capital will be necessarily depreciated as the price of technologically driven expansion. It will lose its value.

Most important of all, Marx observes that the productivity difference between the English worker working with an automated system and the Chinese worker working with a handicraft wheel is immense.[3] Marx speaks of the factors of production being land, labor, capital . . . and science.[4] If we were to substitute 'innovation' for 'science' this is almost Schumpeter before Schumpeter.[5] Yet there is a 'but', for the ecstasies of science and the Faustian industrialism of an unlimited development of productive forces are confounded, in Marx's tortured view, by the agonies of the 'social character' of the 'capitalist form' of modern industry. The latter takes away labor's means of subsistence, makes the laborer superfluous, and generates misery and sacrifice, 'social anarchy' and 'social calamity'[6]: no mean feat. The worker is estranged from the intellectual potential of labor in the same proportion in which science is incorporated into the work process.

What does Marx recommend to fix this? Once you strip away his inflamed rhetoric, his salve is what later evolves into European Social Democracy.[7] First, there's education and training ('technical and agricultural schools'). Second, there's the admission of women and young adults (and also children) into the non-domestic workforce. Third, this process dissolves old family ties making way for 'a higher form of the family and of the relations between the sexes.' Fourth, there's the 'generalization of regulation' – transforming it from the 'exception law' into a law 'affecting social production as a whole'. Fifth, there's the science that industrialists pay for. Marx makes comments in passing in *Capital* on the English system of 'parish relief' for the poor but does not envisage the final plank of European social democracy: the welfare state.[8]

The older Marx's recipe of institutionalized schooling, non-discriminatory employment, the generalization of regulation, and a knowledge economy (i.e., subsidized science) is a formula that has echoed widely in modern progressive opinion. Advocacy of these measures increasingly dominated intellectual writing from 1880 onwards. Step by step, they were adopted into public policy and practice.

The knowledge economy

Nicolas of Condorcet in his *Sketch for a Historical Picture of the Progress of the Human Spirit* (1795) proposed that social evil – Rousseau's bad society – was the result of ignorance. Over time, an increasingly confident knowledge class – made up of educators, academics, technocrats, researchers, and policy makers – argued that it could conquer ignorance and spread knowledge, thereby bringing into reach Condorcet's anticipated perfect society. Yet the horizon of that utopia kept receding even as states increased taxation and spent more on education. The latter pleased the knowledge class, which extracted a high status from the increasingly widespread assumption that a lack of knowledge was the cause of economic and social evils. A familiar economic rhetoric developed: unemployment was the result of inadequate industrial training. Low wages were the consequence of not enough persons graduating from school or (later on) university. Large-scale institutionalized knowledge first took the form of tax-funded classrooms in the nineteenth century. In the twentieth century, it assumed the additional form of large routinized often grant-driven professionalized 'normal science' laboratories and the heavy subsidization by government of mass universities. As spending rose, the level of discovery in society flat-lined and the quality of science decreased.[9]

The knowledge economy classroom model originated in Norway in the 1740s. It was followed in quick succession by Fredrick the Great's Prussian system of tax-funded compulsory primary education in the 1760s, Horace Mann's state-funded 'normal school' movement in the United States in the 1840s, and China's normal schoolteacher training in the 1890s (Table 13.1). 'Normal'

Table 13.1 Public education, percentage of children aged 5–14 years enrolled in state primary schools

Nation	1830	1840	1850	1860	1870	1880	1890	1900	1910	1920	1930
Australia				45%	59%	88%	75%	85%	87%	85%	89%
Belgium					42%	37%	31%	35%	33%	75%	70%
Canada					82%	80%	82%	89%	88%	94%	96%
Denmark						46%	70%	71%	68%	64%	67%
Finland						6%	0%	18%	26%	40%	58%
France		39%	36%	41%	42%	54%	58%	62%	84%	56%	65%

(*Continued*)

Table 13.1 (Continued)

Nation	1830	1840	1850	1860	1870	1880	1890	1900	1910	1920	1930
Germany				71%		71%	74%	73%	72%	75%	69%
Italy				21%	26%	32%	35%	36%	42%	47%	56%
Japan					18%	30%	37%	50%	59%	60%	60%
Netherlands			41%	46%	49%	47%	45%	45%	43%	70%	78%
New Zealand					77%	65%	70%	76%	79%	77%	83%
Norway	68%	71%	64%	61%	60%	59%	63%	67%	68%	69%	71%
Prussia	68%	73%	72%	69%	71%	74%	76%	75%			
Sweden					58%	70%	68%	68%	69%	64%	77%
Switzerland					75%	75%	78%	72%	70%	71%	70%
United Kingdom				52%	55%	54%	64%	72%	72%	70%	74%
United States	54%		68%		77%	80%	85%	88%	89%	85%	83%

Source: Peter Lindert, *Growing Public Volume 1*, New York, Cambridge University Press, 2004, 91, Table 5.1, Students Enrolled in Primary Schools.

signified that instruction in behavioral norms had precedence over reading, writing, and mathematics.[10] Though it was advocated – and even proselytized – in the name of knowledge, 'normal' education was a tacit form of social engineering – and one that was a poor replacement for Calvin's *sola scriptura*, the book alone.[11] It was reading the book for yourself that made Guttenberg's technology revolution so important and that was the essential binding agent that glued the arts and sciences together with a modern market and industrial economy.

The creative economy

The creative economy model has its roots in the work of Henri de Saint-Simon (1760–1825). In *L'Industrie* (1817), Saint-Simon envisaged a society composed of industrious persons as opposed to lazy ones. At the heart of this society was a meritocratic hierarchy of scientists, industrialists, engineers, and managers. In *On Social Organization* (1825), Saint-Simon argued that those 'most fitted' to 'manage the affairs of the nation' were 'scientists, artists and industrialists'.[12] Basically the same idea was recycled by Richard Florida in his influential 2002 work *The Rise of the Creative Class*.[13]

Saint-Simon in 1825 saw French society as a pyramid. At the base of it were 'workers in their routine occupations'. The first layers above that base were 'the leaders of industrial enterprises, the scientists who improve the methods of manufacture and widen their application [and] the artists who give the stamp of good taste to all their products'.[14] That prefigures the image of the world of all subsequent models of a creative economy. As for the rest of French society in the 1820s? Saint-Simon described France's 'upper layers' as 'nothing but plaster' composed of useless courtiers, nobles, the idle rich, and 'the governing class from the prime minister to the humblest clerk'.

Saint-Simon's idea of a creative-engineering economy was re-stated during the American Progressive era by Thorstein Veblen. Veblen argued against
giving the leading role in business to financiers, reserving it instead to those
accomplished in the 'industrial arts', especially engineers. Veblen thought that
'the industrial arts' were at least as important as land, labor, and capital as a factor
of production.[15] He argued explicitly for the superiority of the engineers over
the price system. The industrial arts, he argued, enhance productivity. The spe-
cialized knowledge that they create is beyond the understanding of financiers.
Even the passably efficient management of industry requires this technological
knowledge.

Veblen fantasized that 'a self-selected but inclusive Soviet of technicians'
might one day 'take over the economic affairs of [America]'.[16] This was 1921.
The only condition was that they 'consistently and effectually take care of the
material welfare of the underlying population'. In short the obligation of industry and its technocracy was to create the productive forces that generate wealth
that pays for the welfare state. Veblen's preference resonates today in the high
status accorded to 'the engineers' by America's Silicon Valley technology industries and in the periodic arguments that are made against the financialization of
business. Yet in its actual workings the American model emphasizes markets and
industries in equal measure (Table 4.4).

The post-industrial economy

The generalized regulation of economy and society along with redistributive
state policies had numerous advocates during the nineteenth century and early
twentieth century. But neither policy was adopted to any great extent until the
second half of the twentieth century. The accelerated even aggressive growth of
the administrative state really only begins in the 1970s (Table 13.2). Similarly,
the redistributive state everywhere in 1930 is small (Table 13.3). By 1960, in

Table 13.2 Growth of the Australian administrative state, Commonwealth legislation and
regulation, 1970–2000

Year	Australia's population (millions)	Number of pages of regulations	Number of pages of regulation per million Australians	Number of pages of legislative Acts	Number of pages of legislation per million Australians
1970	12.5	900	72	850	68
1975	13.8	1,200	87	1,100	80
1980	14.6	1,200	82	1,900	130
1985	15.7	1,900	121	2,900	185
1990	17	1,900	112	3,000	176
1995	18	4,800	267	4,900	272
2000	19.1	4,300	225	5,600	293

Source: Michael Ronaldson, *Fighting Australia's Over-regulation*, Policy white paper, Australian Government Taskforce, 2005, Table: Volume of new Commonwealth Legislation and Regulations 1970–2000.

several major economies it had grown markedly. That was true in other cases by 1970 or 1980. The period 1960–1980 is the era of Promethean growth of public spending. At the mid-way point through those two decades, growth of the administrative state takes off.

Strikingly, neither the administrated economy nor the redistributive economy are effects of nineteenth-century socialism or twentieth-century progressivism, even though these political movements hitched their stars to the administrative and redistributive state. Rather, these two statist political economies are a consequence of the era of post-industrialization – as nations searched for alternatives to classic industrialization.

Marx observed that classic industrialism in the nineteenth century worked by replacing labor with machines and then later re-employing labor as adjuncts to machines. As industrial automation grew in sophistication, the latter stopped happening. Machines replaced labor. So new labor markets developed. One model of a new kind of labor market was public-sector employment. This type of employment was funded by the accelerating growth of the industrial arts. These multiplied productivity, whose fruits then were harvested by the state. A number of leading economies emerged in the 1960s that combined high levels of public-sector employment and high levels of public spending as a percentage of GDP. They faced a conundrum in the long term. High productivity generated large tax revenues that funded expansive public sectors whose productivity was low, thereby reducing the level of productivity in society and the capacity of the state to harvest the revenue to fund large public sectors.

The managerial economy

Regulation grew incrementally after 1930. But it came into its own as a Leviathan force in the 1970s. A typical case is Australia. In 1970, the number of pages of Commonwealth government regulation was 72 per million population. By 2000, it was 225 pages per million population (Table 13.2). The pattern was similar in America. In 1936, the number of pages of federal regulations was 20 per million, in 1970, 97 pages per million; in 2012, it was 253 per million.[17]

Rule by administrative rules is the fruit of the growth of the idea of management that took off in the 1930s. Management developed to service organizations that coordinate persons and resources using micro rules in place of orders and commands. Management systemized the practice. It uses a mix of rules, codes, procedures, and rule-based instructions and policies ('legal-rationalism') to coordinate, organize, and direct action. Government regulation applies the same model to the whole of society. It is as if society was a giant firm, which it is not.

A managerial economy is one that is permeated by microscopic instances of rules, protocols, orders, instructions, directives, directions, injunctions, requirements, exhortations, and authoritative requests. Few of these are world transforming in themselves. But cumulatively, as they expand in volume over time, they alter the nature and behavior of economy and society. They represent a distinctive methodology of control. These forms of control operate less on the macroscopic level of society than on its atomic level. The nature of this control is analytic rather than synthetic. It offers dominion by tiny rules, domination by protocols, and control by rulebooks, rubrics, and guidelines. Its authority is communicated not by command but by policy, not by law but by regulation. It operates less by instruction and more by rulings. It is more comfortable with executive decrees than with parliamentary statutes.

The welfare economy

Large welfare states are a product of the era that stretches from 1950 to 1980 (Table 13.3). Welfare, managed well and used modestly, reduces basic social risks and in so doing increases the readiness of persons to assume risk and engage in bolder economic behaviors. Conversely, too much welfare redistribution has

Table 13.3 Social spending on welfare, unemployment, pensions, health, and housing subsidies as a percentage of GDP, 1880–1995

	1880	1890	1900	1910	1920	1930	1960	1970	1980	1990	2000	2010	2015
Australia	–	–	–	1.12	1.66	2.11	7.39	7.37	10.3	13.1	18.3	16.6	18.5
Austria	–	–	–	–	–	1.2	15.88	18.9	21.9	23.1	25.7	27.6	27.7
Belgium	0.17	0.22	0.26	0.43	0.52	0.56	13.14	19.26	23.1	24.4	23.5	28.3	29.2
Canada	–	–	–	–	0.06	0.31	9.12	11.8	13.3	17.5	15.8	17.5	17.6
Denmark	0.96	1.11	1.41	1.75	2.71	3.11	12.26	19.13	20.3	21.9	23.8	28.6	29
Finland	0.66	0.76	0.78	0.9	0.85	2.97	8.81	13.56	17.7	23.3	22.6	27.3	30.4
France	0.46	0.54	0.57	0.81	0.64	1.05	13.42	16.68	20.1	24.3	27.6	31	32
Germany	0.5	0.53	0.59	–	–	4.82	18.1	19.53	21.8	21.4	25.4	25.9	24.9
Iceland	–	–	–	–	–	–	–	–	–	13.5	14.6	16.9	15.5
Ireland	–	–	–	–	–	3.74	8.7	11.89	15.7	16.8	13.2	24.6	15.5
Israel	–	–	–	–	–	–	–	–	–	–	16.2	15.4	15.5
Italy	–	–	–	–	–	0.08	13.1	16.94	17.4	20.7	22.7	27.1	28.5
Japan	0.05	0.11	0.17	0.18	0.18	0.21	4.05	5.72	10	10.9	15.4	21.3	21.9
Luxembourg	–	–	–	–	–	–	–	–	19.4	18.3	18.7	23.1	22.1
Netherlands	0.29	0.3	0.39	0.39	0.99	1.03	11.7	22.45	23.3	24	18.8	17.8	17.7
New Zealand	0.17	0.39	1.09	1.35	1.84	2.43	10.37	9.22	16.2	20.3	18.2	20.4	19.2
Norway	1.07	0.95	1.24	1.18	1.09	2.39	7.85	16.13	16.1	21.6	20.4	22	24.7
Slovenia	–	–	–	–	–	–	–	–	–	–	22	23.4	22.6
South Korea	–	–	–	–	–	–	–	–	–	2.7	4.5	8.2	10.2
Sweden	0.72	0.85	0.85	1.03	1.14	2.59	10.83	16.76	24.8	27.2	26.8	26.3	26.3
Switzerland	–	–	–	–	–	1.17	4.92	8.49	12.7	12.1	13.9	15.1	15.9
United Kingdom	0.86	0.83	1	1.38	1.39	2.24	10.21	13.2	15.6	14.9	16.2	22.4	21.6
United States	0.29	0.45	0.55	0.56	0.7	0.56	7.26	10.38	12.8	13.2	14.3	19.4	18.8

Source: 1880–1970: Peter Lindert, *Growing Public Volume 1*, New York, Cambridge University Press, 2004, Table 1.2 Social Transfers in OECD countries; 1980: 2010: OECD statistics, Social expenditure, % of GDP.

the opposite effect. It discourages everyday risk taking in favor of overly cautious security seeking.

By 1980, several major economies had a pattern of state redistribution that approached or exceeded 30 percent of GDP, including Denmark, Sweden, Belgium, and Germany. One might expect these states to be much more 'equal' than states whose redistribution is around 15 percent of GDP. But this is not so. Lesser re-distributors and greater ones have a more or less identical pattern of Gini coefficients (Table 7.1). A Gini coefficient of 0 means absolute equality (income and wealth is distributed equally among the population). A coefficient of 1 means absolute inequality. One person owns everything and receives all income. Irrespective of levels of social redistribution spending, all the high-prosperity economies have coefficients in the 0.3s and 0.4s – that is mild inequality.

In effect, countries like Denmark and Sweden waste a lot of time and resources on a mythical equality that they never reach. That though begs the question: how do they get to be prosperous societies? In part, the answer is Saint-Simon's industrialism and Veblen's industrial arts. These offset the evident social waste of a redistribution model that has no net positive social effect. There is a tendency among high-performing Continental European and Nordic states to gravitate to versions of the science-technical education-regulation (STER) model. This relies on high productivity that is generated by the application of science to industry to make it feasible. The STER model depends on industrial efficiency – engineering in effect – to support high wages and incomes. The obverse of this is social engineering – the propensity to treat society as if it can be regulated like a machine. But it is notable that it is not only the industrial arts (technology) that offset the down-sides of high levels of state control. There are other systems to consider. In the Nordic case, intact dual-headed households, reading publics, and the aesthetic economy of cities play a key role. In the end, social success is a juggling act.

Notes

1 For what follows, see Karl Marx, 1992 [1867], chapter 14 and chapter 15.
2 Marx, 1992 [1867], chapter 24.
3 Marx, 1992 [1867], chapter 24.
4 Marx, 1992 [1867], chapter 24.
5 Schumpeter, 2017 [2011].
6 Marx, 1992 [1867], chapter 15.
7 See Marx, 1992 [1867], chapter 15, for what follows.
8 Marx (1992 [1867], chapter 24) remarks that at the end of the eighteenth and during the first ten years of the nineteenth century, English farmers and landlords paid 'agricultural labourers less than the minimum in the form of wages, and the remainder in the shape of parochial relief'. The modern welfare state subsumed parish relief into a national system of state welfare, education, and hospitals. The net effect of the latter though is not that different from its parochial predecessor. That is, over a lifetime, it supplements the low incomes of low-skilled workers in order to raise their standard of living to an acceptable social norm.

9 Murphy, 2015, 2019.
10 The paradox of norms, as Durkheim put it, is that deviance from a norm affirmed the norm when a person was punished.
11 On the failure of classroom education compared with book reading, see Murphy, 2019, 155–181.
12 Saint-Simon, 1952, 78–79.
13 Florida, 2002.
14 Saint-Simon, 1952, 79–80.
15 Veblen, 2001 [1921], 19.
16 Veblen, 2001 [1921], 102.
17 Murphy, 2015, 94.

Bibliography

Florida, R. 2002. *The Rise of the Creative Class*. New York: Basic Books.

Marx, K. 1992 [1867]. *Capital*, Volume 1. Harmondsworth: Penguin.

Murphy, P. 2019. *Limited Government: The Public Sector in the Auto-Industrial Age*. London: Routledge.

Murphy, P. 2015. *Universities and Innovation Economies: The Creative Wasteland of Post-Industrial Societies*. Farnham: Ashgate.

Saint-Simon, H. 1952. *Henri Compte de Saint-Simon (1760–1825) Selected Writings*, ed. F.M.H. Markham. Oxford: Basil Blackwell.

Schumpeter, J.A. 2017 [1911]. *Theory of Economic Development*. Abingdon: Routledge.

Veblen, T. 2001 [1921]. *The Engineers and the Price System*. Kitchener, ON: Batoche Books.

14 Paradoxy and economy

Incommensurable

Over the past two centuries, and especially the last century, politics has tended to subdivide into two incommensurable sets of values. One set of values leans towards systems of symmetrical reciprocity. Such systems involve significant components of responsible, self-reliant, self-directed, and autonomous economic and social activity. The second set of values is focused on control. Control as a phenomenon supposes that rather than being patterned economies can be mastered and directed. There are two subsidiary models of control. One is the Romantic model, the other the Enlightenment model. The former leans towards irrational mastery, the latter rational mastery. One idealizes myth and literature, the other science and reason. Combinations of the two – such as 'legalism and paternalism', 'rules and hierarchies', 'rational and irrational mastery' – are quite common.

Typical vehicles for economies of control of the Enlightenment type include the regulatory state, the administrative state, bureaucratized services and benefits, the legal-rational business firm, and the public-sector 'organization'. Often spliced with these will be various residual traces of communitarian charitable 'brotherly love' rooted in thick social ties, kinship, clan and tribal affiliations, and patrimonial habits along with Romantic pantheism, Faustian behaviors, protectionism, and socialism, all offering ideals of irrational mastery. It is not uncommon for each of the latter to gradually translate into bureaucratic idioms or serve as rhetorical legitimations of legal-rationalism.

The conflict of economic paradigms boils down to the clash of Renaissance or Axial economic models with Romantic or Enlightenment models (or often a mix of the latter two). The conflict of paradigms generates well-known cyclically recurring counter-positions of community to society, tariff protection to free markets, customs unions to economic agreements, the big state to limited government, authentic roots to the artifice of industry, and so on. This is the eternal return of modern politics.

The epoch of prosperity can be understood either as a temporal pendulum or as a spatial agon between two images of society. In the past century, most notably we have seen a constant swinging backwards and forwards between the visions of expansive and limited government or managerial and autonomous society. The former stresses the achievement of economic ends through control by means of directing, managing, rule making, guiding, regulating, inspecting, monitoring, surveilling, restricting, checking, auditing, and overseeing. The latter stresses the achievement of economic ends by means of patterns – the productive integration of human action by making the parts of an economy analogies or complementarities of each other, binding them together in ratios, symmetries, lattices, webs, and other pattern-creating media.

Two by two

The animals entered Noah's Ark two by two. So it is with the economically most influential zones in the world: Europe, America, and China. In each case, their economic geography is divided in two. There are two Europes, two Americas, and two Chinas.

The 'two Europes' is reflected in the contrast between sea and land. On the one hand, there are the thalassic states. These range from the 'New Hanseatic League' of Baltic-and-North-Sea edge-states and regions (echoing the old medieval Hansa city-league) along with the island state of Britain. In agonal tension with this is a model of Europe that is earth-bound rather than thalassic. Whether it is the territorial empire of Charlemagne or the foundation principle of the similarly imagined European Union, the social spatial principle of terra firma stands in clear tension with the thalassic principle. The 2016 vote of Britons to exit the European Union illustrates the tension between the two.

The tension between the political economies of the terra firma and those whose spatial orientation is pelagic and hydrographic is rarely a simple either/ or. Both tend to interpolate each other, reproducing the tension between the two in ever-more specific and pretzel-logic ways. For example, the tension between the two competing political economies is reproduced, in a fractal style, within major European states such as Sweden and Germany. These combine export-market-driven, work-focused economies with large per-capita welfare states. Geography (land versus sea, terrestrial versus littoral) and centuries-old forms of religion have mutated into dualistic political economies that are torn between the welfare ethic and the work ethic and between economic cycles and development-state decisions. The almost-even divide within Britain between those in 2016 who wished to leave the Europe Union and those who wished to remain indicates how even (what at its core is) a thalassic island state is still pulled between the two principles.

This dualism is reproduced in the world economy. The 'outer crescent' of the world system is typically less interventionist than the 'inner crescent' or the 'pivot'. Yet all of these political economies, shy of totalitarian examples, interpolate the opposition between interventionism and non-interventionism, controlling free will and cyclical destiny. There have been multitude historical ways of expressing this spatial agon. Time's pendulum swings between

220 Paradoxy and economy

Calvinism and Arminianism, Taoism and Legalism, free trade and technocratic regulation, and so on.

But isn't there a non–dualistic version of this? Does not the idea of a 'mixed economy' synthesize a 'not–two' out of these? Not when the forces of 'state and market' remain a conventional binary pair. They cannot exclude or remove each other. Yet their co-existence is something that is far from the interesting state of 'not–one, not–two'. In the relation between modern politics and economics, to date, the closest we have gotten to a genuine non-dualism is the theory and practice of 'lean government' or 'limited government'. The latter apply pattern principles to structures of power. Self-organizing media such as ratio, scale, economy, symmetry, and productivity are harnessed to the operation of organizational hierarchies with varying degrees of efficacy.

America

Looked at from the outside, America is an 'insular continent'.[1] Looked at from the inside, America divides into littoral and terrestrial parts. The former in turn can be subdivided into dry and wet egresses, including air, rail, road, river, lake, sea, and oceanic portals. In these, wealth concentrates. Wealth – modern wealth – is a function of productivity, itself a function of working out how to do more with less. But wealth creates a temptation, that government can freely use economic wealth to fund programs to cure all manner of perceived social problems. The irony of this – an unfortunately self-defeating irony – is that programs, if they scale above a certain prudential threshold, decrease rather than increase a society's productivity, with the unintended result that the growth of wealth on which programs rely for their existence cannot keep up with the growth of those programs. The consequence is that quietly, almost invisibly, economic dynamism and social prosperity frays.[2]

In the contemporary United States, this plays itself out in the clash between 'two Americas'. Nominally, one America is 'conservative', the other 'liberal'. The two Americas are geographically clustered in different US states. Politically, they are mirrored in two kinds of voters: one is a philosophical voter, the other a program voter. The first prefers government that is limited and citizens who are self-reliant; the second prefers government that delivers benefits, grants, and programs. This political-economy divide is further replicated, like a fractal, within each voter cohort. Thus, American voters can be philosophically conservative yet operationally liberal – and vice-versa. The same applies to the major US political parties. Liberals split between realists and romantics. So do conservatives.

That most American of thinkers, Ralph Waldo Emerson, thought at length about the issue of oppositions of this kind – and how they might be reconciled or mediated.[3] In other words, how can non-dualism emerge out of dualism? Often, the American 'answer' to this question has been simply to allow dualisms such as the philosophical voter and the program voter to exist side by side. Partly, America's continental-scale geography aids this. Its population sorts itself into one or other camp. Those who admire self-reliance move to one state; those who admire programs move to another state. They agree to disagree. Their views, they tacitly concur, are incommensurable. When they cannot avoid each other, as in national politics, deep tensions arise.

Not only that but, as Emerson noted, even when non-dualism in America is practiced, it has a residually militant edge to it. There is a tendency for each side to extract retribution – an eye for an eye, a tooth for a tooth, blood for blood, measure for measure.[4] Emerson tried to get around the idea that the resolution of dueling dualisms amounts to a modern version of Old Testament compensation.[5] The compensation model assumes that in the case of any pairing of opposites, one opposite will invariably cause harm to the other for which compensation is then demanded. If compensation does not occur, then a kind of feuding ensues. This is not premodern feuding, but it is quarrelsome all the same. Grudges, vendettas, strife, rows, and a pervading sense of political bad blood arises.

Emerson envisaged another way through America's dualisms. He was keen not to assume the doctrine of Nemesis.[6] This alternative rested on a sense of the irony of the human condition. Emerson suggests that persons are mistaken if they think that to be great involves possessing one side of nature – the sweet – without the other side – the bitter.[7] In truth, he argues, opposites – means and ends, seed and fruit – cannot be severed 'for the effect already blooms in the cause, the end preexists in the means, the fruit in the seed'.[8] The consequence of this is that the world is ironic. Accordingly a man cannot speak without judging himself and a person cannot do wrong without suffering wrong. Thus, the exclusionist in religion is blind to the fact that in shutting others out of heaven he shuts himself out.[9] The despot and tyrant look to garner riches and powers. But persecution, Emerson observes, is like trying to make water run uphill.[10]

Emerson does not say this but the irony of modernity is that every brutal regime and despotism, of which there has been an un-ending number, impoverishes itself and reduces its own power because economically and socially it tries to make water run uphill. Ideology and violence can enforce a cruel absurdity for a time but eventually its own brutality makes it so dysfunctional that like Ozymandias' kingdom – the kingdom of the king of kings – it ends up as rubble in the sand.

It might sound naïve to say that social wrongs correct themselves but in fact nature including human nature has a paradoxical way of reversing things. Emerson is at his most interesting when he points out that the productive reversals of bad things into good things apply as much to individuals as they do to society. Strikingly, Emerson says that our strengths grow out of our weaknesses and every evil to which we succumb is our benefactor.[11] A person might not be sociable and so not be able to reap the advantages of society. But if this person in order to compensate acquires the habits of self-help, what was negative turns into a positive. Yes, says Emerson, at any given moment, an illness, a disappointment, a loss of wealth or friends seems incapable of compensation.[12] Yet, as years pass by, we realize 'the deep remedial force' that underlies all things. Some of our seeming worst experiences turn out in retrospect to be the best things that ever happened to us.

At the root of all of this, as Emerson observes, everything has two sides: a good and an evil side. Thus in life there is no gain without a loss. In the past century, life expectancy has grown remarkably due to modern medicine. That's a good thing. But a long life for many persons means eventually living with dementia or other chronic forms of debilitation. We may eventually cure those but we are unlikely to cure the loneliness of those who have outlived their spouses, friends, and acquaintances. The great modern delusion is the idea of a perfect world when in reality everything in the world actually has two sides. We might lose our job and look to government to compensate us for this loss by paying us a welfare benefit. We naturally enjoy such compensation. Eventually, though, we realize that had we not taken the benefit but rather moved to another job market with better job prospects we would have avoided being trapped by a low-income benefit. In neither scenario is there an unalloyed good. Both have a good and a bad side.

In America, dualisms side by side are common. Considerable economic and social energies arise from the clash of these – but also illusions. The greatest illusion is the belief that there is good without bad and gain without loss. What follows from this is a delusional pursuit of perfection and the naïve view that things exist without a price or a cost or a loss. Counter to this is the realistic view of life, namely, that success does not exist without failures, nor life without death, deficits without surpluses, sales without profits, investments without forfeitures, or loans without repayments.

The ability to walk the tightrope between these countervailing forces lies at the core of successful modernity. This requires society in the deep background to be able to mobilize enough ironies and enigmas, incongruities and contrarieties, senses of humor and comprehensions of tragedy, metaphors and similes to make possible a recurring productive pattern of tension and relief, stress and happiness, unease and ease. Successful societies are simultaneously driven and relaxed, material and metaphysical, purposeful and meaningful in the same breath.

Maritime East Asia

What is true of Emerson's America applies also to Maritime East Asia. East Asia's most intensive region of industrialism and capitalism is split between a series of 'outer insular crescent states' (Japan, Hong Kong, Taiwan, and Singapore) and the littoral of the region's 'inner crescent', notably Guangdong and Fujian provinces on China's southern coastal rim and the Southern Korean peninsula. Taken as whole, geo-politically, this is a fractured region. Deep suspicions color the relations of the Chinese, Japanese, and Koreans. Each of these societies has its own internal cleavages between dual and dueling political economies. Control versus release is a common battle.

Chinese legalism is a good stand-in for control, as is Japanese state capitalism. These are commonplace and influential outlooks, so much so that a once common explanation for the rise of East Asia nations into the ranks of the most prosperous societies was that it was the consequence of the influence in the region of the idea of a strong controlling developmental 'Confucian' state. That such a control model exists and is influential is not at issue. But it is only half of the story.

We have on the one hand Japan's Meiji-era Prussian model of appointing mainly law graduates to civil service positions in line with the public philosophy of *hoka banno* (omnipotence of the law), or the Japanese state taking a directing role in industrialization through forms of government guidance.[13] Yet, the claims on behalf of such 'legalism' or 'dirigisme' do not account for the equally decisive – and arguably more decisive – fact that Japan produces worldviews like that of Kitarō Nishida, whose 'logic of *basho*' (places) is a non-dualistic logic aimed at overcoming the traditional philosophical subject-object distinction and replacing it with opposites linked in a continuous state of dynamic tension.[14] This 'logic' affirms and denies simultaneously. It prefigures a concept of the divine that is paradoxical.

Such a 'logic' is quite unlike the discursive logic of controlling reason, which directs what to do with reasons. Nishida's 'seeing without a seer', 'seeing the form of the formless', and 'hearing the voice of the voiceless' suggests the way in which creation defies the ordinary linguistic description of a world, namely, one that is analytically differentiated into parts. In the analytic model, one part is causally determined by another part that is outside of it or greater than it. Creation, which is the root not only of the arts or philosophy but also of a modern dynamic economy, is a 'self-identity of contradictories' – or, as Joseph Schumpeter described it, an act of 'creative destruction', that is, in Nishida's terms, a unity of opposites, a co-relation rather than an exclusion.[15]

The development-state model of the Japanese economy obscures the aesthetic nature of the nation's economy – the role, for example, that aesthetic-like miniaturization played in the success of Japan's post-war industries. Japan is not unique in this. A number of powerful economies rest as much on the way in which aesthetics permeate the society. Denmark is a case in point and the Nordic world more generally. The power of aesthetics lies in the self-identity of contradictories, the capacity to beautifully meld the elegant and rough, spontaneous and restrained, simplicity and complexity, as in the Japanese aesthetic of *shibusa*.[16] The influential Japanese industrial aesthetic of miniaturization did something similar. It compressed the macro scale into the micro scale. That launched a thousand consumer products. This was not the developmental state at work.

In spite of the reputation and reality of the directing hand of the development-state, non-dualism resonates through Maritime East Asia. This is the region where the influence of Taoism and Taoism-accented Chan (Seon, Zen) Buddhism is most concentrated. Taoism, the heterodox philosophical-religious strand in Chinese thought, is very old with its roots in the fourth-century BCE Axial Age. Its significance for contemporary economic and social prosperity is threefold. First, it is a style of thinking that is deeply anchored in paradox. Second, its synoptic maxims have a structure that mirrors the epigrammatical structures of the creative imagination. Third, it supports a non-controlling, let-it-be, laissez-faire view of the world.

In the case of contemporary China, there are 'two Chinas'. These are symbolized by the competing economic models of Hong Kong and Beijing, just as there are 'two Europes' and 'two Americas'. In each case, one is 'legalist', the other is 'laissez-faire'. None of these pairs is identical. In each case, society's deep agonal conflicts are expressed differently. In each case, they are shaped by national ethos and specific history. And yet each is similar insofar as one of the conflicted pair emphasizes 'rules' and 'power', the other self-organizing 'nature' and 'order'.

In the classic Taoist view, the most effective way of acting is not to act. That is to say, there is a natural order in society. If government doesn't meddle, this natural order emerges on its own. This supposes a hands-off, do-less-directly, 'don't emphasize governing' approach. Two thousand years ago, Taoist philosophy resolved that if government did not interfere then prosperity would occur spontaneously.[17] Conversely, the more rules there are in an empire, it concluded, the poorer the people are. This is the converse of a state-centric (Communist, Confucian, Legalist, Developmental-State, etc.) view of the world. The latter centrally plans or manages an economy and intervenes in, interferes with, and directs economic and social action to a high degree.

How is prosperity possible?

Alfred Marshall in his *Principles of Economics* (1890–1920) described a business firm that grows and attains great strength and afterwards stagnates and decays. At the turning point, when the firm begins to transition from potency to putrefaction, there is 'a balancing of equilibrium of the forces of life and decay'.[18] Marshall observed the parallels between the 'life and decay of a people' and 'a method of industry or trading'. He compared the balance of opposed forces of economic 'demand and supply' with the opposition of ageing and youth or a stone hanging on an elastic string or balls resting against each other in a basin.

The contrary motion of demand and supply has many forms. The simplest is the balance between desire and effort, when individuals satisfy their own needs with their own direct work. Pleasure is balanced against trouble, weariness and monotony against energy and satisfaction.[19] Equilibrium ranges from this simple though pervasive kind (for who in their daily life does not balance trouble and pleasure?) through the stable equilibrium of 'normal supply and demand' with its gradual adjustments of demand and supply to each other over time.[20] Such adjustments usually oscillate rhythmically but sometimes in a more agitated manner.[21]

Whether stable or unstable, simple or complex, Marshall's equilibria remain one of the great background media that translate trenchant contrarieties into dynamic unities. Self-organizing economies are continually integrating the contrary motions of selling and buying, lending and borrowing, leasing and renting, and hiring and firing. The media for doing so generate mutual advantage, thereby translating self-interest into a common good. Media of this kind are anonymous. They do not behave like the agents of a directing intelligence that commands or intervenes. They adjust rather than direct. Their principal way of working is to mutually adapt and acclimate antipodes rather than order, instruct, stipulate, or require behavior with a view to achieving a specific end-in-view.

The existence of economic cycles is one of the several non-tragic ways that prosperous societies have of resolving the tense interaction of antipodal forces and values. What the cyclical view of things assumes is that economies move not in one direction but in two directions simultaneously. They move up and down at the same time. More than anything, prosperity is not a tragic phenomenon: so production is not sacrificed for the sake of consumption just as consumption is not forfeited for the sake of production. Rather, they coexist as if they were quantum phenomena. The dominant forces in a modern prosperous economy are comic not tragic. They are to material life what paradox, incongruity, ambidexterity, wit, irony, enigma, and humor are to the life of the mind.

This is also why imagination not reason is key to the peak moments of prosperous economies. Reason or rationality has a substantial role in everyday economic behavior. Reasoning is an important way we have of better achieving routine ends and outcomes. But reason also has its limits. We cannot plan a modern dynamic growth economy. It is impossible. This is because reason cannot reason from antinomies, and antinomies are the cognitive fuel of a growth economy.

Antinomy is not a philosophical obscurity. Rather, it is a useful depiction of the way that the human mind operates when it generates things. The imagination is practical. It combines opposites to create things that otherwise do not exist. When in those exceptional moments supply creates demand rather than the other way round, the imagination steps in as a powerful economic force. These moments may be exceptional but they are also decisive. In prosperous economies, the imagination lies at the root of what generates expansion and growth. The propulsive growth of modern economies, almost all of it in the last two centuries, would not have been possible without the contribution of the ambidextrous imagination.

Notes

1 Aaron, 2009 [1974], Prologue.
2 Murphy, 2019.
3 Emerson, 1981 [1946/1841], 165–186.
4 Emerson, 1981 [1946/1841], 175.

5 For example, 'Men do not despise a thief if he steals to satisfy himself when he is hungry;
    But when he is found, he must repay sevenfold; He must give all the substance of his
    house.' *Proverbs* 6:30–31.

6 Emerson, 1981 [1946/1841], 174.

7 Emerson, 1981 [1946/1841], 172.

8 Emerson, 1981 [1946/1841], 172.

9 Emerson, 1981 [1946/1841], 176.

10 Emerson, 1981 [1946/1841], 181.

11 Emerson, 1981 [1946/1841], 180–181.

12 Emerson, 1981 [1946/1841], 185.

13 Among the most influential accounts of the development model was Chalmers Johnson,
    1982.

14 Nishida, 1958, 1987 [1966, 1949].

15 As Nishida (1958, 221) put it, 'As individuals of a world of unity of opposites, we com-
    prehend the world in a creative manner. The historic-creative act grasps reality; this
    means: concrete reason. But herein, the mediation of the logic of judgment is contained.
    "Reason" means: to deepen oneself, from the standpoint of action-intuition. It means to
    grasp reality according to its style of productivity. The "concrete concept" (or "concrete
    notion") is the style of productivity or reality. This is also the basis for scientific knowl-
    edge. The world is apprehended by a creative act; this means it is apprehended intel-
    lectually. The "idea" is essentially the act of creation of the world. Hegel's "Idee" must
    be of this kind. With poiesis at its core, the historical world is confronted with infinite
    past and infinite future. This confrontation and opposition in the present of unity of
    opposites, may be called the confrontation and opposition of subject and environment.'
    Or as Nishida (1958, 179) also put it, 'Where the straight-line is cyclic, there is creation.
    There is true productivity. In the historical world, that which has passed is more than
    something that has passed; there is, as Plato says, the non-being as being. In the historical
    present, past and future are facing and contradicting each other; out of this contradiction
    an always renewed world is born, as unity of opposites.'

16 A key definer of this aesthetic was the Japanese philosopher Yanagi Sōetsu (1898–1961).

17 Lao Tzu, *Tao Te Ching*, chapter 57.

18 Marshall, 2013 [1920], 185.

19 Marshall, 2013 [1920], 190.

20 Marshall, 2013 [1920], 193.

21 Marshall, 2013 [1920], 197.

Bibliography

Aaron, R. 2009 [1974]. *The Imperial Republic: The United States and the World 1945–1973*.
    New Brunswick, NJ: Transaction.

Emerson, R.W. 1981 [1946/1841]. "Compensation". In *The Portable Emerson*. New York:
    Penguin.

Johnson, C. 1982. *MITI and the Japanese Miracle*. Stanford, CA: Stanford University Press.

Marshall, A. 2013 [1920]. *The Principles of Economics*. Eighth edition. London: Palgrave.

Murphy, P. 2019. *Limited Government: The Public Sector in the Auto-Industrial Age*. London:
    Routledge.

Nishida, K. 1987 [1966, 1949]. *Last Writings: Nothingness and the Religious Worldview*. Hono-
    lulu: University of Hawaii Press.

Nishida, K. 1958. *Intelligibility and the Philosophy of Nothingness: Three Philosophical Essays*.
    Honolulu: East-West Center Press.

Index

long-distance 74, 92, 140
long-term phenomenon 28, 84–85, 96–86, 97, 134–135, 137, 142, 204
Loos, Adolf 43, 47
Los Angeles 21–22, 70, 91, 106
Lotharingia 121
love, brotherly 218
low Dutch, language 103
low-fertility practices 93
low-income benefit 222
low wages 211
loyalty 104, 109, 114, 117, 122, 125, 134, 175
Lübeck 91, 122
Luther, Martin 99–100, 104–101, 105
Lutheran 169–170, 184
Luxembourg 4, 40–41, 51, 63–65, 70, 72–74, 80, 114, 127, 166, 215
Lyon 20

Maastricht treaty 121
Macao 71, 80
Macedonia 65
MacFarlane, Alan 92, 97, 104, 108
Machiavellian 148
machines 16, 77–78, 107, 153, 174, 182, 196, 200, 205, 209–210, 214, 216
Mackinder, Halford 19, 28
Macquarie, Lachlan Governor 102
Maddison, Angus 5, 8, 17–18, 30, 49–50, 71, 77, 84, 104, 185
Madrid 70
Magritte, Rene 39
Mahayana Buddhism 52, 150, 173, 179–180
Mainland China 25, 35, 87, 170, 181
Malacca Strait 20–21
Malaysia 20, 35, 42–43, 65, 119–120, 128, 167
Malmo 53
Malta 65
management 51, 61, 106–108, 110, 133, 137, 144, 154, 184, 203, 212–214
Mandeville, Bernard 189, 195–196
Mann, Horace 211
manorial 92, 108–109, 122, 138
Mansfield, Katherine 37, 47
manufacture 67, 71–72, 111, 115, 151, 182, 190, 204, 212
Maoism 56, 115, 179, 203–204
Maritime East Asia 20, 87, 179–180, 182, 222–223
maritime economy zone 181
maritime rim 21, 30–31, 76, 146, 174
markets 12, 14–15, 17–18, 30, 32–34, 55, 58–59, 62, 65–66, 72–77, 85–88,

97, 107, 117, 125, 126–129, 134–136, 142–144, 151, 154, 157, 172, 182, 196, 203–204, 209, 218, 222
marriage 93, 96–97, 103–104, 106, 124–125
Mars 34
Marseilles 157
Marshall, Alfred 98, 133, 157, 225
Marx, Karl 58, 77, 88–89, 131, 135, 138–139, 144–145, 158, 205, 209–211, 214, 216–217
Massachusetts 54
mass-and-void 171
master-and-servant 155
mastery 132–133, 200–203, 207, 218
material achievement 126, 183, 203, 213, 225
materialism 31, 52, 101, 198
mathematical forms 48
mathematics 71, 80–81, 86, 99, 212
Mauritius 65
Maurya Empire 50
May 1968 revolt 56
Mayflower 104
McLennan, Hugh 36
McLuhan, Marshall 82, 89
measurelessness 202
measuring government 71
media 33, 67, 82, 116, 126, 130, 132, 137, 141, 148, 219, 224–225
medicine 134, 173, 222
medieval 15, 40, 54, 106, 109, 121, 158, 219
Mediterranean 20, 24, 31, 34, 110, 149, 179, 183
medium 86, 125, 136, 187
Melbourne 22, 54, 69, 70, 105, 207
membership 13, 117, 182, 206
memories 46–47, 95, 115, 199, 206
mentalities 34, 79, 91, 98, 109, 150, 207
mercantile seapower 40
mercantilism 97, 190, 195
merchants 52–53, 54, 132, 196, 207
merit 58, 133, 156
metaphor 88, 149, 152, 158, 181, 183, 187, 195, 201, 222
metaphysics 16, 31, 33–34, 52, 58, 99, 135, 146, 152, 179, 222
methods, best 176, 224
metropolis 26, 42, 87, 125, 196
Mexico 22, 27, 63–64, 67, 69, 113–114, 119–20, 127, 144
Miami 22, 70
miaphysitism 183
middle-class 198, 207
Middle East 103

Printed in the United States
by Baker & Taylor Publisher Services